CW00859621

For information send electronic mail to books@ethinksystems.com.

ISBN 1-4116-2974-4

For Amy, Amanda & Daniel — their inspiration and belief in me continues to drive me beyond my known boundaries and their capacity to teach me love and patience is endless.

Preface

I'm one of those people who can spend hours at the book store pouring over books, trying to get the essence of their content. Many of the books I choose are technical in nature, and specific about software development. The choice to write, and complete, a book is driven by a decision to share a well-defined set of thoughts and concepts with a reader. There are many people whose unfinished manuscripts remain stored on their laptops or in their drawers.

I've undertaken this complex task because I don't believe that we are, as a society, moving quickly enough to truly valuing the   bits   and bytes we store on our magnetic mediums on a daily basis. Computers can do so much these days! They can render 3-dimensional graphics with speed and resolution that are blurring the lines between reality and animation. At the same time, we still can't gain a consistent and predictable view of all the data that relates to our customers.

Every day, we learn, that data is useless if it is merely collected and stored. It has to be applied to everyday life, in order for there to be a reason to continue the gathering and hoarding process. Today, it is still considered "rocket science" for someone to glean knowledge from a basic set of data. This means that common users cannot leverage the power of the computer to do their jobs better or, perhaps, lead better lives.

I have been present at the early acceptance part of the cycle for every major trend in the computer market since 1980. PC's, dBase III+, client/server, C++, packaged applications, rapid application development, Windows, Java, XML, EAI, Web Services and now EII. I marvel at new technology and I enjoy seeing how quickly I can see how the technology can be used to solve real world problems.

Throughout all these developments, the value of data diminishes in importance in favor of the acts that revolve around the processing of data. For example, it became so important to provide a Web-based interface that developers did not stop to consider the implications of creating new or replicated data sources. They seem not to have stopped to think that some of the data they might be capturing through these interfaces, might conflict with the data captured in paper form at branches, and create downstream accuracy problems.

The silver lining of this cloud, however, is that through all the blunder and mishaps, on both the technical and the business sides, we are gaining a new respect for the value of data and what it can provide us, if we just spend some cycles thinking about what data we should capture. For example, the Enron debacle has driven the need for structure and sharing of financial information in electronic form, as part of an overall compliance program. Given this new profound understanding of the value of data, things will start to move quickly toward the maturation and availability of tools that make it easy for all of us to gather and analyze data, without having to be a trained computer scientist.

Enterprise Information Integration is an early step in that direction. There are many more steps that need to be completed, such as better metadata analysis tools. However, we're on our way toward real knowledge management. By knowledge management, I'm not talking about a content management solution with advanced searching, but the ability to truly understand how our businesses work, or even how the world works.

This book is merely a signpost on the path toward really respecting data and what it can do for us. Having the opportunity to introduce customers to EII has enabled me to also teach them the value that goes beyond simply "hacking" or "band-aid"-ing their current systems to support yet just one more task. Eventually, these approaches will break, and the "house of cards" formed by the layers of poorly architected and overreaching systems will tumble down. Just look how close we came to this in the year 2000. The fact that we didn't have utter disaster due to the change in century should not be perceived as, "See! All those doomsayers were wrong!" Instead, we need to recognize the heroic effort that was undertaken by many companies, and the millions (if not billions) of dollars that were spent to avoid this catastrophe.

To the readers of this book, I hope I can provide a small directional beacon about where to head next, and help you convince those who need convincing, to spend the time and money to organize data into an extensible and reusable framework that will allow computers to deliver on their true potential.

JP Morgenthal
January 2005

About this Book

As one of my favorite salesman likes to say, "This would be a great book if you could get 'what' by reading it?" It's up to you to fill in the 'what' in that question. Are you interested in learning about a new integration methodology or the types of applications that can be built using that approach? Are you designing an enterprise data integration strategy and looking for patterns and approaches that simplify your task? Or, are you just interested in understanding what EII means and how it might impact your investment in Information Technology spending? This book will answer these and other questions.

This book is intended to provide the same pragmatic approach to Enterprise Information Integration that has been used by governments and major corporations. It is designed to deliver knowledge of this subject without overwhelming the reader with technical jargon.

The knowledge in this book is delivered as sets of clearly defined, but high-level overviews that will provide a rapid introduction into the topic space, without drilling down so deep that digesting these materials would require an advanced computer science degree. By the end of this book you should be able to intelligently analyze your current integration problems, ascertain if EII is the best solution for you, as well as discuss potential EII tools and solutions with vendors and developers.

This book is divided up into chapters that examine different components of the EII solution. We will begin with a look at EII as compared to Enterprise Application Integration (EAI), and Extract, Transform and Load (ETL) tools. We will then explore the EII approach to integration, focusing on its key differentiator, which is metadata. In the chapter on metadata, we will look at the various types of metadata in the organization, and identify how they apply to EII and integration. Following that, we will explore the types of applications that EII will simplify the development of, such as portals, executive dashboards, data de-fragmentation, and enhanced querying.

Next, we will look at some of the implementation details associated with EII projects, such as architectures for deploying EII, EII tools, and the role of existing technologies in an EII solution. In addition, the book will provide insight into some of the underlying technologies that enable EII, such as Web Services, UML, XML and other XML-derived technologies. We will look at how XML tagging will impact reuse of the data and how to model the data to deliver more intelligent querying. Finally, the book will look at some best practices around designing an EII solution.

Finally, this book delivers a vision for gaining control of the data within your organization, and harnessing it to achieve your business goals. The glut of electronic data that crosses our desks is forcing us to take new organization and filtering approaches. Spam filtering is a perfect example of the need to limit the digital content we have to process as humans. EII helps enable us to focus our business systems on the data that has enterprise applicability, instead of just departmental or system-wide applicability. It also helps us to turn that data into a structure that informs, versus one that overwhelms.

Acknowledgements

When ideas are formed, they represent the abstract notions of what they will be when they are full-fledged concepts. There are many who helped take my vision for actionable metadata and turned it into reality. First and foremost, I'd like to thank those who helped solidify the concepts behind the best practice, Bill Ruh, Joe Gentry, Nicole Ritchie, Debra Mendes and Frank Saffoori. I'd also like to thank those who were instrumental in the development and deployment of these concepts in the real world, Guido Sacchi, Chuck Papageorgio, Cindy Hayden, Chris Donovan, Ravi Gopalan, Joel Gardi and Puny Sen.

Other individuals who have been of extreme help, in the completion of this manuscript by providing critical content to help clarify this complex area include: John Poole for his extensive contribution on Model-Driven Architecture as it applies to EII, Zvi Schreiber from Unicorn, Rich Ptak and Wayne Kernochan for their contribution on EII and Sarbanes-Oxley compliance. I'd like thank Avaki Software (Linda Thorsen & Craig Muzilla), Composite Software (Mike Abbott & Peter Tran) and TakeCharge Technologies (Debbie Hamel) for providing real world case studies of EII. I'd also like to thank Rick Bridges of Telus for allowing us to see inside his QuickWin team to illustrate how Business and IT can work well together.

Finally, I'd like to thank my technical review team. Kevin Dick, who really went the extra mile with his extensive suggestions and introduced me to the concept of meta-events, Andrew Johnston, David Linthicum, Ankur Laroia, Bryan Quinn and all those who provided great input into the development and structure of this book through their valuable reviews.

Foreword

What you hold in your hands is an excellent description of one of the most surprisingly useful technologies that I have run across in 35 years in the computing industry.

Four years after I helped coin the term Enterprise Information Integration, and six years after the first EII startups began surfacing, I still tend to get the following reactions from a wide swathe of people unfamiliar with EII:

1. "Yet another bit of software infrastructure? Isn't my life complicated enough???"
2. "Oh, you mean EAI. Aren't they the same thing?"
3. "It sounds like Old McDonald's Farm. Is object-oriented EII called EII-O?" (sounds of rolling on the floor laughing at one's own joke)

As hopefully this book will show, the answers to these questions are:

1. EII has both short-term and long-term positive effects that should actually simplify your life. In the short term, as real-world project after real-world project is now demonstrating, EII (by bridging disparate data sources) can have a surprising and significant effect on the bottom line, getting new key information to key decision-makers or empowered employees quickly. In the long term — and even more significantly — EII creates "globalized metadata" that gives a far better view of the organization's information assets and a superb platform for leveraging those assets better in application after application — or, as this book would have it, it turns the less-than-useful data in many modern organizations into meaningful and far more useful information.
2. No, they aren't the same thing, nor are they competitors. In fact, as this book makes clear, the EII, EAI (Enterprise Application Integration), and ETL (extract, transform, load)

technologies are all complementary, and when combined are worth much more to the business than the sum of their features.
3. Actually, I haven't thought of an answer to this one. I just look (and feel) pained.

So, from my point of view, how can this book help? Well, I (and some other analysts, but never mind them) provide a broad overview of the EII market, with particular attention to what EII tools are out there to help you with your job. What this book does is draw a line between the business benefits of EII and real-world technologies and standards that real-world implementations should consider. It goes deep, where deep is useful; but it doesn't lose sight of the forest for the trees (I love these mixed metaphors). Above all, it relates the theory of EII to the practicalities of *your* business, *your* IT organization.

A classic New Yorker cartoon has a man staring at the fancy mess on his plate just served to him by his wife, and saying belligerently, "I say it's spinach, and I say the hell with it!" Substitute "infrastructure software" for "spinach," and you have the reaction of some in the past to technologies like EII. But that reaction is wrong — not necessarily about the spinach, but definitely about EII. EII is not an old technology in fancy marketing dress; it is here to stay; and it continues to prove its usefulness in project after project. In fact, here are a couple of new uses that recently showed up at my front door:

a. The real-time enterprise. Wouldn't it be nice if you could query and get the latest key data of all types as it arrives in your organization, instead of waiting for it to show up in the data warehouse?

b. RFID. Wouldn't it be great to ask "What happened to my customer's order?" by issuing one query across RFID, POS, and customer data, instead having to ask someone to code separate queries and then combine them?

I believe that EII repays closer examination tenfold and a hundred-fold. This book is a great place to start.

Wayne Kernochan

Data is not information, Information is not knowledge,
Knowledge is not understanding, Understanding is not
wisdom. –
Cliff Stoll & Gary Schubert

Introduction

An organization that has a modern IT infrastructure, but can't rapidly answer questions about its business, is like an explorer who has a map, but doesn't know how to read it! Information and knowledge are the best tools for navigating an increasingly competitive business environment.

There's data everywhere you look. It's on your receipts when you go food shopping. It's on the monthly financial statements and bills you receive by mail. It's even on the front and back of your car. Before there were computers, there was data. Now, the only difference is that we've taken to storing much of that data electronically, so that we can access it more quickly and easily.

It should be no surprise that information technology departments within organizations have been ignored in favor of sales, marketing and finance. Computers were created to increase the productivity of all other departments. When we increase productivity, we increase output without increasing the cost of producing that output. Hence, computers are just an enabler for creating more wealth, and they've accomplished this mission well. We've tripled the size of the economy since the first mainframes came online[1].

---

[1] Based on real GDP from 1959-1996

Productivity, however, is no longer providing leading countries with enough growth to maintain the competitive advantages they have come to rely on. Influences from globalization, such as lower costs of labor in developing countries and fluctuations in currencies, mean that companies need to produce higher quality products, and products that meet individual customer demands, even if meeting these requirements entails extensive customization of the product.

For example, the auto industry has gone from the famous Ford statement, "You can have any color you'd like, as long as it's black," to auto manufacturers using colors as a market differentiator, as part of an assembly line process, to customers having a car built to their specification and delivered to their door. This need to move away from the assembly line mentality, to a service-oriented mentality has permeated all industries and is causing a revolution. As a result, business leaders are now required to pay attention to the data in those systems that merely provided automation of routine tasks in the past, to glean intelligence about the industry their in, and the customers that they do business with.

Unfortunately, many of the systems we're relying on today, to provide us critical business information, were not designed with this task in mind. Many of these systems were designed for the sole purpose of increasing productivity. Thus, only the data necessary to produce the intended increase was incorporated into the system. Fortunately, the need for greater and greater productivity has forced us to change systems or build new ones to meet the demand. This process has resulted in data accumulating in rough layers that have been loosely knitted together, to provide us with many of the answers we need today to remain competitive. However, these layers have become so fragmented and isolated, that it requires Herculean efforts to make sense of it.

To drive this point home even further, the CEO of a major logistics and transportation company called his efforts to obtain a consolidated view of all business done with a particular trucking company across all business units, a "Chinese fire drill". This quote indicates that his information systems do not support his needs, and instead, require the chaotic process of humans manually pulling data and consolidating it, in order to obtain the values this CEO needs.

If we're looking for greater productivity in our organizations to increase net profits, here's a prime place to start. Of course, there are two ways to approach this information problem: 1) rip & replace, or 2) integrate. Neither is perfect. Both are expensive. However, since rip & replace is not a one-for-one replacement, it requires that all new systems be developed, deployed and parallel-tested for at least six months before they can be relied upon in a production environment. By the end of this process, two to five years might pass, along with changes in the market and economy, without having been accounted for in this strategy.

The alternative approach, integration, can be performed on an as-needed-basis, continually delivering value of the current system in a production-level manner, while meeting the needs of the users for new data structures and applications. However, bringing together the layers of data that have been accumulating for years, will present a daunting challenge that requires a novel approach. This approach is known as Enterprise Information Integration (EII). It includes specialized software that is designed to meet these challenges.

Another Integration Strategy?

If you're reading this book, you're most likely interested in identifying better ways to leverage the data assets within your organization. You may be concerned about the emergence of yet another approach to integration, after significant dollars were already spent on integration technology. You may find it interesting that, in survey after survey, Chief Information Officers consistently define integration as one the problems that keep them up at night. As other industry leaders in the integration space have noted, there are no "silver bullets" when it comes to integration. Each new approach hopefully brings with it, the ability to satisfy integration requirements faster, less expensively, and with fewer resources.

While we will explore the benefits of EII in relation to other integration technologies in the next chapter, let's now look at some of the business drivers that have lead to a need for EII. Most Information Systems in production today suffer from these major drawbacks:

- Require IT assistance for end-user access
- Difficult for end users to identify relevant information
- Overload of data delivery
- Provide only partial answers to questions
- Often present out-of-date information
- Contain enormous amounts of redundant data
- Expensive to develop and maintain

The truth of the matter is that we're delivering data, not information. Notice that we're being very specific by not using the terms *data* and *information* interchangeably. Most people speak of data and information as if they are the same thing. This confusion of terms is one of the leading causes of the problems in information systems, as noted above. These are distinct concepts, as we will see shortly.

EII is an approach to integration that has arisen out the need for organizations to identify and correlate related, but separate, data. It allows users to derive new data structures and information models without having to understand the nuances of underlying data structures, data locations, data types, etc. In essence, EII solutions provide access to the data without the hindrances of the underlying technology selection.

One common problem EII has been applied to is identified as a single view of the customer. If you consider the IS infrastructure of any modern mid- to large-sized organization, you will find a number of legacy systems that have related and, sometimes, replicated data. The reasons for the emergence of these differing systems include: performance, response times, data governance, etc. However, the pragmatic approaches taken by IS to respond to users' needs has resulted in an inability for the company to see clearly and accurately across these systems.

18

While integration techniques such as Enterprise Application Integration (EAI) and Service-Oriented Integration (SOI) exist, there are requirements to harness the mounds of raw data within our organizations and enable users to more easily identify, correlate, process, and reuse this data within the business's processes. That is, EII may have emerged because of requirements, such as single view. However, the integration technique answers the much larger need for making data more digestible and accessible regardless of one's role within the organization.

This book is intended to satisfy the needs of those who want to quickly gain insight into EII as a new approach toward integration, and to better understand where and how this technology can be applied to solve complex data problems.

What is Information?

MIT Scholar Geoffrey Brooke sums up the relationship between people and information best. "The more information there is, the more time you have to spend converting it (into knowledge). We've made it easy to produce, collect and transmit information. We haven't made it easy to consume information. Consuming information is just as slow as it always was."[2] Enterprise Information Integration is an architectural approach that not only makes it easier to create, but also consume, information.

Information is defined as the communication or reception of knowledge or intelligence. If you receive a table of numbers with no headers and no explanation, you've received data, not information. It isn't information until the headers and other metadata are aggregated with the data, that you have information.

The Aberdeen Group explains this as the task of strategic information management. They describe the short-term goals of strategic information management, as the ability to deliver available information in a consistent manner, on demand. They also describe

---

[2] MIT Management, Spring 1992, P.50

Enterprise Information Integration: A Pragmatic Approach

the long-term job of strategic information management to identify, manage, add, and support the leveraging of the information resources of the organization.[3]

An EII solution was recently implemented in response to the requirements of a major credit card company in the United States. The solution needed to meet the company's overall goals. They included:

- Support dynamic integration of new portfolios
- Overall corporate agility
- Alignment of Information Systems with the goals of the business
- Increase effectiveness in managing portfolios
- Become more efficient in the use of corporate information

Clearly, this company understands the impact that information and Information Systems has on corporate growth. However, this company also realized that their existing Information Systems infrastructure was a hurdle to achieving their goals. They needed to align the employees and applications around a common business vocabulary to drive consistency and transform their data into information.

A recent IDC report lists "single customer view across channels and offerings," as one of six CEO-Level business priorities that will drive IT spending growth.[4] This is one of the driving factors behind implementing EII today. This report goes on to say, "In 2004, regulatory mandates, deregulation, consolidation, and more sophisticated, segmented channel management will increase the urgency." Thus, EII solutions will have a major role to play in fulfilling the demands in this area.

There are a number of processes that data might undergo on the way to becoming information:

---

[3] Enterprise Information Integration, The New Way To Leverage E-information, Second Edition, July 2003
[4] IDC Predictions 2004: New IT Growth Wave, New Game Plan

20

- *Aggregation* – the process of combining data from disparate sources into a new structure
- *Consolidation* – the process of summarizing groups of related data
- *Transformation* - the process of turning one set of data in a given structure into one or more sets of data in potentially different structures
- *Filtering* – the process of identifying and removing pieces of data that are not relevant to the current process
- *Validation* – the process of ensuring the validity of the data by comparing its structure and content, against a pre-defined set of criteria
- *Cleansing* – the process of ensuring the validity of the data by meeting canonical specifications

Moreover, data may pass through each of these processes multiple times, as part of a single business process, or an information gathering exercise.

The implementations of these processes constitute only part of a complete EII solution. They are merely operations performed on data in order to prepare it for other uses. There is a higher level component to EII that manages the correlation of data. Correlation is what allows us to connect fragmented islands of data sets into a coherent whole.

When developing a normalized relational database, the wonderful thing is that all the tables can operate from a common key. In contrast, when operating against fragmented, disparate data sets, different conventions may be used, in order to establish the identity of a single logical record. EII's correlation process facilitates mapping identity conventions across data sets to each other, and provides the necessary rules for synthesizing logically coherent records.

The following scenario illustrates this problem. A single company with three acquired business units may have three different ways to identify their customers. The parent company's ability to identify the total business they are doing with any one customer necessitates an information engineering exercise, to map the entities in a common approach. For example, the parent company will first have to develop the ways and means of identifying that Company ACME in Business Unit X, is the same as A.C.M.E in Business Unit Y (see Figure 1). The implementation of this may be as simple as using a lookup table that associates a Business Unit customer number with a corporate customer number.

Are these the same companies?

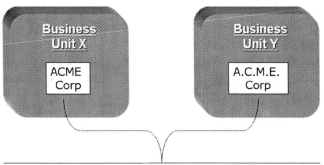

Figure 1: Identifying related data across differing data sets

However, there is a requirement here for a human to sit down and look at the attributes of the customers, such as name, address, billing contacts, etc. to determine that ACME Corp. truly is the same as A.C.M.E. Corp. String matching will help in some cases, but more advanced data cleansing tools may be needed in order to determine that these companies truly are one and the same. It is a very realistic scenario that each of these business units might each use different representations, in order to identify the same company.

In a nutshell, these are the types of problems that EII attempts to solve. For the businessperson, EII removes the barriers to accessing enterprise data and provides a common infrastructure to transform that data into usable information, usually on demand. For the technologist, EII simplifies the longstanding data integration problem by applying a "semantic veneer" over the complex physical data layer.

EII increases the productivity of front office personnel by:

- Providing high-quality data
- Simplifying access to data from front office applications
- Providing well-understood meaning around the data across the organization
- Delivering context around the data

As we will see in Chapter 2, EII shares common traits with other integration approaches. If, as you read the previous paragraph, you thought to yourself that you could accomplish this today with the integration tools that you have, you would be correct. However, the remaining questions are how easily you can do it, with the integration tools you have now, and whether it would be more easily done with a tool designed specifically for the task of turning raw data into powerful, reusable information? Throughout this book we will continually revisit these questions as we learn more and more about the EII approach.

What is Knowledge?

Knowledge is what we now seek from our information management systems. In 1994, Shlomo Maital predicted in his book, *Executive Economics,* that "the knowledge economy will radically change the way executives make decisions about labor, capital and knowledge."[5] One of the factors that lead him to this conclusion was that knowledge expands, the more widely it is shared, and the more intensively it is used. He also noted that knowledge is created, shared, and disseminated faster and better in smaller organizations rather than large ones. Hence, our information systems must now provide us with more than just basic automation. They must help us understand our world. They must convey knowledge.

Knowledge has been defined as the body of truth, information, and principles acquired by mankind. This definition shows that information is just one component of knowledge. EII solutions do not address knowledge directly, but they are an important step toward creating it. The patterns and facts that we learn or derive by examining information provide us with the knowledge we need to make good decisions. Figure 2 illustrates the hierarchy of reasoning necessary to distill knowledge from raw data.

---

[5] Executive Economics, Maital, P.114

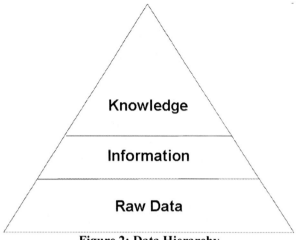

Figure 2: Data Hierarchy

EII will take us from raw data to information. We still require analytic tools, such as inference engines, to help extract knowledge from the information we create. For example, EII can provide us insight into our customer base by consolidating the customer information into a single structure that can be analyzed simultaneously. This is the benefit of information integration, but EII does not provide us the ability to readily identify that the customer tends to shop on Monday, which is the day after the flyer is delivered. Analytic tools are designed to look for these patterns, but they need the structure derived from the EII solution to be able to have enough supporting data to make such an assertion.

Why Invest In EII?

Today's science fiction movies and shows are filled with references to a world where computer systems dynamically communicate with no human assistance. The virtual information screens that Tom Cruise combines at will in "Minority Report," and the ability for Star Trek's Enterprise to analyze even the most obscure and unfamiliar ship upon first contact, are just small examples of this capability. In a perfect world, there would be no need for EII software, because all data would be available to even the most novice user, with little or no effort.

However, the world we live in is comprised of systems that run on different hardware platforms, use different operating systems, have proprietary data formats, and run applications without external interfaces. In short, our data is fragmented and accessible to only those who have the capability to unlock it from its imprisonment.

With EII, we can take steps to provide novice users with the means to view data from a perspective that matches their specific needs. For example, allowing newly merged companies to create a comprehensive view of the combined customer base only weeks after the merger, instead of months, or help health and human services case workers recognize inappropriate child placements prior to unfortunate events.

Moreover, EII provides a foundation layer for the eventual incorporation of context-dependent uses of data in new applications and business processes. For example, once a set of data has been absorbed into the EII layer, the workflow and business process management tools can start to leverage the vocabulary that has been captured as the primary means of creating units of work. That is, instead of business analysts struggling to understand technical interfaces to applications and services, analysts can focus on a vocabulary that they understand and work with everyday, as a means to drive new business automation.

We will explore this concept throughout the book, but it is important enough to reiterate now, that EII provides a means to drive automation that hides (or abstracts) the underlying technical services from the tools and products that will consume data, which is all that the business is eventually ever interested in. Business process re-engineering is even analyzed and reviewed for success, as a series of metrics that underlie that change.

Key Concepts

1. Organizations need to gain control over their data, if they want to maximize growth and productivity
2. The terms data, and information, should not be used interchangeably. Information is data that's been processed, and is accompanied by a supporting context and has implied some intelligence or knowledge.
3. The operations that help create information from raw data are aggregation, consolidation, transformation, filtering, validation and cleansing
4. Analytic tools are required in order to create information and knowledge from raw data, but EII tools can provide the base from which knowledge can be discussed

*"To the man who only has a hammer in the toolkit,
every problem looks like a nail."*
— *Abraham Maslow*

Integration: The Three-Legged Stool

This chapter introduces general integration strategies, and compares and contrasts them to satisfying overall integration needs within an organization. There are going to be many different requirements for integration, such as application integration, metadata integration, services integration and data integration, within an organization. As we become more distributed in our implementations, more of these integration requirements will arise at different times. Therefore, the number of tools available to the market increases with each new integration requirement or technique, which makes the job of selecting the lowest cost alternatives more difficult.

Information integration helps end users gain access to data that is critical for decision making, and provides the basis for turning that data into something that provides more immediate value in that decision making process. Where ETL and EAI are both developer-level integration techniques, EII is a technique and a best practice that is shared by both the business and IS user alike. This chapter explains the value that each integration technique provides, and discusses how they work together to provide a comprehensive integration strategy.

Integration as a Best Practice

Integration is a practice, and not a technology! When we submit to this line of reasoning, it becomes easy to see why integration is so complex. Software does not exist that automates implementation and execution of best practices; however, certain tools can make it easier to follow one. That is what the Extract, Transform & Load (ETL), Enterprise Application Integration (EAI) and Enterprise Information Integration (EII) tools do for the integration problem.

In general, these tools do not solve integration problems if they are not used in tandem with a method and discipline. We use the analogy of a three-legged stool to represent our best practice for integration, and each leg corresponds to ETL, EAI and EII. These three legs share many common features, but the one key differentiator between them are the types of problems they are best at solving and their approach.

Figure 3: The three-legged integration stool

There is a reason why "simple" is a word that is hardly used when discussing integration, unless you are a software or hardware vendor. Integration is complex. Some of the reasons why integration is so complex include a lack of knowledge of what is being integrated, a lack of understanding of current data formats, political and technical hurdles in accessing the data where it resides, and a limited perspective on the role of the integration now, and in the future. Assuming all these factors were eliminated, integration would still require skilled individuals who are capable of approaching an integration problem from a business perspective, and select the best integration technology, or set of technologies, to solve that problem. More often than not, the choice of integration technologies leads to failure and overruns for the integration project, more than any of the other technical hurdles mentioned earlier.

In the end, the success or failure of an integration project depends on the experience of those responsible for requirements gathering and architecture. These people will need simultaneous breadth and depth in integration implementations, tools and technologies. That which seems simple to the non-practitioner can be fraught with complexities.

For example, one of the complexities of selecting an integration technology stems from the multitude of approaches to that problem. Message-Oriented Middleware (MOM) is a simple and straightforward approach to systems integration. All that is required to integrate two systems is to create a communications conduit between them; this is often a queuing mechanism. Once the queue is created, software formats the data for delivery and sends it to the queue for retrieval by the second system (see Figure 4).

Figure 4: Point-to-Point integration

As simple as this approach is, it is not without its problems. For example, queue-based integration creates the formation of a master/slave relationship between two systems, and architecturally establishes one system to be of higher priority. Later, this dependency will make it difficult to either move this system to a new platform, or rewrite it entirely.

To further demonstrate the increasing complexity of integration, we will modify the problem so that there are two systems that must be fed by the same system of record. The integrator will have a choice to make to either continue with the queue-based approach and create a separate conduit between each system that needs to receive updates from the system of record (the Point-to-Point approach), or apply a different solution using a different tool. Selecting the point-to-point approach will make maintenance and management issues more difficult in the future, as well as introduce increasingly poor performance, as the number of conduits increase (see Figure 5).

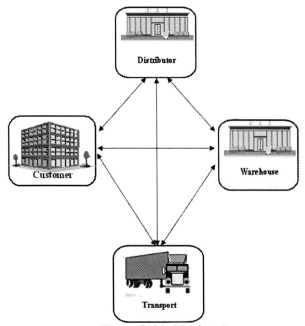

Figure 5: Multipoint chaos

An alternate approach is to broadcast the message to all interested parties. This can be done with a publish/subscribe messaging technology. Publish/subscribe technologies allow the master application to publish the message once to multiple applications, in a near-simultaneous manner. The publish/subscribe middleware handles the distribution and delivery of the message to systems that subscribe to receive updates from the master (see Figure 6).

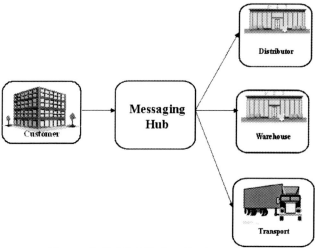

Figure 6: Publish/Subscribe integration

To illustrate the difference between the queue-based and publish/subscribe-based approaches, you could think of the point-to-point approach as similar to a telephone network. Each time a call is made, a connection is made between the caller and the recipient. Thus, in order to notify two or more people of an event, you would have to call each one individually. In contrast, publish/subscribe technologies are more analogous to the radio. The transmitter broadcasts a radio signal on a particular frequency, and all those interested in hearing the broadcast can tune their radio to that frequency. In the former approach, you can ensure that each person has received the call and acknowledged receiving the message you sent them. In the latter approach, you can reach more people simultaneously, but won't know whether they tuned in, or that the message was even understood.

The approaches discussed above are still relatively simple given our requirements for integration. In one case, the requirements mandate that one system, the master, send data to another system based on a given event, such as the master being updated. In the second requirement multiple slaves need to receive the same updates from a single master. Using this very simple use case, we can show varying levels of complexity and discuss the integration technology selection process and its downstream implications.

The following scenarios illustrate certain complexities associated with sending data between systems. The goal is to illustrate how the requirements and existing environment make integration complex. They also illustrate the breadth of understanding that an integration architect must have, in order to successfully overcome these hurdles. In these scenarios we assume that the selection for building the conduit has already been made.

Issue: Each slave system runs on different hardware architecture than the master.

Response: Differences in hardware have typically been some of the more painful hurdles in integration. For example, mainframes use a different coding scheme (EBCDIC[6]) than open systems (ASCII[7]). Chip architectures use different byte ordering schemes, known as big endian and little endian. If the system of record and the recipient systems use different architectures, as listed above, then the data that the system of record formats could prove to be useless and unintelligible to the recipient.

Recently, the industry settled on XML and Unicode as common ways to represent data for integration purposes. This does not solve the problem completely because we still need to convert existing data into XML. This may require a change in applications or the development of special adapters that perform this conversion for us. Moreover, these transformations lead to more "moving parts" in the integration solution, which, in turn, result in higher maintenance costs and greater opportunities for failures.

Issue: Message sizes are very large.

Response: This type of integration scenario is common in commercial service industries, such as telecommunications, where monthly statements must be delivered to the print

---

[6] Extended Binary-Coded Decimal Interchange Code
[7] American Standard Code for Information Interchange

service and made available over the Web. The issue is that the telecom bill for a medium to large sized corporation for one month could be upwards of thirteen megabytes. Large messages can cause big problems for message-based integrations because the data must be stored in the interim, until it can be dispatched or retrieved. It doesn't matter if you're using a queue or publish/subscribe, there's going to be a backlog of messages awaiting delivery, just because of how long it takes to transfer each message. In addition to the backlog, larger messages are more prone to failure during delivery, since an error in delivery can cause the entire sending process to fail, particularly if the solution is not designed to break the message up into smaller-sized blocks.

Issue: The receiving system misinterprets the structure of the data received.

Response: The problem is probably more indicative of an unaccounted version change, but may also arise if the implementation guide (specification) was not followed perfectly by the developer. The worst part of this scenario is that the exception will probably now be recognized at the application level, which requires application-level handling to generate an appropriate response to the sending system, that the message received cannot be processed. In the previous two scenarios, it is possible for the exception to be handled by the infrastructure software that performs the exchange of data, and therefore, is managed in a consistent manner. Once the exception reaches the application layer, however, both parties have to have processes to deal with the issue.

Here are just a few examples that demonstrate the levels of complexity that underlie a seemingly simple solution, and can turn it into an IT support nightmare. Unfortunately, scenarios like this are not uncommon and the fault lies nowhere. Even if integrators do their job correctly, lack of integration experience could lead the integrator to miss a requirement that will lead to problems in the future. Integration checklists and solution patterns can limit these types of downstream problems, but nothing can replace real integration experience.

Integration Best Practices

The selection of the appropriate integration practice is critical to the success of an integration project, where success is defined as the stability, reliability, and maintainability of the solution. If we look at the classification of integration patterns, there are three primary best practices—ETL, EAI & EII—each of which has a distinct property set that makes it appropriate for solving different types of integration problems. However, due to the fact that there is overlap in these classifications, there is also the opportunity for integration disasters as each one of these can be viewed as satisfying the requirements of the other two. But, when an inappropriate selection is made, the costs of integration skyrocket, as the inefficiencies of the tools become apparent.

It is only recently that the third leg of the stool—EII—was added and introduced as a formal best practice. Before then, users attempted to use ETL and EAI patterns to perform pure data integration, with varying levels of success, and usually high costs. It is the addition of EII that balances out the integration portfolio and gives our stool the balance it needs.

In the following sections, we examine, in more detail, each pattern's properties and role in integration.

Extract, Transform & Load

In the early days of computing, applications were written for single purposes, such as accounting, inventory, etc. The tasks were simple, and duplicated where necessary. For example, updating the accounting system to reflect a purchase of inventory would lead to two separate entries in two different systems. At the time, this approach to application development was state-of-the-art. (If you can identify your organization's approach in this statement in the 21st century, don't feel alone).

During the rise of the PC and minicomputer server markets in the early 1980's, the IT industry saw the rise of the first coming of process re-engineering. The second coming is here now and it's called Business Process Management. This re-engineering of an organization's processes led to unprecedented increases in productivity levels, as much of the duplicate entry work was replaced—along with the existing systems—by expensive packaged applications. These applications promised fully integrated data and processes through the use of a homogenous application platform. It is this early migration away from existing applications to the new packaged applications, that helped spawn the ETL market.

Extract, Transform & Load (ETL) was the first integration best practice to emerge. As organizations started to migrate away from their obsolete custom-built mainframe applications or packaged applications in favor of newer, up-to-date packaged applications, it became obvious that porting data from its existing locations and formats was going to be one of the most complex parts of the migration. Hence, ETL emerged as a batch-oriented tool that would handle the one-time loads of new systems, and ongoing updates, as needed, so long as these original systems remained in operation.

ETL's started appearing in the market to help support these migrations, typically, toward new SAP or BAAN enterprise resource planning (ERP) systems. These new ERP systems provided organizations with a pre-integrated set of functionality, such as accounting, manufacturing, shipping, & logistics. However, since ERP systems consolidated data from what was typically stored in three times as many systems, it was going to be necessary, as part of the migrations, to extract the data from the current systems, consolidate and transform to meet the requirements of the new ERP, and then load the data into the new ERP systems en masse. A major benefit of the ETL systems is their ability to perform this last function with a high-degree of performance.

Over time, ETL tools also began to be used to update systems from tape and optical media that, typically, were delivered to the company from external partners and suppliers. Normally, organizations use custom code to perform this function, since the media formats often changed over time. ETL has proved to be a solid and powerful solution and allowed organizations to respond to changes quickly, and less expensively. Additionally, these tools have become the backbone of data warehousing projects because they can consolidate data and load it into the data warehouse en masse.

A typical ETL tool, such as Informatica or IBM/Ascential, usually comes with a powerful graphical user interface that allows integrators to describe the inbound and outbound data sets and then perform operations to combine and transform the inbound to become the outbound. These combinations and transformations are then downloaded into a middleware server that handles the operation, and reports on failures and errors. Some ETL tools are also capable of assisting with data cleansing. Data cleansing means looking for pattern variances between disparate data sets that should be congruous, and then reporting on these variances so that the newly formed data set doesn't carry across the same errors and problems as the legacy environments.

Since ETL was the first of the integration best practices to appear, products began to focus on helping customers solve the problem of integrating their silos of applications by adding a real-time document processing capability. Due to ETL tools' strong ability to parse data and then recombine it through transformations, it seemed a natural extension to then do this inside business processes, such as purchasing, by implementing Electronic Data Interchange (EDI) handling. This is an example of systems integration using a document paradigm; that is, documents are sent to each of the systems, and it becomes the responsibility of the receiving systems to read and process these documents and taking the appropriate action.

> ## ETL is best for providing data extraction, cleansing, consolidation and loading of large, and sometimes disparate, data in a batch manner

Enterprise Application Integration

The Enterprise Application Integration (EAI) practice emerged during the late 1990's. As we move forward in our story, we find that the packaged application vendors diversified, based on some vertical strategy. SAP is strong in manufacturing. PeopleSoft is strong in Human Resources, and Oracle is strong in financials. So, line-of-business management made decisions based on the needs of their department, without forethought as to how this information would roll up to provide a complete picture of the organization. At the time, departmental financial data was typically the only data that was consolidated across the enterprise, and this was accomplished using common formats, such as comma or tab delimited. As packaged applications started taking hold in the enterprise the number of outdated and too-tightly focused applications was greatly reduced.

Problems with this approach became glaringly clear when finance and budgeting executives identified irreconcilable totals due to the fact that each department was managing its own accounting systems. This inconsistency occurs when systems are not updated across the board, as part of the same transaction, and therefore, errors are introduced through data entry or lost changes. Enabling these systems to operate within a single unit of work, as we had been doing on the mainframe years before, would require the formation of a new integration best practice that focused on making disparate applications look like one single, cohesive application.

Once again, a new class of software was required to correct our lack of cohesive transaction processing. EAI emerged to ensure that transactional integrity is maintained across systems. For example, when a sales order is paid, the amount needs to be deducted from what the customer owes in the ERP application, and the commission paid on that invoice needs to be issued to the payroll system, which, in most organizations, means two or more different applications.

Early version of these packaged applications provided only rudimentary and proprietary interfaces to access the data, which made integration and customization expensive and difficult. With changing times and increased need for greater levels of productivity and data, it became clear to the packaged application vendors that they had to open their systems up to simplify integration, or suffer a declining user base as customers moved to packages that were open.

Those with open access provided it via application programming interfaces (API), which exposes access to system data programmatically. This was a major improvement over having to access the data in its raw form or through a database management layer. These APIs also allowed EAI solutions to be developed more easily, since the tools could be made to operate with a number of different packaged applications.

It is for this reason, that most successful EAI platforms sell adapters, code modules that expose raw data sources in cases where an API does not exist or is overly complex, in order to further the programmatic metaphor. In addition, EAI products also have transformation, aggregation and data exchange components. These components emerged out of the need to incorporate data that was still running on older, legacy systems that were not replaced by packaged applications, but still housed critical information to their operation and function.

By the end of the 1990's, the EAI pattern had generated a significant amount of interest, and sales of EAI tools were soaring.   In contrast to ETL, EAI implementation techniques were hotly contested by the experts at the time. That is, some experts believed that EAI should be implemented using asynchronous messaging technologies; while others believed EAI was squarely in the domain of linking together programmatic interfaces.

This debate that formed among integration experts was over the best way to integrate all these enterprise applications. The rift between integration professionals mimicked the rift between the disciplined mainframe application developers and rapidly-moving client/server application developers.   The former group was concerned with the robustness, reliability, and consistency provided by following well-defined interfaces, while the latter was concerned with the speed and flexibility provided by loosely coupling applications.

Out of this debate, two primary approaches emerged. One approach is the asynchronous document-based approach, where two systems send documents back and forth to each other as a way to share and exchange data. An example of this is Electronic Data Interchange (EDI), which is the most popular method of application integration across departments and firms. Another approach is to expose the behavior of a system as a set of interfaces, and force systems integration to take place as an exchange of fixed, strongly-typed, lists of parameters.

The former approach offers tremendous flexibility as the interfaces between the two systems is based on a document structure that can change over time, or be sent to different applications. This approach also requires a significant amount of investment up front, to ensure that the document meets with the criteria of a valid document.   The latter approach overcomes the validation requirement because all the parameters are tightly-bound and can easily be checked at the time the data is sent. Unfortunately, this approach is very rigid and does not always meet with the changing demands of business.

Both of the aforementioned approaches may be used in a single integration, depending on the requirements for throughput, scalability, and security.

Regardless of the underlying technologies, most EAI architectures were in general agreement with the one illustrated in Figure 7[8]. These EAI architectures advocated the creation of an integration hub through which the work of integrating one system into the hub could be leveraged across multiple integration projects. This shift was an important change for Information Technology, because they were no longer integrating systems in a "one-off" manner, using point-to-point approaches, but were realizing that the cost and time to integrate one endpoint could be averaged into the total cost of all integrations.

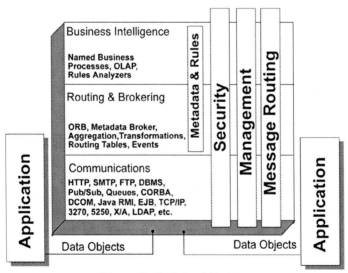

Figure 7: EAI Architecture

---

[8] "Lowering Total Cost of Change for Enterprise Application Integration with VAA", EAI Journal, May/June 1999

Further increasing the trend toward enterprise application integration was the advancement of the World Wide Web and the need for companies to build new processes that provided direct access to those back office applications and communicated directly with the customers, suppliers and partners. This audience didn't care that the organization had its data stored in different systems, or was using different systems for procurement of different product lines. They wanted access 24x7, over the Web, and they wanted it integrated.

More than ever the transformation, aggregation, and data exchange capabilities that overlapped with some ETL capabilities, become a required to overcome gaps in data or structural formats from the sending system.

By the end of 2002, many companies were at a loss to see an increase in productivity or a decrease in expenditures due to the cost of integrating all these systems, and also due to the high cost of the tools and skills, and the long project completion times. The task of driving new processes around e-business required both data and application integration best practices, and, often, low-level programming was required to satisfy the needs of basic information integration. This need for additional programming, in addition to the EAI tools, caused many to believe that EAI wasn't living up to its hype.

> EAI manages transactional context across two or more systems as part of a single business event

Enterprise Information Integration

The truth is that the emergence of the EAI pattern puts the cart before the horse. The EAI pattern deals with the lack of ways to implement new business processes, using existing information systems. For instance, let's consider the ability to create a Web-based sales system that allows the buyer to determine if the item is in stock, before completing the purchase. In existing brick and mortar companies, this often requires process integration across multiple systems.

However, for many organizations, process integration is the end goal. But, before the process issue can be addressed, the data must be organized in such a way that the new processes would provide the right information at the right time. Thus, issues of data quality quickly arise, to impairing attempts to drive process integration. This forces organizations to face years of operating without data management discipline, and developing application silos with redundant data.

Furthermore, by the time this need becomes apparent, the Information Technology department will have been under pressure from the business to respond to the increasing costs in the front office. These increased costs are due to the extra effort required to format and cleanse the data before it can be used. The Enterprise Information Integration (EII) practice emerged to help organizations deal with the pressing need to increase data quality, and make it available to front office users. Since the remainder of this book is about EII, we'll just provide a quick overview here, and show how it differs from ETL and EAI.

EII simplifies access to enterprise data from the front office, and it complements our other two integration strategies perfectly. Our ETL best practice provides us with the tools for integrating legacy and external data sources into our existing applications. The EAI best practice provides a way for us to integrate existing applications so that they operate in unison. Meanwhile, EII provides a way to access existing data in unique and dynamic ways.

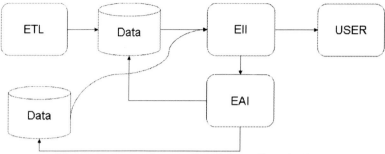

Figure 8: A sample complete integration strategy

Figure 8 above illustrates how the legs of the stool work together to provide a complete integration strategy. In this strategy, ETL provides data consolidation and loading capabilities. This may be needed if some of the data is available only through batch application interfaces, or is only available in a transient form, for example from a clickstream event. EII provides the user with a consolidated view of data across disparate data sources, and EAI provides the capability to manage updates across the distributed architecture, in a transactional manner.

Another key property of EII is that the data remains in the systems in which it currently resides, but incorporates that data into new structures, as needed. This process typically focuses on normalizing fragmented data sets. For example, customer data may be stored in the sales system, and the customer resource system. This fragmented view of customers limits the organization's ability to have a consolidated view of all the touch points with their customer base, which leads to missed opportunities and potentially poor services. In turn, de-fragmenting data leads to an ability to satisfy new business processes and develop new applications, while building upon all the prior integration work that has been done over the past years. Additionally, it allows data to be exposed to the business users as information-critical for driving the business. This saves the company the very expensive process of requiring its IT group to have to develop a new application, every time a new view of this data is required by the end users.

Enterprise Information Integration is the automated process of turning data into information

Comparing the Legs of the Stool

As you can see, EII, EAI & ETL are three very different approaches to integration. When used together, they can provide significant advantages for simplifying an integration project. When only one approach is used for multiple tasks as the hammer and all integration projects are treated as nails, the project is at-risk of undue complexity and potential failure. However, without the benefit of the experience of having used all three approaches, selecting only one approach can be a difficult task.

Figure 9 below illustrates the overlap between these approaches. There are two common attributes across all three approaches—data aggregation and transformation. In addition, each one of these three approaches shares one additional overlapping attribute with the other two. From this picture it becomes clearer how one tool might be used in place of another, in an integration project.

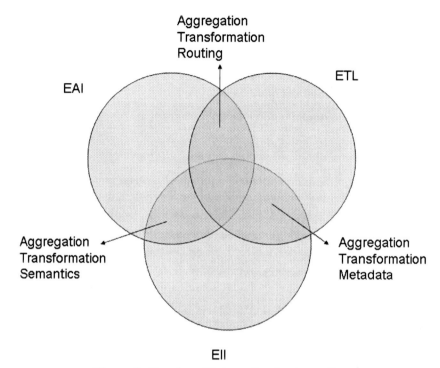

Figure 9: Overlap of integration best practices

Let's now explore these overlaps in more detail. We'll start with the general overlap of aggregation and transformation. In all three best practices, we're dealing with a publisher of data and a recipient of that data. If all systems used the same underlying structures and formats for their data, integration would not be as difficult a problem as it has become. However, since they do use different formats, either the publisher or the recipient has to establish the requirements for the integration.

The need for aggregation is a given across all three best practices, because all the data is not available from one system. For example, a tape with names and addresses for a targeted marketing campaign will not contain data that indicates if someone is already a customer. This requires us to aggregate the tape's data with our own customer management data. The combined data set can then be used by the marketing application to modify a message to current customers.

Transformation is required because of the incompatibilities that arise due to field sizes, or ordering of the publishing or receiving system. An example of this is that our shipping system requires a nine-digit zip code, while the sales order system only uses a five-digit zip code. Therefore, we need to transform the zip code field so that it meets with the requirements of the shipping system.

Now, let's explore the individual areas of overlap. First we'll review the overlap between EAI and ETL, which is routing. Both of these systems need to have defined for them, which system is the recipient of the data. In the case of ETL, we will route the data to the underlying data model of an existing application, for example, from one database table to another database table. However, in EAI, we route the data to either a programmatic or asynchronous interface. If your primary goal is to get data from point A to point B over an asynchronous interface, it's not difficult to envision using an asynchronous messaging adapter with an ETL tool as the endpoint of the loading stage. However, this is not the preferred approach.

EAI and EII share an overlap in the area of semantics, or meaning. With EAI, semantics pertain more to the combined behaviors of two systems working together, as it would be if we integrated our shipping and inventory systems to ensure that an item taken out of inventory is delivered to a customer. With EII, semantics provide users a way to commonly refer to a particular piece of data located somewhere in the company. It is not difficult to make an EAI tool handle both behavioral and business semantics, however, this is not an EAI tool's specialty.

The trick with successfully implementing an EAI best practice is to avoid using it to define both front office and back office semantics. For this latter requirement, we have learned that the audience is less technical and more aligned with the needs of the business. Therefore, the semantics need to be more closely aligned with the business, whereas we rely on EAI to provide the semantics of the systems themselves.

Finally, EII and ETL, which are the two most similar best practices, share a common layer of metadata management. Metadata will be defined and fully discussed in Chapter 4, but suffice to say here, that it enables ETL tools to know about all the databases and all the fields that can be used as part of bringing data online. EII uses metadata to deliver an understanding of the data that is available to them for use in their front office applications. In the case of ETL, we're dealing with metadata that represents the physical data stores, while EII deals with metadata that represents the business world. However, one could easily be made to provide the function of the other.

In each of these cases, it's easy to make the tool deliver the functionality we need to mimic one of the other tools. However, tools alone do not make integrations successful. We need to follow a pattern for the particular integration, and the tools should support the use and implementation of those best practices.

Table 1 shows one final comparison of the three legs of the stool. This representation compares the best practices without reference to a particular tool. Through this chart, we see that the best practices are very different, regardless of how we can make the underlying tools fit their needs.

	Enterprise Information Integration	Enterprise Application Integration	Extract, Transform & Load
Goal	Turn data into information	Allow multiple applications to act as one	Bring legacy and external data sources online
Data Flow	Data stays with the applications	Data moves to and between applications	Data flows into applications
Architecture	Bus	Hub & Spoke	Point-to-Point
Impact on Systems	Preserves systems of record	Modifies systems of record	Modifies and creates new systems of record

Table 1: Comparison of integration best practices

We should also not lose sight of the fact that at its root, all computing amounts to, is the input-process-output model. Therefore, while we can point to some basic functional differences and overlap between these approaches, the benefit can be seen when we look at the levels of productivity that each approach provides.

While it seems that each of these tools can deliver some of the functionality of the other approaches and may even be used to develop solutions that the other is better designed to do, it is the increased productivity that comes from using the right tools—shorter development cycles, ease of maintenance and lower cost of development—that is the real difference between these approaches.

Key Concepts

1. Integration is not a technology, it's a best practice.
2. ETL best practices are better at providing data extraction, cleansing, consolidation and loading of large, and, sometimes, disparate data
3. EAI best practices manage transactional context across two or more systems as part of a single business event
4. Enterprise Information Integration is the automated process of turning data into information
5. The three leading patterns for integration all share common attributes, but upon deeper examination, they are specialized in certain areas that make one better than another depending upon the task
6. Because each of the patterns share common properties and have similar components, selection of an integration solution is difficult and confusing. Experience and training are the only ways to avoid common mistakes
7. The legs of the three-legged stool can work together to create powerful integration solutions in shorter time than ever before. For example, you could use EII to create a new structure that represents all known customer data, EAI to render changes made to this new structure back to its source of origin, and ETL to consolidate this data for loading into a data warehouse.

"The Semantic Web is not a separate Web but an extension of the current one, in which information is given well-defined meaning, better enabling computers and people to work in cooperation."
— *Tim Berners-Lee*

"The research rat of the future allows experimentation without manipulation of the real world. This is the cutting edge of modeling technology."
— *John Spencer*

Modeling, Semantics and EII

As a whole, our planet works under a framework of common understanding. For example, all people have a way to express the concept of the sun, body parts and land masses. The reason we can express these concepts is because they are represented by physical attributes of our world that we instinctively know by sight, smell or feel. That is, the words and pictures that represent these physical attributes are all universally known.

However, once we start to apply meaning to things that are outside of our shared physical reality, there is no common basis to ensure that a meaning make sense. For example, the concept of a customer to a U.S.-based corporation would be completely foreign to an Aborigine tribe in Africa. While this is an extreme example, this concept is relative to culture, geography, and even ethnicity. It is this relativity of meaning that makes automation difficult to achieve, when it comes to the meaning of things.

In order to move toward understanding the meaning of the terms and nomenclature of our everyday business, we need to devise a framework in which things can be described. These frameworks need to allow an entity to be described by a set of attributes and properties that are common across similar entities, but remain unique enough to differentiate this entity from all other entities. Moreover, this framework allows things to be described based on existing, well-understood things, which means more complex descriptions need to be based on simple or atomic descriptions in order to achieve agreement on meaning, and the context in which it is being used.

This chapter looks at two key frameworks that are used to define objects in our universality: modeling and semantics. Modeling provides us with abstract descriptions of entities and how these entities relate to other more basic entities, as well as other complex entities. Semantics provide another framework for understanding, but is based on language and the meaning derived by combining simpler words and concepts together, to create more complex concepts.

Modeling Information

Modeling is a key component of automating the processing and management of information. The models that are created to enable the storage, query and in-memory representation of data, define the meaning of that data within the given context of a process or application within the organization. Unfortunately, many of these models are very low-level constructs, such as a relational database models, and offer little in the way of defining meaning or context, but were intended to provide electronic "cubby holes" for data.

Entity/Relationship (E/R) modeling was devised, in 1976, as a way to unify network and relational database views. E/R modeling is a way to describe how one entity relates to other entities, within a given context. Context is an important part of establishing meaning in a digital world. It establishes usage of the entity, which has the ability to change meaning as context changes.

Slang is a great example of how context can impact meaning. When someone says, "What's up?" in the context of greeting another person, they are not asking them what is above them. Likewise, an entity/relationship model establishes how one entity relates to another in the context of a particular process or organization. A context can be as large in scope as the universe, or as small in scope as a single task.

In addition to context, E/R modeling establishes meaning through the uniqueness of the relationship's characteristics, such as its cardinality, attributes, degree, direction, existence and type. E/R modeling also supports the concepts of generalization, which allows two or more entities to share common attributes.

The following illustration provides an example of E/R notation, which is a visual representation of an E/R model.

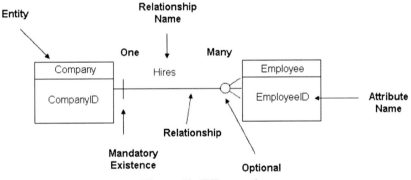

Figure 10: E/R notation

Object-Oriented (O-O) modeling is concerned with establishing meaning through the creation of a taxonomic structure and behavior. Indeed, it extends the power of generalization found in E/R modeling significantly, by allowing the designer to quickly create larger, more complex objects from simpler more atomic objects. However, the primary difference between E/R and O-O modeling is behavior.

E/R modeling is primarily concerned with the organization and structure of data only, and does not include semantics to describe the behavior of an entity. O-O modeling has enhanced capabilities for extending meaning to the entity (or object) by incorporating its behavior, along with its attributes, into the definition.

Figure 11 below illustrates the difference in modeling using E/R and O-O notations. This diagram also introduces the concept of generalization as PublicCO and PrivateCO are subtypes (or subclasses) of Company. These two new classes share the relationship with Employee that the parent class has as well as its behaviors and properties.

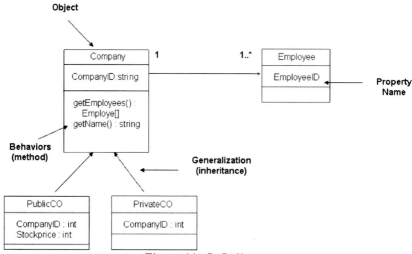

Figure 11: O-O diagram

E/R and O-O modeling provide us with good static models for information. However, they don't meet the requirements for modeling information that is unstructured, or for which the structure is not known in advance. Indeed, these models are predicated on their ability to bring structure and strong type definition to data management and data processing.

As an integration technique, Enterprise Information Integration crosses the boundary between the static modeling worlds and the unstructured data world. On one hand, EII needs well-defined structured information to use as the basis for generating new information sources. The E/R and O-O models form a basis for automating the extraction of data from existing legacy environments. In fact, unstructured and untagged data limits the selectivity that EII can place on the existing data. On the other hand, EII solutions will generate structured, semi-structured and unstructured information as output of its work. Therefore, EII needs a way to model the information it will produce, such that it can be interpreted and processed by downstream processes.

As alluded to earlier, information is relatively unstructured, recursive and chaotic. It cannot be modeled by traditional data modeling techniques due to their rigidity and closed—that is, it cannot be expanded further—architecture. Instead, what is needed is an open architecture that can flexibly model data and its relationship to both behavior, and other data. The most common approach taken to fulfill these requirements is the triple.

The triple is a simple construct that ties two entities together through a link. In this scenario, an entity can be an atomic or complex object, where an atomic object is fully defined and the complex object has links to other objects. This approach has been successfully used to model metadata, which tends to be very dynamic and very difficult to model statically, without continuous maintenance on the model. It also can be used to model sets of properties and attributes (see Figure 12).

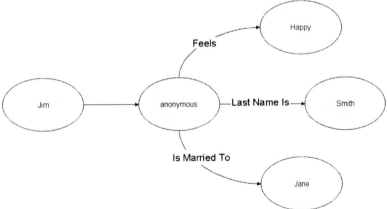

Figure 12: Triple-based model

In the above model, we can quickly identify a number of properties about Jim, such as his mood, last name, and wife's name. Using this model, we can add properties about Jim ad infinitum. However, this model also implies some level of ownership or containment of these properties, such that they belong to Jim and no one else. Using this method, we can provide meaning to Jim through the set of relationships and properties that are assigned to him. In the above figure, the anonymous node represents an unnamed place holder that acts as a container for all sub-connected properties.

Moreover, while the model shown in Figure 12 is unidirectional, it is not a requirement for all information models. Indeed, the above model can be amended to show that Jane is married to Jim, which would result in the model represented by Figure 13, which introduces the ability for the model to be recursive and, thus, extremely complex to process and requiring special logic to ensure that links already crossed, are not crossed multiple times.

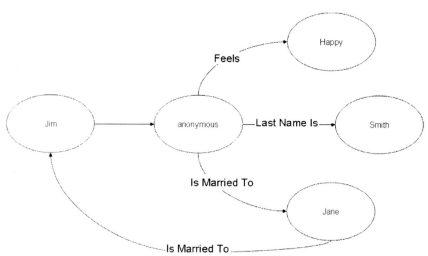

Figure 13: Recursive information model

Again, the key to modeling information in this way is the openness that allows the model to change dynamically and continue to expand without requiring constant maintenance to the applications that processes these models, or the metadata that represents them. You should take notice, however, that E/R or O-O modeling techniques can be used to successfully model the triple architecture. In this case, the resulting model would merely be the basis for supporting future development for a single information model.

According to Zvi Schreiber, in Unicorn Solution's white paper entitled "Semantic Information Management (SIM): Solving the Enterprise Data Problem by Managing Data based on its Business Meaning," a well-organized information model (ontology) consists of five layers: organization layer, entity layer, property/attribute layer, business rule layer and descriptor layer. Each of these layers is further defined below:

Organizational Layer

The Organizational Layer divides and subdivides the Information Model into different packages, reflecting different parts of the business such as customer, product, etc., and reflecting ownership of different parts of the model. In EII, this layer is the business vocabulary.

Entity Layer

The Entity Layer captures the entities or "things" that play a role in each area of the business. Examples include people, documents or products. The Entity Layer should capture the business at different levels of detail and specialization. The general concept of "product," a specific category of products, or a specific product might all be captured as entities. In modeling terms, this is also known as generalization.

Property/Attribute Layer

The Property/Attribute Layer captures the characteristics used to describe each entity and related entities. For example, it captures the fact that every customer is associated with a contact person or that a product is associated with a price. In EII, this layer is known as ontology.

Business Rule Layer

The Business Rule Layer allows the Information Model to centrally capture business rules relating alternative vocabularies. This layer enables EII solutions to extrapolate and reuse business rules across many applications, instead of having them hard-coded in individual applications. Examples of rules are look-up tables, and logical/arithmetic rules. This layer might also capture aliases across vocabularies, such as relating annual revenue to quarterly revenue, or capture role-based constraints over data.

Descriptor Layer

The Descriptor Layer ensures that all concepts in the other four layers are documented in a structured way, providing definitions, synonyms, aliases, examples, and, where needed, foreign language representations.

Applying Information Models to EII

Much of today's organizational data resides in silos that are separate and distinct from one another. Each year, organizations spend millions of dollars trying to integrate these silos to make them deliver against real business goals, such as advanced analytics or better communications with their customers.

Some of these projects are successful, but many are either terminated before they are finished, or delivered too late to provide the intended value. A common reason for these failures stems from the fact that the information model, which includes the key relationships between data, is captured inside of the applications directly, instead of reusable models that the applications are developed from. That is, integration across the silos of data is implemented as application logic, in a high-level programming language that is intimately tied to the physical data structures and locations of the disparate data, whereas, conceptual models would have provided greater reuse, and protected the investment against future technology changes.

This does not imply that developing application logic is never necessary or does not provide specific business value, such as providing a customer service representative with the customer's purchasing history. However, the application has trapped inside of it the knowledge of how disparate pieces of data are related within the scope of a particular topic; for instance customer service. An alternative approach to the problem of integrating silos of data is to leverage the information mode—the ontology, the taxonomy and the semantic definitions—to provide the instructions for aligning the data with the goals of the business.

Developing this information model will require you to capture the relationships between data as metadata; typically focused around your everyday business vocabulary. For example, how would you define the relationship between a salesperson and commission? The salesperson *earns* a commission when they make a sale. Thus, "earns" takes on specific meaning in the context of a sale. Capturing these relationships as externalized entities instead of snippets of application logic, facilitates the reuse of these relationships among many applications, thereby reducing the cost of development and maintenance of these applications. For example, once "earns" is defined, it makes it possible for any new application being developed to include sales along with their corresponding commissions as a new data structure.

There are six key relationships that must be captured as illustrated by the Table 2. For purposes of this table, we will define the business vocabulary metadata as a "business term", the metadata of the physical information assets we will call "physical terms," and business process metadata we will call "process terms". The chart shows examples of the types of relationships that might be shared across each of these terms.

From/To	Business Term	Physical Term	Process Term
Business Term	• Contains • See also • Refer to	• Represents • Points to	• Required • Used by • Resolved by
Physical Term	• Represented by • Stored as	• Adjacent to • Related to	• Used by • Stores • Input to • Output from
Process Term	• Represented by • Uses • Implements	• Uses • Stored as	• Subsequent to • Follows • Precedes

Table 2: Key relationships

In each of the cases above, there could be unlimited numbers of relationships that can be formed. Your applications and your business will dictate the names and directions for these relationships. A good metadata management tool will enable you to capture these relationships in a simple manner, so that they can later be combined with the instance data as part of a downstream process. We will see more of exactly how the relationship metadata can be leveraged, in later chapters.

As you start to capture the relationships between these three components, the metadata will form a map of the lifecycle of data within your organization. To demonstrate, the following explores mapping based on the need to aggregate data from a customer management system and a transaction clearing system. The former contains the customer profile data, while the latter contains the up-to-the-minute actions against a particular customer's account.

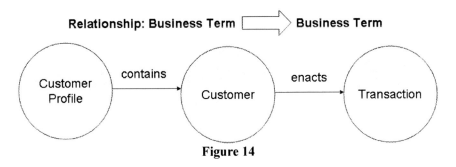

Figure 14

Based on the relationship illustrated in Figure 14 we know that *Customer* is "linked" to *Transactions* through the customer enacting a transaction. Since *Customer* is contained within the *Customer Profile*, the taxonomy extends the "enacts" relationship to the Customer Profile as well.

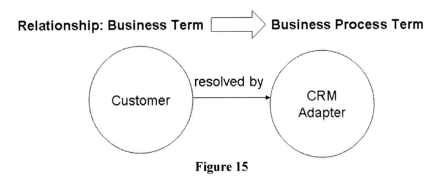

Figure 15

This relationship in Figure 15 identifies the code associated with retrieving customer data from the customer resource management system.

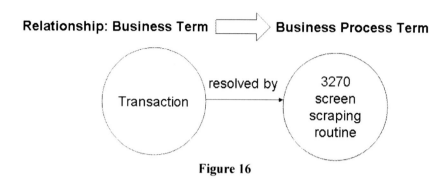

Figure 16

The relationship in Figure 16 identifies the routine associated with retrieving transactional data from the mainframe application.

With these pieces of metadata, end users can now request a customer profile, and the underlying infrastructure is able to determine that the requester is asking for the aggregation of the customer data from the CRM system, and transaction data from the mainframe application. The infrastructure "understands" the associated routines needed to retrieve that data.

Of course, this is an oversimplification of what is really required to obtain this end result. However, it suffices for the needs of explaining how the information model can be applied to integration requirements. We will see how to further apply information models for integration, later in this book.

Semantics

Semantics are defined as the study of meaning, where meaning is the mental representation of a "thing" and the words and phrases used to describe that thing, in communications with other individuals. Integration is primarily a problem of semantic dissonance, which is a fancy way of saying that two systems do not represent the same piece of data by the same name, type, size, etc.

Overcoming this hurdle is currently an expensive and time-consuming task, due to the need for human engineers to have an intimate understanding of the two entities being integrated. In the future, by way of semantic science, we will be able to develop software that can automate the more tedious parts of the integration exercise, leaving engineers to focus on the solution to the problem, using more than one system or data source.

The field of semantics is wide and covers a large range of associated topics, such as:

- Conceptions of meaning
- Words and lexemes
- Denotation, connotation, implication
- Pragmatics
- Ambiguity
- Metaphor, simile and symbolism
- Synonym, antonym and hyponym (a word that is more specific than a given word)
- Etymology (word origin)
- Polysemy (words having two or more similar meanings)
- Homonymy, homophones and homographs (one of two or more words spelled and pronounced alike but different in meaning)
- Lexicology and lexicography
- Thesauruses
- Epistemology (the study or a theory of the nature and grounds of knowledge especially with reference to its limits and validity)

Each of these sub-fields represents additional tools that can be applied to the semantic dissonance problem that hinders the ease of integration.

444444

The Semantic Web

The Semantic Web is an extension of the current World Wide Web infrastructure that enables machine understanding. The use of the word semantic in the name extends from the ability of the Web pages to impart meaning about that page's content to some machine-based processing agent. The long-term vision and goal of the Semantic Web, is to turn the Web into a large and navigable information space that has the ability to locate and retrieve information that matches a loosely-defined set of constraints.

For example, today's Web searching is primarily based on text-based constraints and logical operators. The results can be scored based on relevance to the query, but is still highly reliant upon the query's form. Moreover, the search itself is based on page content, which can be easily duped by simply placing keywords on the page that may be picked up by the search engine's search agents.

While the latter problem will always be delegated to a trust model and an agreement to play fairly in the Web community, the Semantic Web overcomes some of each of these limitations by tagging Web content more specifically with semantic markers that impart meaning about that page's content. For instance, an airline's Web page can embed meta-tags on the page that identify that particular page on their site as containing airfares, travel rules, routes, etc. This will result in more applicable information retrieval for someone looking for airfares from New York to England, and will not also get someone's Weblog entry for their recent vacation. Moreover, these semantic markers also improve both automated and human navigation of the Web, since both implicit and explicit linkages can be more easily established.

The foundation of the Semantic Web is the provision of key metadata stored with the Web content in the form of the triple information model discussed earlier in this chapter. The triple information model is critical here, so as to ensure that the Semantic Web does not impose specific requirements on how a Web page must express its meaning to the overall Web; a key requirement of both adoption and flexibility.

Without the triple information model, the Semantic Web would have to establish and diligently maintain a specification for the expression of meaning; an improbable task.

Semantic Integration

Behavioral semantics have played a very large role in integrating disparate systems and data for a long time now. Integration is a complex process that requires the ability to make two discrete unattached entities operate as if they were designed to work together. This is different than assembly, in which the parts are discrete, but designed to be put together. It is also different than interoperable, which means they stay discrete, but can pass "stuff" back and forth.

We can best describe semantic integration as the elimination of the nuances between systems, due to an agreement on vocabulary as it relates to analyzing and understanding data. At a simplistic level, one could say that EII and semantic integration are one-and-the-same. So, often, one of our biggest barriers to integration is the vocabulary or terminology we used to identify data within various systems. Semantic integration uses existing integration techniques to neutralize the barriers caused due to inconsistent naming and typing, and, thereby, simplifies the act of making systems work together more seamlessly.

An EII solution presents us with an excellent platform for the capture, management, and use of industry-standard taxonomies. Industry consortiums invest heavily on the definition of data that is widely shared across an industry, such as bar codes, product numbering, business documents, etc. The reason that organizations invest in creating and supporting the consortium's efforts, is because it eases the burden on them in receiving and sending this data across the industry, and it lowers the costs of vendor-based solutions that implement these standards.

Many of these data standards implement a common taxonomy for data to assist in the classification process. Examples of these include standards organizations include Dunn & Bradstreet, International

Standards Organization, XML Business Report Language, and OASIS. Their taxonomies are used heavily within the electronic data sharing framework, and, in some cases actually represent the format for the data being exchanged.

The metadata management component of the EII solution is a perfect adjunct to modeling these existing taxonomies, and, in some cases, may even provide the platform for producing industry standard documents directly from the EII solution. The key to successfully using this metadata lies in the process of mapping/integrating it into your existing environment. This requires you to undergo a process called a gap analysis, in which two or more data sources are analyzed to see how they can be mapped into the new, required structure. Out of this process come two results: a) a mapping of known fields and b) a list of fields that have no corresponding equivalent in the original data sources.

This mapping process exists in all fields of semantics, not just in systems integration. Both translating and interpreting spoken and written language requires a similar process. The following table lists the types of processes that are applied in a semantic mapping or interpretation exercise:

- Word <-> word. Example: door (English) -> porte (French)
- Clause <-> word. Example: noodle soup (English) -> Nudelsuppe (German)
- Clause <-> concept. Example: "what's up?" -> greeting
- Concept <-> word. Example: greeting -> "wassup?"
- Concept <-> concept. Example: greeting -> salutation

As you can see from the above list, the gap analysis is not always a straightforward one-for-one comparison. Indeed, it's very possible that it may take multiple fields and some additional logic to create the translated value required. Dictionaries, thesauri, and other lexicons assist in the mapping and translation process. However, if you've ever been on vacation in a foreign country, and attempted to create a sentence using individually selected words strung together, you may have noticed that the person you were speaking with still had no clue what you were saying. Even though you successfully mapped your language to theirs, you were unable to map the clause to a related concept.

How does all this relate to systems integration? To successfully map or translate data from one structure to another, we need to be able to apply the same concepts and processes for mapping language. The following list shows how mapping and translation occur at the systems level:

- Field <-> field.
- Structure <-> field.
- Structure <-> structure.

At the systems level, structures represent both the clauses and concepts within spoken and written language.

The key to semantic integration is to establish a unique meaning and representation for each component of data that is critical to the organization. For instance, the word 'hat' in English only means one thing—a head covering. It doesn't mean floor covering or boat covering, because these inconsistent meanings would hinder the use of the word and cause confusion instead of convey a message. We need to do the same thing for our organization's data.

Once we establish for our organizations a common vocabulary, it then becomes the basis for all other systems to communicate with each other. However, if we think of the common vocabulary as English and our systems as French and German, then we realize that there must be a translation layer between our systems so that our native systems can understand the messages being sent to them. This mapping becomes part of the overall semantic integration solution, which takes data in its current structure, translates it to the common vocabulary, routes the data according to various business rules and then translates the data for recipient. Figure 17 below depicts this type of solution.

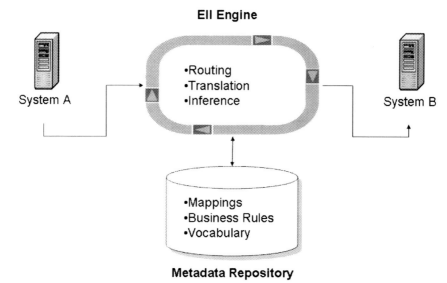

Figure 17: Semantic integration solution architecture

In this scenario, the EII solution is comprised of the collaborative efforts of the Metadata Repository and a routing, transformation and inference engine. There may be other components that actually handle the execution of business rules and applied mapping that the EII engine will rely on for additional processing..

It is important to note that, usually, the biggest hurdles to success in building these types of solutions are data governance and cooperation across departmental boundaries, to establish a common vocabulary. In the most successful cases, a senior executive sponsored the creation of a separate group empowered to exact cooperation from each department in the research and creation of this vocabulary. Consequently, the costs associated with creation and staffing of this group paled in contrast to the cost savings achieved on individual integration projects, which typically were completed faster and at a lower cost.

Key Concepts

1. Modeling is an important way to abstractly provide meaning to intangible or culturally different entities.
2. Closed modeling techniques, such as O-O and E/R cannot support the needs of dynamic information modeling. Instead we need open models like the triple.
3. Semantic structures are also an important part of conveying meaning. The Semantic Web intends to convey meaning of Web content to human and machine agents.
4. Semantic integration brings systems and data together through establishing a common understanding.

"One man's data is another man's metadata"
– Anonymous

The Role of Metadata in EII

Savvy information technology professionals are often frustrated by the lack of investment in turning the organizational data—a lazy or non-performing asset—into an asset that yields a return. Sometimes, this savvy IT professional is reminiscent of a toothless miner during the start of gold rush of 1849, who, standing in front of his executives is heard crying out, "There's gold in them thar hills!" Those who were open-minded and listened to the miner became very wealthy. Those who dismissed him as a crazy old coot soon found themselves on the back end of that gold rush, paying more for equipment, and working harder to extract the small left-over deposits that remained, once the easy pickings were gone.

Like those who dismissed the miner, not establishing a strategy to turn your data into an asset yielding a return means that you will be playing catch-up with your competition in the future, paying more to get it done faster, and having to dig deeper to gain back a competitive advantage.

The right data can identify where more investment is needed, how to spend less to achieve the same results, and improve our processes overall. However, trying to leverage data as an asset without capturing and organizing the critical metadata surrounding it is akin to mining for gold with your bare hands. Metadata is a critical component for understanding and mining the data you have, while also describing the role of the data within processes in the organization.

Understanding Metadata

If you work with data for a living, then you are bound to cross the fine line that divides data and metadata, no matter how much you try to avoid it. Answer the following question for yourself, "Is the address at the top of a business letter data or metadata?" There is no right or wrong answer to this question; it depends on your perspective. If you perceive the body of the letter as the data, then, to you, the other parts of the letter, such as the date and the address would be metadata. However, if you are the recipient of the letter, and interested to know where to send a response, then you might view the address as data; being that it is key content, not supporting data. This now leads us into the discussion on defining metadata.

When people try to define metadata, they often say that metadata is data about data or data that describes data. In a basic and elementary way, this is a true statement, but it is highly generalized and remiss in explaining that metadata assists in establishing context around data, without having to change that data.

> Metadata is data that helps both people and machines to come to agreement on what is being analyzed or discussed.

The following example illustrates how metadata delivers context around data. If you live in the United States of America and look at any financial statement, you will most likely notice a '$' in front of dollar amounts. The dollar sign is metadata that is pre-pended on to the data to make it clear to anyone viewing this number that it represents US dollars. A '€' placed before that amount changes the context—the value—of the dollar amount significantly, but does not change the actual amount. Thus, $123.00 is not equal to €123.00 unless the exchange rate from US dollars to Euros is 1:1. This still represents 123 something, but the metadata identifies what that something is.

Additionally, we can change the $123.00 from money we have to money we owe with the addition of a '+' or '-' placed in front of the value. These symbols denote a context of credit or debit. Thus, metadata does not always work in isolation, but instead, there can be multiple metadata components, working together, to provide a complete context, and thus convey information or intelligence about the data being discussed.

It is for this reason that some people say that:

Data + Metadata = Information

When both components—data and metadata—are provided the results deliver contextual understanding of the overall data. Suppose someone offered to sell you a car for ten-thousand. Would you accept? Hopefully, you would not. At least not without first capturing the critical metadata you need to make that decision, which is ten-thousand what? Dollars? Rubles? Pesos? Making decisions without the right information can land you in the poorhouse. Yet, everyday, millions of organizations make critical decisions without first having the proper information—information that is derived by having the right supporting metadata.

An additional value of capturing metadata is that it can make data more reusable, which adds to the return on data as an asset. Assume that an article discussing a budget deficit prints "$300 billion"; the way we'd expect to communicate this to a reader. However, just because the printed result tightly associates the data and the metadata, does not mean that the systems that authored and printed that article have to follow suit. Indeed, we can capture the metadata as an annotation in the source for the article using a tagged-based language like the Extensible Markup Language (XML) in the following way:

> The budget deficit for 2003 is now <amount currency="USD" multiplier="1000000000.00">300</amount>

Now the publisher can develop automated rules to deliver this same content to a European community whereby the dollars values would also be represented in Euros. For example:

> The budget deficit for 2003 is now $300 billion (approximately €375 billion)

Capturing metadata enhances the value of your data by allowing it to satisfy the needs of multiple audiences. Capturing that same metadata in a way that automated processes can identify and use increases the level of reusability across processes.

Metadata also helps us achieve increases in productivity. These increases are the result of first capturing the metadata, and then being able to relate it with the underlying raw data, later in time. In this particular case, we have two pieces of metadata that are important to us: the metadata that directly describes the underlying data, such as the dollar sign we discussed earlier, and the rule that describes how to apply that metadata. In this case, the rule would be "apply the dollar sign when the value represents US dollars."

The best way to explain how the use of metadata increases productivity is to illustrate it based on the needs of a health and human services case worker. The job of the case worker is so difficult because of the complex relationships between humans. For one child, the case worker could require the files for an additional two to ten individuals. It's then the job of the case worker to develop a map of how all these people relate to each other, and what impact they have to the case. The map that the case worker develops, which describes the relationships between all parties involved with a particular case, is the metadata for that case. Once that metadata is compiled, the case worker can efficiently make decisions about child placement, guardianship, etc.

Here are some additional examples of metadata in our information universe:

- The author of a word processing document, the annotations on a collaboratively developed text
- The comments in source code
- The attributes in XML documents
- The computational models in a financial spreadsheet

Taken by themselves, these pieces of data have meaning only to the process that they are a part of. However, as a whole, these pieces of data are valuable assets toward understanding data lineage and organizational processes. As we will see later in this chapter, it is important to create a structure for capturing and evaluating these pieces of data in their entirety.

Metadata and EII

The more metadata you are able to capture that corresponds to how your data is used, where it resides, and what is looks like, the more likely it is that you will have a successful EII initiative. As stated in chapter 2, EII is the automated process of turning raw data into information. Accomplishing this task requires a comprehensive "roadmap" that tells us what data to start with, where that data is, what processes and contexts the data relates to, and how that piece of data relates to other pieces of correlated data in a group. Hence, we rely on our foundation of metadata to provide us with the roadmap we need to make this transformation.

Since EII is just now emerging as an approach to data integration, an EII solution will have many different facets. Some EII solutions are going to be very low-level, which means that they will operate at the physical layer of data storage and representation. These solutions will require metadata that provides an understanding of the structure and location of the raw data to perform their tasks. Moreover, these solutions will require more manual intervention in the formation of the roadmap, and the metadata helps provide input into that development process.

More advanced EII solutions will provide support for incorporating semantics with the raw data, in order to provide meaning and context. Advanced solutions usually require less human intervention, and attempt to integrate data more dynamically; therefore, they require more metadata to guide them in this process. These solutions will require some of the low-level metadata, in addition to semantic dictionaries, taxonomies, and ontology. Metadata plays an important role, regardless of your approach toward data integration.

The rest of this chapter will focus on where to look for metadata and the types of metadata you should be paying attention to with regard to EII.

Start With a Focus on Business

Why do we hire individuals with experience that is specific to a particular industry? One of the reasons we hire them is that they understand the vocabulary—the lingo—of the business environment in which we operate. At the end of the day, it is the understanding of industry vernacular that makes the difference between a person who must climb a learning curve, and one that can jump right into action. It is not an understanding of the business processes, since these are often radically different from organization to organization, but, instead, the ability to know how the industry semantics relate to a business process that, ultimately, makes them valuable.

Having a command of the business vocabulary enables us to communicate around the needs of the business. The following is a true story that illustrates how losses and expenses occur in business due to misunderstandings that are rooted in the semantics of business terms.

> Recently a customer requested that their travel agency book a ticket for him on a flight the following week, but when he arrived at the airport he was bewildered as there was no ticket waiting for him. As it turns out, to

the travel agency, booked means reserved, not ticketed. To the customer, booking the trip implied both reserved and ticketed. Ultimately, the travel agent suffered a loss due to this misunderstanding, and had to reimburse the client the additional cost of purchasing a ticket at the last minute.

Most businesses have little or no idea how much money they lose every day because of misunderstandings like these. We see them most often in services industry outlets such as restaurants, repair and retail, where the ambiguity of a word or phrase can result in the business having to assuage the customer's anger or frustration; usually at a loss. If this happens often enough, it will impact the bottom line!

Believe it or not, the most important metadata is the set of words and phrases that you use to describe your business and business activities. If you're in the health care industry, term such as *"vaccine"* and *"insurance waiver"* provide the basis for communication with other employees, suppliers and customers. Yet, most organizations never realize the power of capturing and organizing these terms in a way that they become the active ingredients for integration of all data and systems within their organization.

Given the tendency of many businesses to view their Information Technology department as an expense rather than an investment, it is understandable that developing staff and software to support the notion of vocabulary management would not be a priority. Yet, all of their business processes and information systems rely on these terms in some form or another. Following through with our healthcare industry example, this usage may take the form of a schema in a database, where the name of a field is *vaccine* or the schema is called *insurance waiver*. These terms also appear on our reports and on the input screens used by humans to enter data into a system.

As ubiquitous as these terms are within and around our systems, business spends relatively little on understanding where terms like use of vaccine or insurance waiver are used as part of existing automated processes. Moreover, the term within the organization can become ambiguous depending upon the system and department that it is used in. Often times, this can end up impacting a business, as we illustrated at the start of this section.

CompuCredit of Atlanta, Georgia is an excellent case study in the value of understanding and capturing the vocabulary of the business. Their drive for speed, efficiency and ability to quickly and easily integrate newly acquired portfolio information provided fertile ground for the exploration of new integration technologies. By capturing and using their metadata, they not only created and solved their portfolio data integration problems; but they created an entirely new way to use their data across other processes and applications.

CompuCredit is in the business of providing credit to high-risk candidates. Growth in this business can occur in two ways: 1) direct marketing and 2) acquisition of existing credit card portfolios. In the latter case, integrating a new portfolio of existing credit card customers into an existing set of services can be a daunting task. However, because CompuCredit has taken the time to capture and categorize their key business terms, they are able to quickly integrate new portfolios by mapping their data into CompuCredit's common representation.

Step one in capturing your business vocabulary is to establish a registry of terms that can be used as part of downstream processes. By capturing these key terms, the organization can work from a common understanding and ensure that there is a unique description for each term within the business. As we will see shortly, terms will refer to different parts of processes, or contain different attributes depending upon context, but they should also have single meanings to the organization as well. The explanation shown in Figure 18 may help to clarify how this is possible.

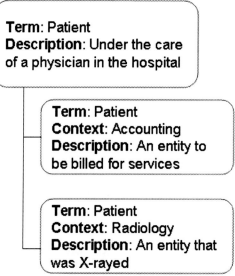

Figure 18: Business term hierarchy

For many hospitals, the term *patient* is used ambiguously depending on whether you are communicating with Accounting or Radiology. However, for the hospital administrator, who is responsible for the hospital's profitability and is interested in the patient as a holistic entity, he/she wants everyone working in the hospital to recognize that a patient is one thing and one thing only—someone under the care of the hospital.

Registries of business terms make for excellent references for new employees, as they will have a place to search for terms that they may not be familiar with, as they come across them in their everyday dealings. It becomes a customized dictionary for the business.

More importantly, a registry of business terms becomes the basis for the organization's logical representation of all data going forward. Through this logical abstraction, data can more easily be accessed and integrated without reliance on specialized programming skills. This logical abstraction also insulates our applications from change.

The database world has used this technique for years to insulate applications from changes to the physical database structures.

Database management systems allow administrators to create logical views. These views provide application developers the façade of working with the underlying data, but instead they are accessing the data through a level of indirection (see Figure 19).

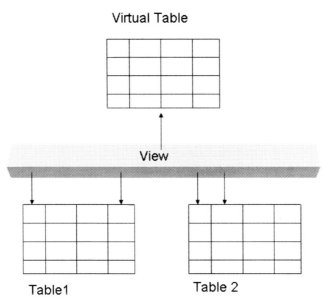

Figure 19: View of multiple database tables

A logical abstraction provides transparency for the organization. Transparency is important because it insulates us from changes in the physical implementation and has been an active goal for the computing industry since the advent of the network. The concept of the Internet only works because a layer of transparency was added to allow us to substitute human-readable monikers for what would otherwise read as complex and technical Internet addresses. The Internet and the World Wide Web would not have become as ubiquitous as it is if you had to remember 216.109.118.68 instead of Yahoo.com.

EII uses metadata to provide a transparency layer which hides the data formats, structures, and locations behind middleware that manages these details on behalf of the application. Thus, the user of the application can focus on using business terminology instead of arcane field names. In turn, transparency minimizes the need to update software and applications whenever the underlying data structures and data sources change or move, thus lowering the overall cost of developing and maintaining these applications.

Additionally, the business terms that comprise the transparent layer can be defined as either a single term, or they can be an aggregate structure composed of a hierarchy of business terms (see Figure 20). It is this hierarchy that provides us with context surrounding the use of the business term in our organization. For instance, we can define "Total Balance" globally across the company to mean the total amount outstanding on an account. However, when this term is further incorporated into the context of a "Billing" hierarchy, the "Total Balance" can take on additional meaning that means the total amount at the close of business on a particular date. A misunderstanding between semantic differences between these two, at least in this particular case, can have both legal and financial ramifications for the business.

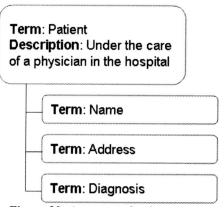

Figure 20: Aggregate business term

Within each of these terms, either fixed or user-defined attributes are contained to allow the transparency layer to provide more intelligence. Examples of these attributes include: a description, data type, the author or creator of the term, the list of users who can modify these attributes and the term's definition. This last attribute, the term's definition, is especially meaningful to the business term, as we will see in later chapters

There's an interesting side effect that occurs when you start with a business focus—the business has to be involved. Organizations that have been wildly successful at using Information Technology as an enabler to grow their business, understand the importance of a close alignment between business and IT. UPS is one such company. It has spent a significant amount of effort to ensure consistency of business terms across its organization. This effort has enabled them to ensure that technology does not become an inhibitor to change, in a fiercely competitive environment.

Unfortunately, UPS is not a typical case-study where IT and business work hand-in-hand, with the side-effect often being that the line-of-business develops their own information systems without IT involvement. Other times, IT is involved, but there is a genuine lack of understanding of the nuances of the business, which, in turn, translates into applications that cause the business users frustration.

Putting business first forces IT and the business to work closely together to define and establish the base of terms that will become the model for all downstream processes, as well as, the development of new applications. Hence, business is leading the way and defining a core component within the application development lifecycle.

Metadata: Helping IT and Line-of-Business: Working Together

In a majority of cases, the IT organization within a company is seemingly disconnected from the line-of-business. This disconnect can take many forms. For example, line-of-business is procuring and implementing its own information solutions around their function. Then, the IT department is developing new applications, based on requirement that they've misunderstood. Oh, and there are battles going on over data governance within this organization. However, as more senior executives begin to realize the reliance that the company has on its digital assets, such as data and metadata, the heavier the emphasis they begin to place on having a better working relationship between IT and line-of-business.

An example of one company that has invested heavily in enhancing the relationship between IT and line-of-business is Telus, Inc., Canada's largest telecommunications provider. Telus has created an entire team—called the QuickWin Team—that is focused on bridging the gap between IT and line-of-business. Telus is successful because they do not expect IT and line-of-business to put aside their political and philosophical differences overnight. Instead, the role of the QuickWin team is to work with line-of-business to develop a stop-gap solution to their information needs within a short period of time, usually within 90 days. This solution, along with a full analysis of the line-of-business needs produced by the QuickWin team, provides the basis for IT to develop a robust and maintainable solution, using traditional life-cycle management and software development techniques. In essence, the QuickWin team is formulating the set of metadata that line-of-business and IT will use to communicate when the long-term solution is developed.

CompuCredit is another company that realizes the value of their digital assets and has worked hard to develop a strategy for bringing IT and Line-of-Business together. In CompuCredit's model, line-of-business is responsible for capturing the business terminology and processes, in a clear nomenclature that is represented using an abstract notation. This abstract notation will then be implemented by IT professionals. This is in contrast with the older model of requirements gathering being led by the IT group, followed by a period of "develop and then deliver."

CompuCredit's model uses an abstract notation that both business and IT can share and understand. The shared notation is a critical component that provides a common basis for IT and business to agree upon. Once the shared notation is captured, all future work will be based on this notation, which minimizes the opportunity for misunderstanding and speeds the time for delivery of solutions.

Understand Your Data

In the information technology universe, the physical world where data is physically stored, there is a complex environment comprised of varying media, storage formats, data formats, and access methods. This complexity requires discipline, methodologies and technologies to keep it organized and managed. However, due to the nature of rapidly changing business environments, believing that homogeneity is the answer is a faulty grail that will lead to unnecessary delays and potential failure.

Thus, creating silos of data that are dedicated to a particular business function, helps us to keep pace with these ever changing needs. Therefore, lack of visibility across these silos should be an expected side-effect that requires us to integrate as needed, to meet the needs of the larger entity—the enterprise. Meeting this expectation will require us to have deep knowledge of the metadata that underlies each of these silos.

There are two steps to meeting the requirement to understanding our data. The first step concerns capturing and cataloging our current data assets so that we have a solid understanding of our existing systems environment. The second step concerns adding new processes and systems on top of our existing environment with full knowledge of what we already have, and additions we may want to make in the future.

Let's explore these steps through an analogy of transportation systems. Imagine that you are tasked with renovating a city to relieve traffic congestion. The first thing to realize is that there is a number of modes of transportation all running in the city already, such as trains, roadways for buses and cars, bike paths and sidewalks. It's not realistic to believe that you can replace all these with one type of transportation for the entire city, just as it is not realistic to believe you can replace all data facilities with a single one. Therefore, the area to concentrate on is how these systems work together, and then provide better methods of transferring from one mode of transportation to another. It also means that you may have to change some transportation routes in the process. As a result, you are integrating your transportation systems.

This is primarily a knowledge engineering task that requires human effort to analyze the existing transportation systems and understand their metadata requirements, such as requirements for power, contribution to pollution, proximity to business centers and schools, etc. We will use tool to help catalog this metadata, and we will use it in helping us build models for simulation. In the metadata world, these are our metadata repository and data/code analyzers.

Still, tools do not remove the need for humans in this process, which means that it is not very scalable and could be very expensive. Would you undertake modifying the city transportation systems without first understanding these issues? Probably not. Yet many organizations undertake similar efforts around their information systems, without the equivalent levels of supporting data. This is yet another reason why investing in metadata management is critical to the organization.

Now that we've handled the case of our legacy transportation we can move forward. The city council has decided, that in addition to the current modes of transportation, it wants to add a monorail system to alleviate further congestion. How will you integrate this new mode of transportation? As you can see, it is not going to replace the existing modes of transportation, just as you're not going to decommission any of your legacy data sources anytime soon. However, you do have hindsight, which means that during the design of the monorail system, you're going to think about how it can integrate with the existing transportation systems. This is exactly what we're going to do with our new systems moving forward. You're going to create another transportation silo, and that is okay, because it has added value to the city as a whole, just as your new silo of data will have added value to the organization as a whole.

As we saw with our first step above, you effectively have to reverse-engineer the current set of transportation systems. Reverse-engineering is a time-consuming task that has significant downstream repercussions. To further illustrate the level of complexity surrounding this reverse-engineering we will review the requirements needed to accomplish this with one of the oldest data management systems—VSAM[9].

VSAM is a very low-level interface for data storage, typically used on the mainframe. Since it is such as low-level interface, all the data management functions are delegated to the application, which means that all the metadata about the structures, fields, record ordering, etc. are locked away in the programming source code used to develop that application. While VSAM has extreme versatility and speed as two of its characteristics, it is notorious for its lack of understanding about what it manages.

It is a less arduous process when we need to do this with newer technology, such as Relational Database Management Systems (RDBMS), which usually have a method of accessing the field names, data types, and indexing metadata for requesting applications. While having access to this type of information can make the reverse-engineering process easier, it does not obviate the need to also examine programming source code for the meaning of this data. That is, one of the key premises of RDBMS technology is data normalization for purposes of reducing data redundancy and improving reusability. However, this process breaks the explicit relationship among data, thereby forcing the application to impose these relationships instead. Thus, one cannot necessarily understand the structure of the database even though the metadata is readily available without reverse-engineering the code for the application.

One of the biggest problems with developing EAI solutions is that the packaged application environments typically impose intricate relationships on data elements, making it very difficult to access the underlying database management system directly. Thus, in addition to the type of metadata that the RDBMS provides, we also have to understand the semantic conventions of the packaged application in order to have a complete understanding of the data and how it is used.

---

[9] Virtual Storage Access Method

On the positive side, there is a number of tools that can help with the reverse-engineering effort, by examining the data structures trapped inside the source code and assigning meaning to them. This data can then be captured for association with downstream processes and related business terminology. We will see in an upcoming chapter exactly how this is accomplished.

Understand How Your Data Is Used

All organizations have processes that dictate how they do business. Sometimes these processes are well documented, and other times they are evolutionary patterns passed from employee to employee, like folklore. In many cases, we achieve increases in productivity and scale by automating some of these routine processes. When we do, we create business process metadata, which are effectively the models for implementing these processes in a digital form.

Incorporated into these models are the inputs to the process, the rules for when the process gets executed (also known as an event), a description of the process (also known as the logic) and the outputs expected from running the process. Embedded in these processes are references to the data that we have already captured and catalogued. Thus, by understanding our business processes we can begin to understand how data is used within our organization. Armed with this metadata, we can derive the implementation for executing this model dynamically.

Unfortunately for most organizations, this all important business process metadata is often locked in obtuse programming languages, which can only be understood by those skilled in deciphering its code. To clarify this point, all developers cannot decipher all programming languages. A COBOL developer cannot read a C++ program and understand its content. Thus, as technology progresses and we create systems with diverse language sets, we increase the cost of keeping those systems in production by requiring the availability of programmers for each language we use.

The requirement to have programmers skilled in certain programming languages will not dissipate in the short term, but we can make it easier and less costly to maintain the code if we capture the business process metadata the code implements, in a reusable form. Therefore, our goal should be to extract the business rules from the applications and allow them to be defined using a common business terminology.

The following programming code example helps clarify this point.

```
char * thisCodeWillForeverBeTrappedInMe(char *p)
{
    // ensure that the string doesn't break
        // the corporate standard for addresses of 55 characters

    if (strlen(p) > 55)
       return substr(p, 0, 55);
    return p;
}
```

In this example, we have a module of C programming language code that ensures that street addresses will not exceed a fifty-five character limit; a limitation probably imposed to support a legacy data structure. Notice that this rule is hard-coded, which requires a programmer to make the modification, should this limit change in the future. Additionally, it is extremely difficult to identify and locate all the modules of code that are managing these types of policies for all the data in the organization. The greatest real-world example we have of this to date, is the Y2K problem and there are undoubtedly similar snafus that will emerge over time.

The effort to extract the business rules metadata from existing code is similar to the effort to extract the structural metadata from the physical stores that we discussed in the previous section, with one exception. Programming languages all follow a well-known grammar, which enables us to more easily develop tools to scan and extract business rules in an automated fashion. But, many of these tools assume the presence of the original source code in order to complete their task. In the event that the original source cannot be located, source can be built using the machine language executable, but this usually produces less than favorable results.

Optimally, the following example would be how we would like to have our business process metadata captured:

Address Length Rule

CHECK *address* LENGTH <= *address_length*
ON TRUE CONTINUE
ON FALSE TRUNCATE *address*

Where the words in all capital letters represent pre-defined functions, the italicized words represent either literal values or business terms that will be resolved at the time of execution. Consider the difference between these two sentences to determine if a credit card company should provide a credit limit increase:

> *Connect to database, read record for key [account number], subtract account balance from credit limit, if result <= 20% of credit limit, increase credit limit by 10%.*

and

> *If account_balance <= 20% of credit_limit for account [account number] increase credit_line by 5%.*

The first sentence is highly technical and writing it requires specialized skill, whereas the second sentence could be generated by a subject matter expert. This is the value of capturing both the business vocabulary and the business process metadata outside of traditional programming methods.

One of hurdles facing the industry at the time of this writing, with respect to capture of business process metadata, is that the industry has not chosen a major candidate to standardize representing business process metadata. One standard that has been put forth is RuleML (www.ruleml.org), which was designed to help interoperability between business rules engines, such as ILog JRules, Microsoft

BizTalk, Jess, etc. At the same time, the business process management market has matured quickly, yielding its own approach to capturing business process metadata with its forthcoming standards, such as the OASIS Web Services Business Process Execution Language (BPEL) (www.oasis-open.org). Now that these standards have emerged, so will the tools to support making capture of this metadata easier.

Context Can Be Defined By Events

Organizations are often driven by internal events, such as your manager telling you to complete a task, or external events, such as a customer calling with a complaint. Each of these events has metadata associated with it, such as the actions that need to be taken due to the event, and the data associated with the event itself.

Event metadata represents the relationship between an event, the data that generates an event, and the processes that act on an event. For example, in the case of the event identified by a person turning fifty indicates a state change in the raw data usually identified by age. Assume that a US organization recognizes that reaching the age of 50 entitles a person to join the AARP Foundation, which provides senior citizen benefits. The organization may have to offer different pricing for services they are currently offering this customer, or risk losing him to a competitor. The meta-event here, is the relationship between the state change—person turning fifty—and the set of events that need to be triggered because of this change in status.

Incorporating event metadata is an important part of identifying the context in which data is used within your organization. Thus including event metadata in the set of captured metadata directly relates to what data means to your organization. For instance, given the types of metadata we've discussed capturing so far, if we use "Birth Date" as the business term we wish to define, we can provide the following:

- The business taxonomy metadata surrounding this term, such as a description and properties
- The physical declarations of "Birth Date" in our existing data sources, data models and applications
- Which business processes require "Birth Date" as part of their execution

At this point, we cannot tell why "Birth Date" is captured by the organization. There is a reason why we take the time to capture the birth date of a person in our information systems. These reasons are far-ranging, from legal requirements to understanding market dynamics, but many of these reasons have associated events. In our birth date example above, the event associated with birth date is related to a change in status, which indicates that an action, such as providing the customer with a letter outlining benefits offered to senior citizens.

The model for capturing event metadata is:

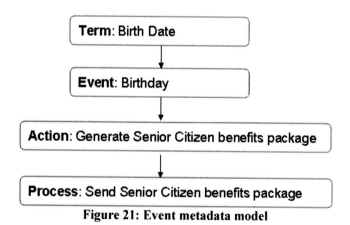

Figure 21: Event metadata model

In this model, there are relationships between Term and Event, between Event and Action, and between Action and Process. We will see, in the next section, how to capture these relationships. Suffice to say that our interest with regard to event metadata is to understand how a particular business term maps into the business drivers for the organization. That is, it is the event metadata that tells us how a discrete piece of data can impact our organizational structure, productivity and processes.

Additionally, like our business process metadata, if we can capture event metadata in a machine readable format, then it is possible to drive proactive management of these events. In turn, this can generate new information sources that help us to better manage our business by actively monitoring the effort expended in dealing with certain events.

Case in point, every time the assembly line stops in an auto manufacturing plant, losses mount quickly. This is because profit estimates take into account all the processes from managing the supply chain, to delivery on the dealer lot. When there is a change in the number of cars produced, or the time to produce these cars changes, so does overall profitability. In the case of an automobile manufacturer, such as General Motors, this type of event metadata can directly lead to shorter delays in manufacturing process, thus yielding more cars in the same time and generating expected, if not, more revenue.

Build Relationships between Your Metadata

Creating an information model that is closely aligned with our business goals, enables the transformation of the raw data distributed across the organization into usable information. A comprehensive information model includes the taxonomic structure of the business terms that apply to a particular organization and the relationships between the various silos of metadata that we have captured.

Hence, there is value in capturing and understanding the metadata that forms the foundation of our systems and data, but that value can be increased by also capturing the critical relationships between key business elements. Eventually, this leads us to being able to provide metrics around, and understanding the value we are gaining, from leveraging our data assets—our return on assets.

There are two ways we can describe our information model: as a taxonomy or as an ontology. Each of these is described in more depth below:

Taxonomy

Taxonomy—from the Greek word *taxis* meaning arrangement or division and *nomos* meaning law—is the science of classification according to a pre-determined system. The resulting catalog can be used to provide a conceptual framework for discussion, analysis, or information retrieval.

A trait of taxonomies is that they tend to be linear and tend to be represented as hierarchies (see Figure 22).

Class: Mammalia

Subclass: Theria

Infraclass: Eutheria

Order: Carnivora

Family: Canidae

Genus: Canis

Species: lupus

Figure 22: Mammal taxonomy for wolves

Other everyday examples of taxonomies include search engine results, yellow pages, Dun & Bradstreet and the United Nations Standard Products and Services Code (UNSPSC). Each of these orderings helps provide us with a finer granularity with which to represent a known entity.

In EII, taxonomy plays multiple roles. It enables us to organize our metadata into a class structure. However, it also provides us a means to represent our data relative to that class structure. In doing so, our data will have a greater context and thus, transfer more knowledge and information to a recipient. For example, since a wolf is of the class Mammalia, then we can infer that any other animal that is also Mammalia has middle ear bones, hair and mammary glands. Or, for a more business-oriented example, if a person is of the class account holders, and accounts have a credit or debit balance property, then we can infer that any account holder has a credit or debit balance.

These concepts have been heavily employed in information modeling and object-oriented programming (OOP). Indeed, taxonomy of classes is the basis for OOP technology and provides the concepts of inheritance and mutation of data structures.

Ontology

Whereas taxonomy provides us a means to categorize data within a given model, so as to be as coarse- or fine-grained as needed, ontology provides a method of defining and capturing an entire information model; this includes the taxonomy. For example, ontology can map a trained-by relationship between whale and trainer, but whale could be mapped into the classification of mammals within a taxonomy. Thus, a trained-by relationship would hold for whale or any mammal. Hence, ontology and taxonomy work together to form the structure of the model.

When we take disparate pieces of data and we bind them together through the use of a predicate structure—a set of well-defined relationships—we create what is known as an ontology. An ontology is an information model, usually limited to a particular domain, which includes all the terminology for that domain and the associated relationships between each term. Recently, there has been a significant rise in interest in ontology science as people have begun to realize that silos of data are far less informative than data mapped into a particular ontology. Data mapped into an ontology facilitates topological navigation of the data relative to other associated data and enables one to answer logically drawn questions.

For instance, if we are developing an ontology for a case worker in child protective services, it should model visibility across agencies with the goal of fully understanding a child's situation. This may mean that we need motor vehicle records, law enforcement records, justice records, hospitalization records, etc. Additionally, we will want to collect these pieces of information for any family member that could act or has acted in a role of guardian for the child.

To implement this information model we need to define the relationships between the child and the guardian(s) and the guardian(s) and these various agencies. Through these relationships we bind the metadata components together into a cohesive fabric that can be traversed and that ultimately delivers a structure capable of allowing automated inference. For example, in Figure 23 below, we can answer questions, such as "Was Jimmy's uncle ever in Jail?" or "Has Jimmy's uncle held a full-time job for the past two years?"

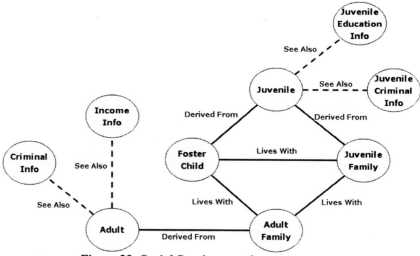

Figure 23: Social Services ontology

As you can see by the above figure, ontologies are often represented by directed graphs versus a hierarchy as we have seen with the taxonomy.

No greater example of this exists than the incidents leading up to September 11, 2001. As the factors leading up to these disastrous events unraveled, it became increasingly clear that the Federal Bureau of Investigation, Central Intelligence Agency, and local and state governments each evaluated reports in an isolated manner. A terrorism ontology did not exist to express potentially dangerous associations, such as flight school, Afghanistan and karate.

Of note, we're not implying that even if this ontology existed, the events in question were stoppable. We're just illustrating how important it is to understand the relationships between key pieces of data, in addition to the data itself, in making an informed decision. Additionally, developing an ontology is a heuristic process. It grows over time, based upon human experience, which means that it is unlikely that we might have even understood the implications of these relationships until the events of September 11 occurred.

Other benefits derived through the development of ontology include:

- Enabling reuse of domain knowledge. Ontology provides a framework in which those creating and using domain knowledge can share that knowledge with each other in a consistent manner.

- Analyzing domain knowledge. As an ontology develops, users of that ontology can use that body to quickly understand the state of knowledge surrounding that particular domain.

- Sharing common understanding of the structure of information among people or machine-based agents.

Ontology forms the basis for common understanding of principles and entities.

- Making domain assumptions explicit. Ontology has the ability to capture domain knowledge explicitly, which allows built-in assumptions to change more readily and allows new users to climb the learning curve faster since they are more quickly introduced to these assumptions. For example, if we had a sales ontology and in it we captured that sales refers to the person or entity that physically receives the product or service as the "Receiver", then this assumption can be captured as part of the ontology. Likewise, it can be aliased with other terms also used to represent this entity, such as "Customer" or "Ship To".

- Separating domain knowledge from the operational knowledge. Ontology allows us to define the separation between the instance and the form. For example, we can generically describe the components of a car and the algorithm for assembly of discrete components in the ontology, but we probably would not model the specifics for building a particular model.

There are two primary methods of ontology development: Top-down and bottom-up. Neither of these approaches is correct, the choice depends upon which information is most prevalent at the time of creation. The top-down approach starts with more definition of the most general categories first, before creating specialized classes within that category. This approach works best when all the details are not known in advance. For example, the Department of Motor Vehicles (DMV) might create an ontology for the types of vehicles that they register. The *vehicle* category could be specialized into *truck, SUV, and sedan.*

The bottom-up approach works best when many details are known about a particular domain, but the process of identifying similarities between or across the details will be worked out in the future. An example of this would be the creation of *light trucks, SUV, heavy-duty trucks and 18-wheelers.* Here the Department of Motor Vehicles may know the types of vehicles they've registered in the past, but is unsure how they want to classify the data due to the impact it could have on registration fees and license requirements.

Regardless of the approach you use, you can formulate relationships between the categories. There are two primary types of relationships in an ontology: implicit and explicit. Implicit relationships are those formed through the classification scheme itself. Sub-categories have an implicit relationship with their parent categories. Explicit relationships are formed across categories. For example, the DMV may want to create an "owns" relationship between the *vehicle* and *driver* categories. As we can see by this example, the predicate that binds the two categories together can be arbitrary; however, the act of defining this relationship is what creates semantic value. Thus, if these relationships are nonsensical then their value to the exercise will be nullified.

Semantic Metadata

Any language, computer or spoken, is made of two key components: Syntax and semantics. Syntax is the rules for putting linguistic elements together to form clauses or phrases. Thus, syntax allows us to form sentences, such as, "The boy has a blue hat." However, it is semantics that allows us to understand that the subject of the sentence (the boy) has (the predicate or relationship between the boy and the hat) a hat (a piece of clothing worn on the head) and the hat is colored (a property of clothing) blue. Therefore, semantics is the study of meaning based on the context formed by the sequence of known labels or symbols. In the sentence above, the labels that we understand are boy, blue and hat. Changing any of these words will change the meaning of the sentence.

Given that meaning is provided by context created by sequence, then it follows that meaning changes depending on how shallow or deep one of the labels falls within a particular taxonomy. For example, when a trainer is training a whale there are certain assumptions that can be drawn about the trainer, such as they probably work in an aquarium. If we say that the trainer trains mammals, then whale training satisfies this statement as true. However, we can no longer assume that the trainer works in an aquarium.

Thus, each level, deeper within a taxonomy, provides more detail about the subject matter. The combination of taxonomy and ontology, together, provide us with context (semantics) that can be analyzed by software to assist us in drawing out information from our raw data, and perhaps even creating knowledge about a particular subject. The following is a realistic example that brings to light the importance of having captured the required metadata for ontologies and taxonomies.

Law Enforcement Example

A red Toyota with the Virginia license plate X12-J32 and a cracked headlight was seen traveling north on I-495 in Rockville, MD at 2:45pm. A red foreign car was seen leaving the scene of an accident in Reston, Virginia at 2:18pm. Are these the same cars? Only inspection will determine this for sure, however, is there enough evidence for the police to pull over the Toyota?

1. Toyota is a Japanese car (via taxonomy)
2. Japan is a foreign country (via taxonomy)
3. Red is a color (via taxonomy)
4. Cars have color (via auto parts ontology)
5. Cars have license plates (via auto parts ontology)
6. The headlight is part of a car (via auto parts ontology)
7. Headlights can crack when hit (via traffic accident ontology)
8. Reston, Virginia is a place (via taxonomy)
9. Rockville, Maryland is a place (via taxonomy)
10. Rockville is north of Reston (via geography ontology)
11. There is a distance between Reston and Rockville (via geography ontology)

Based on these assertions, the question can be rephrased as: "If a red foreign car that was once involved in a traffic accident can travel from one place to another place, in a certain direction, in 27 minutes, then there is ample evidence for the police to pull over that car to examine it further."

As humans, our brains evaluate the original question without going through the minutia. However, taxonomies and ontologies allow software to infer automatically across continuous streams of information—something that the human mind is easily overwhelmed by. While we see the two statements presented together in a single paragraph, it is possible that these were actually alerts that were received independently of each other. Being able to assess the possible relationship between these pieces of information, using the power and speed of computers, allows us to enhance our lives by providing greater security, delivering swift justice, or saving a life.

Active and Static Metadata

So far most of the metadata we've discussed in our examples are of the static variety. That is, that they don't change often and when they do, it is part of a major change or replacement process. However, metadata can exist in two states: Active and static.

Active metadata is volatile, which means that it has the tendency to change often. This means that active metadata must carry with it an added dimension, which is time. Active metadata is designed to represent dynamically changing aspects of your system. For example, the Domain Name Service (DNS), which powers the Internet, is effectively a mapping to a particular machine located over the Internet. However, this mapping can change within minutes if a new domain is added or a server changes addresses.

If you're new to working with and capturing metadata, it would not be uncommon for you to overlook volatile data as a metadata source. Most people would classify this type of data differently because of the rate at which it can change. However, volatile metadata can sometimes be a critical component toward information integration as the time axis may be needed for proper context.

Key Concepts

1. Organizations should invest in managing their metadata because it reduces the cost for development and maintenance of information systems
2. Your metadata management strategy should align with the goals of the business rather than the needs of the Information Technology department
3. Treat the vocabulary of the business as a critical piece of metadata that should become the cornerstone of building an information model for the organization
4. Creating a logical view of your physical data will insulate future applications from change, simplify maintenance and enable end-users to more easily interact with the organizational data for increased productivity
5. Use the metadata to help you to understand the current structure of your information systems
6. The key to making your metadata actionable is to capture how the metadata relates to other data, processes, events and metadata
7. Leverage your metadata assets for both design-time and runtime functions within your organization

"Become aware of internal, subjective subverbal experiences, so that these experiences can be brought into the world of abstraction, of conversation, of naming, etc., with the consequence that it immediately becomes possible for a certain amount of control to be exerted over these hither unconscious and uncontrollable processes."
 – *Abraham Harold Maslow*

XML, SOA and EII

The title of this chapter may look like an attack of the three-letter acronyms, but these three technologies are an essential part of delivering an information integration infrastructure. These three technologies share a common attribute; they all provide a standards-based abstraction layer between the implementation and the users; an important aspect for integration of data. It is this layer of standards that simplifies the access, representation and delivery of data for purposes of informing and imparting knowledge.

There are many quality books on the market that focus explicitly on the Extensible Markup Language (XML) and Service-Oriented Architecture (SOA), so this book will provide only a brief introduction to these technologies, or just enough to help relate their usage within an overall EII solution.

Introduction to XML and SOA

In 1998, the World Wide Web Consortium (W3C) produced a recommendation for a new way to mark up data. XML is based on the principles of an older and more complex markup language called the Standard Generalized Markup Language (SGML). These languages provide the basis for us to "tag" data within a document so as to provide additional information about the tagged data. Initially, this tagging process provided instructions for printing machines to produce the tagged documents with the correct presentation format. With XML, this concept was extrapolated to the Web and, eventually, all types of data within our organizations.

The following is an example of a well-formed XML document:

```
<?xml version="1.0">
<Book>
     <Title>Enterprise Application Integration
          with XML & Java</Title>
     <Author>JP Morgenthal</Author>
     <Publisher>Prentice Hall PTR</Publisher>
</Book>
```

This book document provides the details on a single book. Since XML was used to distinctly encapsulate the text of this document, we can identify the title, author and publisher by simply viewing the document, but more importantly, we can also identify them by having a machine process the document. Hence, tagging data enables machines to identify parts of documents as easily as humans, and thus, illustrates the power and popularity of XML.

As XML became ubiquitously accepted as a way to represent data, both internal and external to organizations, it was a natural step to use XML to exchange data between applications. Initially, this was done in an ad-hoc manner. Eventually, standards evolved around inter-application communications based on the XML standard. Thus, Web Services was born.

The industry has not reached accord on a definition of Web Services, however they typically have the following attributes:

- Atomic—Web Services are an encapsulated software entities with clearly-defined interfaces
- Accessible—The same Web Service can be exposed via a variety of network transports
- Declarative—The Web Service interprets the steps for processing based on conditions defined by the input
- Composite—Web Services can be aggregated into more complex Web Services

Essentially, Web Services provide the basis for a loosely-coupled distributed application architecture, or as it is commonly being referred to these days, a Service-Oriented Architecture.

Of course the concept of a SOA is much more comprehensive than just an intra-application messaging scheme. The SOA covers multiple layers of the computing infrastructure, including data access, transformation, routing, business process management and line-of-business functionality (see Figure 24). However, the concrete description of SOA will continually be refined by the market, but can be defined by the following properties:

- SOA is a design pattern for applications
- SOA is loosely-coupled
- SOA applications can be bound at runtime
- SOA is platform neutral
- SOA is distributed
- SOA is point-to-point

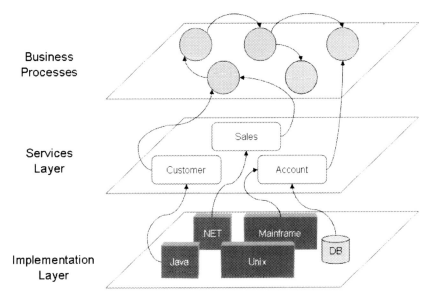

Business
Processes

Services
Layer

Implementation
Layer

Figure 24: Service-Oriented Architecture

Non-SOA EII

In the post-XML and Web Services world, it is an accepted fact that
SOA shall be an important component of any information integration
solution. The primary reason for this is that SOA provides an
abstraction in front of the various data formats and data access
mechanisms, so that accessing data can be viewed homogenously. Of
course, without SOA experience, this definition can sound like a bunch
of hocus-pocus nonsense. After all, there are few, if any,
organizations that are apt to say that their integrations were easy and
inexpensive. One way we can view the impact that SOA has on EII is
to examine our options for delivering an EII solution without Web
Services.

Note that there are many organizations that are using the approaches
we're about to discuss to deliver data aggregation and integration
within their organizations, without using SOA. However, experience
is beginning to demonstrate that SOA can simplify and speed the
execution of this type of work.

Straight Coding Approach

If you have the coding talent on staff, one of the most straightforward ways to undertake an information integration task is to develop an application specifically for this task. This approach follows a typical application development process. First, the requirements that will indicate which data needs to be integrated are gathered. For example, data required to support a customer service representative or health services case worker may reside in various applications and database management systems.

The most common approach to the fragmented data problem is to take extracts of the existing systems data and load it into a new database specifically designed to support this one task. The downsides to this approach are identifying and correcting dirty or outdated data, and the high overhead required to keep the databases synchronized and/or highly available once the right data is identified.

An alternative approach is to access the data directly from its current system. However, this introduces yet another set of complexities for the developer. First, the developer will need the capability to access the data across different platforms, such as a mainframe "green screen", flat files, non-SQL databases and SQL databases. Given that the developer can access the data directly, she can then focus on the task of retrieving the data, organizing it for display, and developing the routines to update the sources, should there be an update capability provided.

Assuming that all has gone well, this task probably will have taken a single developer more than two weeks per data source to develop and test. At the end of this process, the application can be deployed to the users, and all is well. However, one-off applications such as this one tend to exist in isolation and do not feed the reuse needed in order to support additional and similar applications that will no doubt be required in the future.

ETL Approach

The primary difference between the ETL approach and the straight coding approach is that instead of developing special applications for cleansing, aggregating and transforming the data into a new data source, you will use a commercial off-the-shelf tool. Since this approach typically works off of extracts of existing systems, timeliness of the data is often called into question. Again, there is nothing wrong with this approach, if timeliness of data is not a concern. In most of the EII applications that are being developed today, timeliness of the data is key. Sometimes, EII is even referred to as a "real-time" solution.

Of note, there is an emerging class of ETL that has many of the facets of EII associated with it. In this class of ETL, users are leveraging the capabilities of ETL to move and transform data in a real-time manner. That is, they are using newer and updated ETL tools that have dynamic and programmable interfaces, to execute an ETL process that generates views of disparate data. Classic ETL users will be quick to respond that they are using ETL to perform data aggregation in real-time, based on this capability. But in keeping with our definitions of the three practices of integration, it seems more likely that this approach is simply a case of tools functionality being confused with the role of the practice. In essence, these solutions are EII based upon our set of definitions within this chapter, but implemented with an ETL tools set.

EAI Approach

For purposes of this discussion, let's rely on our definition of EAI in Chapter 2, and not rely on the functionality of some of the products that support EAI implementations. The distinction is important, as you've seen earlier. Indeed, the EAI approach shown here will not be greatly differentiated from the SOA approach; except that SOA relies on more widely adopted standards.

Enterprise Information Integration: A Pragmatic Approach

The EAI approach to data aggregation requires the installation of adapters for each unique data source or application that will be included in the integration. Since EAI is about behavioral semantics, each adapter will expose a set of programmatic interfaces, typically based on the function of the application housing the data. For example, an accounting system will most likely have functions for retrieving balances, posting transactions and getting details of transactions. A well-designed adapter, if you're lucky, will include a set of "get all" functions, such as "get all transactions", but most will require multiple calls to a basic "get" function to retrieve the required data.

In addition being tied to a tightly-bound interface for accessing the application data, you are also bound to the formats in which the data is provided. For example, if the application's developers decide to provide the transaction date as a number that represents the number of seconds since some arbitrary start date, then you will need to have software that can transform that number into a date format that can be used by the application.

With the introduction of XML, several vendors redesigned their adapters so that they are now much more focused on document-based interfaces, in addition to the behavioral interfaces. However, this only proves the value of SOA for these types of approaches.

As you can see from these three approaches, information integration solutions can, and are, being developed without the use of Web Services and SOA. The primary benefits of SOA to an EII solution are abstraction and loose-coupling. Web Services and the supporting components of a SOA hide many of the low-level intricacies required to locate and access data as part of aggregating data from disparate data sources and applications.

Components of a SOA

An SOA is more than just using Web Services for application development. It's also a pattern for software development, based on loosely-coupled components, and it is supported by a growing number of standards and software components. The following discussion provides an overview of some the basic components of a SOA.

Web Services Platform

Probably the most important component of a SOA is the Web Services platform. This is the scalable component that will handle the receipt and execution of Web Services requests.

The platform component is the most basic of all parts of the SOA. If using a SOAP-based Web Services approach, then the Web Services platform will be responsible for opening the SOAP envelopes, processing any pertinent headers and extracting the body for passing onto the implementation. For more information on implementation, see the Sidebar entitled "Approaches to Web Services: SOAP vs. REST" below.

Approaches to Web Services: SOAP vs. REST

A discussion of Web Services cannot be complete without addressing the issue of how Web Services are implemented. The two major approaches to implementing Web Services are SOAP and REST.

Simple Object Access Protocol, or SOAP, as it is known now, was first introduced by Microsoft. SOAP defines an XML structure for enveloping a Web Services request and a protocol framework for exchange of SOAP-based messages. This means that the SOAP approach defines the format for encapsulating a message for submittal to a Web Service, acceptable values for submission, the format and values for responses, and acceptance and denial of the submission from the Web Service.

An additional component for SOAP-based implementations is that they are not necessarily tied to using Web-based protocols for communication. Indeed, SOAP-based implementations can also use Simple Mail Transfer Protocol (SMTP) and Java Messaging Services (JMS), in addition to HTTP, as acceptable protocols for delivery of SOAP-based Web Services requests.

REST stands for Representional State Transfer. REST is an architectural approach to implementing Web Services that leverages the protocol and simplicity of using the Web as a means to implement a services-oriented architecture. In a REST approach, the XML message body, which might be found in our SOAP implementation, would simply be POST-ed to a Web address. The key point for REST fans is that the approach is compatible with existing legacy applications and adheres to basic Web standards, thereby increasing the chances for interoperability.

While some in the industry are adamant that REST and SOAP are conflicting approaches, they are not significantly different; especially if SOAP uses HTTP to deliver its SOAP requests.

More information about SOAP and other Web Services standards that are part of the core platform can be found in "Appendix A: Core Technology Overview."

WS-Stack Implementations

Web Services is a rather simplistic approach to distributed computing. The predecessors to Web Services, such as CORBA and DCE offer a much more robust set of supporting services, such as naming, event management, addressing and security. However, the advantage of Web Services over these existing, robust distributed computing mechanisms is its simplicity, openness and lightweight nature.

The community responsible for continued enhancements to Web Services and SOA realizes the need for the robustness described earlier, but it needs to be done using the same premises that have driven the ubiquity of Web Services. To this end, vendors and standards organizations have been working to deliver additional specifications to support reliable messaging, event management, event notification, security, addressing, and transactions. Together, these, and other standards that will eventually be developed, will comprise the Web Services stack. Several of the stack's components are described in more detail below.

WS-Reliable Messaging

A Services-Oriented Architecture is fundamentally based on the ability to route and deliver messages in a reliable manner. In the absence of standardization for reliable messaging, many companies are satisfied to use HTTP in a synchronous manner as the primary messaging vehicle for their SOA, as this provides them the greatest level of openness. Others that are less concerned with openness, mainly because they have committed to a Java-based architecture in their organizations, have been able to use a Java Messaging Service implementation for their SOA.

Once agreement is reached on the WS-Reliable Messaging (WS-RM) standard, and enough products incorporate the standard into their Web Services platforms and Enterprise Service Buses, it will most likely become the primary means of ensuring reliability, regardless of the underlying transport mechanism.

WS-RM is designed to overcome lost, duplicated, or reordered messages. It does this by establishing a protocol that is shared between endpoints that either acknowledge message delivery or raise errors. SOAs can rely on one of four types of delivery assurances:

- AtMostOnce. With this type of assurance, messages will be delivered at most once, without duplication, or result in an error. However, it is possible that some messages in a sequence may not be delivered.
- AtLeastOnce. With this type of assurance, every message sent will be delivered. However, some messages may be delivered more than once.
- ExactlyOnce. With this type of assurance, every message sent will be delivered without duplication.
- InOrder. With this type of assurance, messages will be delivered in the order that they were sent. This delivery assurance may be combined with any of the above delivery assurances. It requires that the sequence observed by the ultimate receiver be non-decreasing. It says nothing about duplications or omissions.

WS-Notification/WS-Eventing

WS-Eventing offers a novel approach to handling latency issues in data aggregation within an EII solution. Most EII solutions take a very synchronous approach toward aggregation. In cases where a system cannot respond, because it is down or because the query takes time to process, it may be useful to allow the aggregation engine within the EII solution to subscribe to the data source, to be notified when the data is available. Additionally, this capability can be made available directly to the requesting agent, allowing the application to continue in the absence of an immediate response.

While WS-Notification and WS-Eventing may eventually support distinct roles in a publish/subscribe messaging architecture, their relation is close enough to be discussed in the context of a single topic. The goal of both of these specifications is to provide an open and interoperable method of allowing applications to subscribe for notification of systems events.

The following is a list of requirements for version 1.0 of the WS-Eventing specification, which, at a minimum, will become the basis for WS-Notification.

- Define means to create and delete event subscriptions.
- Define expiration for subscriptions and allow them to be renewed.
- Define how one Web service can subscribe on behalf of another.
- Define how an event source delegates subscription management to another Web service.
- Allow subscribers to specify how event messages should be delivered.
- Leverage other Web service specifications for secure, reliable, transacted message delivery.
- Support complex events topologies that allow the originating event source and the final event sink to be decoupled.
- Provide extensibility for more sophisticated and/or currently unanticipated subscription scenarios.

Additionally, WS-Eventing supports only a push-based asynchronous delivery mode, but does define a means for extending delivery modes within implementations as well as allowing these extensions to be expressed to subscribers.

WS-Addressing

WS-Addressing (WS-Addressing) increases overall interoperability across Web Service implementations by defining a consistent method of expressing endpoint references, which are a typical component of transport protocols and messaging systems. An endpoint represents a facility that can handle and process Web Services messages. Endpoints do not necessarily also have to process the Web Service request, but they can be responsible for routing and delivery to other endpoints.

WS-Addressing also defines a set of message headers that assists in the delivery and handling of Web Services messages. The types of properties that WS-Addressing defines in this regard include destination endpoint, source endpoint, reply-to endpoint, fault endpoint, Web Service action, and message identifier.

The following example illustrates the use of these mechanisms in a Web Service message that represents a call to a purchasing service.

```
<S:Envelope
   xmlns:S="http://www.w3.org/2003/05/soap-envelope"
   xmlns:wsa="http://schemas.xmlsoap.org/ws/2004/08/addr
   essing">
   <S:Header>
    <wsa:MessageID>
      uuid:ABCDEF01-ABCD-01234-ABCD-ABCD1234ABCD
    </wsa:MessageID>
    <wsa:ReplyTo>
    <wsa:Address>
      http://www.mybusiness.com/POAckService
    </wsa:Address>
    </wsa:ReplyTo>
    <wsa:To>
      http://www.yourbusiness.com/Purchasing
    </wsa:To>
    <wsa:Action>
      http://www.yourbusiness.com/SubmitPO
    </wsa:Action>
   </S:Header>
<S:Body>
```

114

```
    . . .
</S:Body>
</S:Envelope>
```

WS-Security

The WS-Security specification establishes a standard way to incorporate integrity and confidentiality into Web Services: specifically, at the Web Services messaging layer. Integrity ensures that information is not modified in transit, while confidentiality ensures data is protected so that only authorized parties can view the data. The WS-Security specification establishes a way to consistently encrypt, decrypt and digitally sign Web Services SOAP messages.

WS-Security can operate with a simple authentication in which there is a trust relationship established between the sender and receiver. An example of this would be if the sender and receiver establish a shared password to use for encryption and decryption. However, approaching security in this way can prove to be a daunting management task. An alternative approach is to use a trusted authority to provide the distribution of keys and an infrastructure to resolve their uses. For example, Verisign provides digital certificates that can be used for digital signing and for public key/private key encryption and decryption. In this particular case, Verisign will also verify that a certificate is authentic.

WS-Policy

In a distributed architecture, one of which is a Service-Oriented Architecture, it is very difficult to manage a group of distinct components as if they were a single managed entity. WS-Policy is an extensible grammar for expressing a policy that can be applied to multiple components, in a distributed architecture, in order to simplify use and management.

A policy can express the capabilities, requirements, and general characteristics of an entity, or group of entities. For example, a policy can specify privacy, transport protocol selection, authentication scheme, access levels and quality of service. These policies are established as a set of assertions that can be interpreted by the various agents that will process these policies at time of use. For example, a policy may specify the role that is required to use a particular Web Service, but it is up to the Web Service platform to handle authentication, role assignment and role checking before executing the Web Service.

Additional specifications that have been developed under the WS-Policy framework include:

- WS-PolicyAttachments – defines mechanisms for associating policies with policy subjects.
- WS-PolicyAssertions – a common set of assertions that are needed by all Web Services.
- WS-SecureConversation – defines mechanisms for establishing and sharing security contexts, and deriving keys from security contexts, to enable a secure conversation.
- WS-SecurityPolicy – indicates the policy assertions for WS-Policy that apply to WS-Security.

WS-Coordination, WS-AtomicTransaction and WS-BusinessActivity

Some EII solutions will rely on the capability of systems to derive data on demand, as part of a long-lived transaction, business activity, and workflow or business process. This places a requirement on the SOA to support the implementation of these actions in a consistent and atomic manner. An SOA without these capabilities places a burden on the EII solution to manage coordination and fault management across a set of services that will be used to aggregate or publish data. For this reason, the WS-Coordination, WS-AtomicTransaction and WS-BusinessActivity specifications have been developed.

WS-Coordination, WS-AtomicTransaction and WS-BusinessActivity are three distinct, but related specifications that provide a Service-Oriented Architecture with the capability to manage Web Services communications in a transacted manner. That is, it provides the SOA with assurances about the state of a service call, or coordinated service calls, and provides consistent failure and recovery semantics. Figure 25 illustrates the dependency among these three specifications.

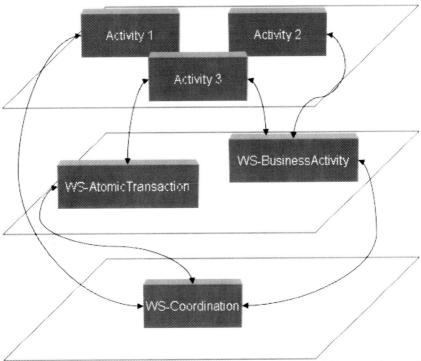

Figure 25: Dependencies for WS-Coordination, WS-AtomicTransaction and WS-BusinessActivity

The WS-Coordination specification is the base specification for WS-AtomicTransaction and WS-BusinessActivity. It describes an extensible framework for providing protocols that coordinate the actions across distributed applications. The goal of this framework is to provide a consistent way for applications to reach agreement on the outcome of distributed activities. A coordination service implements the protocols defined in this specification, to manage and propagate activations across a group of services.

The WS-AtomicTransaction specification implements transactional semantics, such as prepare, commit and rollback, but provides only an

117

all-or-nothing outcome. Each service that participates in a transaction will register with the coordination service. The coordination service, in this instance, will act as a transaction manager, notifying registered resources at each stage of the transaction, and returning a single outcome to the client application.

The WS-BusinessActivity specification provides a protocol for managing agreement across loosely-coupled services. It differs from the atomic transactions in that the entire activity may continue, even if there is a failure within a single participating service, and the exception handling is typically managed by an application, instead of the coordination service. Additionally, business activities may have long durations and a requirement to expire if they run past a certain date or length of time. EII data aggregation is a good example of a business activity that requires this type of coordination. It may be useful to have a partial data set return even if all the participating data services do not succeed.

Universal Description, Discovery, and Integration (UDDI)

Initially, UDDI was designed with the belief that it was going to be the master directory for all Web Services available on the Web. Indeed, there is an implementation of UDDI, called the Universal Business Registry (UBR) that is designed to act as a directory for publicly available services. The UBR is currently managed by four companies, Microsoft, NTT Com, IBM and SAP.

However, due to a greater level of adoption within companies than across companies, interest in using UDDI as an internal or private registry arose more quickly. Now, as a technical committee within the OASIS organization, the UDDI technical committee manages one common specification that facilitates the implementation of both private registries and the UBR, and facilitates communications between them.

The purpose of the UDDI in the SOA is to provide a service for location transparency of Web Services. When applications need to use a service, instead of wiring in the service information at the time of development, a service consumer can call upon the UDDI service to provide the location of the Web Services Definition Language (WSDL) files which describe the inputs, outputs and message structures of a Web Service. Once the application has the WSDL, it then figures out how to connect and use the service. This is often referred to as the Find, Bind and Execute model (see Figure 26).

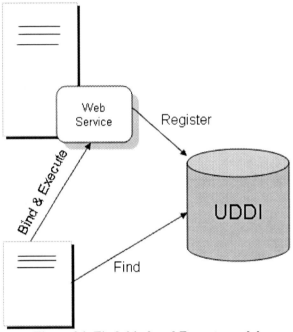

Figure 26: Find, bind and Execute model

Does UDDI obviate the need for a Web Services Metadata Repository?

The title of this sidebar is a common question that arises when analyzing the role of UDDI in a Service-Oriented Architecture. Many have found that UDDI is cumbersome to use and that its original design purpose—as an Internet directory for public Web Services—does not satisfy the need to centralize, control access, and manage Web Services on a large scale.

Indeed, if one delves into the inner workings of a UDDI repository, one is likely to come to one of two conclusions: a) the model is so loosely-coupled that it can be used to represent anything; or b) the model is too convoluted to easily develop new applications on top of. Developers who come to the conclusion described by option "a" have recognized that the abstraction was designed into UDDI in order to ensure future extensibility. The problem with this design is the lack of rigidity in defining how to "fill the model in," which leads to the inconsistent use of structures within a UDDI repository, and makes it very difficult to write applications that can leverage this metadata. Developers who come to the conclusion described by option "b" are most likely looking for a simple directory mechanism in which they can store WSDL and XML Schema documents, and to assist with deployment and location issues.

Regardless of which conclusion is drawn about UDDI, it does satisfy the basic need of find, bind and execute. However, this functionality comes at a high maintenance cost, complex search interfaces, loosely-defined rules for structure usage and a lack of support for access control, deployment and measurement.

The Role of SOA in EII

Since we have expressed the goal of EII as automating the process of turning data into information, there are some basic infrastructural requirements for making this happen:

- Data access – provides access and the capability to query data regardless of its location. This access can come in many different forms, such as application programming interfaces, proprietary messaging interfaces and directly reading the data from storage.
- Metadata – provides an understanding of the structure of the data we're working with, how that data relates to current organizational processes and what data is needed to provide a complete context.

- Aggregation – provides a means of taking disparate data and organizing it into a structure that can impart knowledge and context.

Web Services and SOA make it easier to implement these requirements. Primarily, Web Services offers an abstraction of both the underlying implementation for a service and hides the details of how that implementation represents data. Therefore, our data access requirement is simplified by providing a homogenous interface for retrieving data. That is, in addition to providing a consistent interface for the request and delivery of data from an underlying data source, the data can be normalized to be represented by standard XML Schema data types.

Of note, other data abstraction facilities, such as Java Database Connectivity (JDBC) or Open Database Connectivity (ODBC) provide a similar benefit, but in order to do so, they require our applications to integrate with low-level programming libraries. Web Services allows us to communicate with our data access facilities, using ubiquitous messaging facilities, such as HTTP and SMTP.

Web Services also provides an environment that is rich in metadata. For example, WSDL documents are all defined in XML, which allows any application to inspect and bind to a Web Service remotely. Additionally, these descriptions are important pieces of metadata that will help us provide more context about where the data came from, what processes the data is a part of, and the structure of the data.

Additionally, and this point is not limited to Web Services, XML Schema, which is used to define the structures that will be conveyed across Web Services, establishes a set of semantics that will be used upstream. It is the *Customer* schema that will define what elements of data are comprised within a structure that represents a customer. We will see, later in this book, that EII is a process of associating meaning and resolving instances within a particular context. Web Services offers us a basis for providing a one-to-one relationship between a word and resolving that word to its underlying meaning.

Finally, because Web Services uses XML as the format for receiving and responding to service requests, the process of aggregating data from disparate sources is greatly simplified. Indeed, since we know the structure of all the data from the WSDL files, we can map entire subsets of the resulting XML documents into a new document that will be used to satisfy the EII requests.

Key Concepts

1. A SOA is a design pattern for developing applications using loose coupling of components called Web Services.
2. Developing an EII solution without using a SOA is possible, but more complex and time consuming than using a SOA.
3. A robust SOA requires services, such as security, transaction management, policy management and event notifications.
4. XML and Web Services provide a means to simplify EII solutions development by abstracting the physical data formats, locations and types into a single homogenous access mechanism

"Our Age of Anxiety is, in great part, the result of trying to do today's jobs with yesterday's tools."
— *Marshall McLuhan*

Applied EII

Like all integration solutions, EII is very broad and can be applied to a wide array of problems. Primarily, EII offers organizations the ability to gain control over their disparate data and think about new ways to organize and view that data. Ultimately, EII enables applications that assist in digesting and understanding information. In this chapter we examine the types of applications that EII solutions enable.

EII can solve problems for multiple audiences. For data architects and software engineers, EII provides the means to capture, organize and leverage existing metadata, and drive reuse across applications. For business analysts, an EII solution provides a means to explore the types of data that the organization has been storing, and formulate new strategies for organizing and manipulating that data for tactical and strategic planning. Finally, for the IT organization, the EII solution can speed the delivery of data to internal and external customers
The following sections cover specific uses for an EII solution through case studies, and explore the overall requirements for EII in each problem domain. Characteristics of these examples are taken from real-world scenarios; however, they can apply liberally across all of examples provided in this chapter. Therefore, do not look at each of the sections below as separate silos that EII applies to in a unique way; especially since the most unique feature will most likely be the output or result of applying EII. Instead, notice the patterns of requirements that EII is attempting to satisfy.

Compliance Reporting

Compliance reporting is a diverse and confusing problem domain that is significantly data-driven. There are many areas of compliance that requires data correlation and aggregation solutions. Most often, compliance is a government requirement to ensure that individuals and companies meet government regulations. However, sometimes industry will also require compliance reporting, as a way of governing itself, as in the securities and credit card industries.

Two of the most pressing compliance requirements, today, are Sarbanes-Oxley and Basel II. Sarbanes-Oxley is also known as the Public Company Accounting Reform and Investor Protection Act. It was signed into law on July 30˙ 2002, and introduces new rules to protect investors by improving corporate reporting accuracy. However, for many public companies, the requirements for disclosure require the capture and auditing of data, which, for many, is not centralized, or even organized, in a way that facilitates easy access. See the reprint of an report by Ptak, Noel & Associates and Infostructure Associates entitled "Enterprise Information Integration and Sarbanes-Oxley".

Enterprise Information Integration and Sarbanes-Oxley

The real world is messy, and implementation of Sarbanes-Oxley reminds us just how messy it really is. As we have noted for years, most organizations keep their information in "archipelagoes" — multiple databases and data stores that are loosely related to some, but not all, other data stores. Data needed to show Sarbanes-Oxley compliance can show up anywhere — in the data warehouse, in the CFO's spreadsheet, in the company Email used to communicate financials, in the text files that the CEO's administrative assistant has created to draft the press release about results, even in the custom data store of the company's ERP system.

So when the auditor shows up to certify compliance, or (heaven forefend) an SEC lawyer shows up for discovery, how do you allow them aggregate and access to the data? For that matter, how do you yourself aggregate and access the data to see whether you will pass scrutiny?

Alas, for all too many companies today the answer takes the form of a slow, manual slog through each separate data store or each archipelago. Even when, as a previous piece has noted, proactive enterprises have bought and installed configuration control and infrastructure relationship mapping solutions, actually getting at the data requires separate access to separate systems. Not only does this annoy the auditor or SEC enforcer; it can cost real money, as the lawyers' billable hours for discovery skyrocket.

Consider the characteristics of an ideal solution to this problem:

- It should provide access to all your data stores of whatever type — Email, text, relational data, and custom data stored in applications, spreadsheets and graphic data.
- It should allow the auditor or discovery lawyer to issue one query across all these data stores — "Find me all instances of the word 'cover-up''.
- It should automatically adapt to change in the company's data stores, as when new types of data such as RFID inputs start showing up.
- It should scale to query across the terabytes of data in the typical large enterprise's information base in a reasonable time (less than an hour).

Oddly enough, a technology already exists that meets these requirements: Enterprise Information Integration (EII). EII provides a "veneer" or "façade" that looks to the outside like a full database management system, accessing a wide variety of data types. EII can:

- Provide access to a wide variety of data types, including relational data, flat files (text and spreadsheets), graphics and content (video and audio), Email, and even Web URLs, both inside and outside the company.

- Support the ability to issue one SQL-standard query across all of these data types.
- Auto-discover (and auto-rediscover) the company's data, once the company tells EII what data stores are out there (hence the need for configuration management).
- Scale, according to IBM tests, at least as effectively as the enterprise writing tuned queries to each of the data stores and then combining the results — and, remember, the enterprise's proprietary queries will have to be retuned and the combining operation rewritten constantly as each data store evolves independently, while EII adjusts to all that automatically.

So why hasn't EII yet become prevalent in Sarbanes-Oxley implementations? Well, for one thing, it remains less than visible to most CTOs, much less CEOs. Only IBM among major vendors is pushing EII for Sarbanes-Oxley as of yet; and even their business compliance marketing does not stress EII. And for another thing, most of today's EII implementations are point solutions, not spanning the entirety of an enterprise's data sources. Meanwhile, some business compliance solutions are "reinventing the wheel", writing their own EII-like functionality that typically spans fewer data types and is less scalable than today's EII engines. In other words, the opportunity is there, but few realize it.

However, as users gain experience with Sarbanes-Oxley, a "killer argument" for EII is becoming ever clearer — Email. More and more users are finding out that auditors do want to see an enterprise's hundreds of gigabytes of Email over the last five years; but today's querying systems are not well adapted to querying Email data. EII is.

About Infostructure AssociatesAs the first analysts to identify and report on EII, Infostructure Associates continues to track the evolution of the EII market, including its extension into areas such as business compliance. Our recent publications on EII include "Wanted: the Virtual Real-Time Enterprise; Needed: EII+ODS=VOS" at www.valleyviewventures.com. Additionally, competitive data on EII vendors can also be found at this Website.

About Ptak, Noel & Associates
With a belief that business success and IT success are inseparable, Ptak, Noel & Associates works with clients to identify, understand and respond to the implications of today's trends and innovations on the future of IT Operations.

www.ptaknoelassociates.com

Basel II is a framework that sets out details for adopting more risk-sensitive minimum capital requirements for banking organizations. Initiated to stem the tide of bank failures, Basel II was put forth by The Bank for International Settlements (BIS), an international organization, which fosters international monetary and financial cooperation, and serves as a bank for central banks. The Basel II framework reinforces these risk-sensitive requirements by laying out principles for banks to assess the adequacy of their capital, and for supervisors to review such assessments to ensure banks have adequate capital to support their risks. It also seeks to strengthen market discipline by enhancing transparency in banks' financial reporting. This combination of risk management and financial reporting traditionally requires up-to-the-minute data; another indicator that EII would be an excellent adjunct to delivering on these requirements.

Note: EII does not make a system Sarbanes-Oxley or Basel II-compliant, since these compliance requirements extend beyond data management, and focus on multiple orthogonal issues.

Real-time Customer Relationship Management

Customer Relationship Management (CRM) software covers a broad array of functionality. However, its primary role in the organization is to manage all the data pertaining to customer touch points, from

128

introduction through support. In many organizations, the touch points with customers are distributed across multiple departments, each with their own applications and software, to assist them in their job.

Due to the realities of customer interaction, CRM is not a panacea for many organizations that, instead, opt for an integration strategy across many customer data systems, sometimes using the CRM as the central aggregation facility. This is not unlike any data mart or data warehouse strategy, only with the downside that the CRM data is often stale. Recently, organizations have decided to move to integration solutions that provide them up-to-the-minute data. Hence, real customer management requires that data be aggregated together on-demand. This is also known as creating a single view of the customer.

The choice to go with a real-time data solution is more than just a "nice-to-have" in today's competitive business climate, and, in many cases, can be a must-have requirement. For example, in the areas of banking and telecommunications, it is imperative that a customer be able to call and receive information about recent activity on their account at the time of the call; this is especially true of issues like theft and fraud. In these cases, it's okay if the customer's phone number or address are not correct because a change has not yet been replicated However, it's unacceptable if a bank is unable tell a customer, within a minute or two of the call, the last time their ATM or credit card was used, where it was used, and the amount charged or taken out.

Moving from a data mart/data warehouse approach to up-to-the minute, CRM requires the ability to directly access the transactional systems, or, alternatively, immediately replicated versions of those systems. Of course, there is a number of serious hurdles and complexities associated with accessing these systems directly. We will cover those in detail in Chapter 8. Still, EII solutions simplify the accessibility of transactional data by providing the required pathways to the most up-to-date versions of the data, and structuring it for immediate use, as if it were being pulled from a data mart or data warehouse. Yet, we need to be careful not to confuse this with a virtual data warehouse, since this data has not necessarily gone through cleansing or consolidation. This approach focuses on providing users with a more accurate and timely view of information in the organization.

Major Insurance Company (Avaki Software)

Creating a Single View of the Customer

A major property and casualty insurance company has many different insurance products, a line of financial services, and many geographic locations. In addition, they have data centers in multiple locations that support operations, including relationships with insurance agencies across the country. The company's employees, customers, and agencies use a variety of CRM tools including Siebel, self-service portals, agency management, and other applications.

The Challenge: Need for Unified Customer Information

The company's size, geographic distribution, and wide array of products make it difficult to provide support for the straightforward relationship customers and agents want to have with the company. Efforts to improve customer service are hampered by the lack of unified customer information. Today, for example, the Property & Casualty and Financial advisory services are entirely separate businesses, and so the data is not easily accessible across divisional boundaries. In addition, the various types of insurance are separate from one another. Integrated customer information is needed for a variety of applications. For example, business line managers wants to put systems in place so that the customer (or agent) who asks a self-service portal to "show me my open claims" or "show me my policies" to receive information about claims or policies for any type of insurance they have purchased with the company—not just claims for one type of policy. An improved architecture for this information is valuable for the company's selling efforts as well; the people who sell or market insurance products—either inside the company or throughout its network of third-party agents—need to be able to know what products customers already have, and which additional products they might be open to purchasing.

Architectural Requirements: An SOA for Data

The company's architects were moving toward a service-oriented architecture (SOA) approach across the organization, with the goal of simplifying and streamlining application development, maintenance, and management. As part of this evolution, they hoped to create an SOA for data resources, making data available to applications through a layer of services. The data access and integration framework also needed to integrate with web services on both the front end and the back end. The company had been using ETL technology and some limited, point-to-point application integration solutions, but with major expansion initiatives underway, they required not only a substantial integration effort but also a solution that would scale as the company grows organically and by acquisition. The current point-to-point solutions would not be able to scale.

The Solution: A Data Service Layer

Regardless of which exact technology the company chose to help create their SOA, the architects realized they first needed to define the specific data access and integration requirements based on the existing applications and data sources. First, they worked with business users in order to specify in detail which data was needed by each application, and in which form. Then, they determined from which existing data sources data needed to be gathered, and how it needed to be transformed, integrated, and aggregated to create the forms needed by the applications. This was a mapping and modeling process that resulted in a clear understanding of how data would flow to the applications from the data sources where it was currently stored. While each application that required data would have its own, very specific needs, the company wanted to provide basic customer information through a unified set of services that conformed to a common logical data model. This would help ensure that each application obtained the same information from the same source, and that the data would be integrated in standard ways where possible. As a result, application developers (and users) would be working with a "single view of the truth" while providing data in the specific forms needed by individual departmental applications. Examples of data views that would be accessible to multiple applications included: Customer Overview, Policy Summary, Policy Billing Status, Claim Summary, and so on.

The technical environment included several different geographic locations, and information was generally divided among the geographies, based on the location of the agency. In addition, each data center had multiple database technologies including DB2, SQL Server, and IMS. Because the organization was moving toward an SOA, they planned to provide some of the data through web services, and required a specific XML header that would conform to their IT standards.

The solution approach involved creating a layer of individual data services that could be called by applications. With the EII software, the company's applications would be able to access a single virtual data source (the Avaki domain) and would not need to specify the individual data sources. Data integration logic is encapsulated in data services that are defined in the Avaki data layer. These data services in turn perform the task of accessing and integrating the appropriate data from the original data sources in a pre-defined way.

Once the data requirements were defined, it was a simple matter to define the appropriate services and create them in the data layer using the software's graphical data integration tools. Specifically, multiple layers of data services were defined, where lower layers conformed to enterprise standards and data models, and where application-specific layers ensured that data was made available in the appropriate format for a given application.

The company then needed to determine exactly how the data would be delivered. In its initial assessment, the company had determined that centralizing all the data was not practical, and that performing all data access and integration "on the fly" would not meet performance requirements. One of the ways the company balanced their needs was to take advantage of the EII system's comprehensive caching and scheduling features, in order to schedule the execution of integration logic and cache the results on a periodic basis. This can be done on a service-by-service basis so that architects can balance multiple factors:

providing fresh data to applications vs. protecting operational databases from uncontrolled or excessive access.

While this company chose to make data available through services, the EII system also provides the ability to make data available through a SQL interface, in which application queries can either execute joins on tables made available in the data layer by the EII system, or query a virtual table that is composed of information from multiple data sources. A SQL interface can be helpful for prototyping or for situations where applications generate SQL. In contrast, services provide more predictable data access and better performance.

For this company, important aspects of the chosen EII solution included:

- **A common data layer** compatible with a Web Services architecture, because the company was evolving toward greater use of service-oriented architectures and web services.
- **A variety of data integration approaches** sufficient to handle the wide range of data access and integration requirements discovered during the data analysis and mapping phase.
- **A scalable distributed architecture** in which multiple interoperating servers form a single EII system that services application requests for data. Applications and data sources can be added incrementally, and capacity can grow incrementally as requirements expand.
- **Ability to address performance requirements** on a case by case basis, such as the ability to schedule data service execution and cache results, the ability to balance execution load across multiple servers, and so on.
- **Compatibility with the company's security architecture**, including directory services.

Business Benefits: Flexible, and Scalable Data Access and Integration

Through the data service layer, the company can provide access to standard views of enterprise data, thereby breaking down silos between different departments and data centers and making data available to any application that needs it. Benefits of this improved data infrastructure include:

- **Practical data management.** Data owners retain control over their data sources and can determine which queries are run against these sources and how often.
- **Data consistency and freshness.** Applications share a common data integration infrastructure, and layers of services have been designed so that applications requiring the same data go through the same integration services.
- **Streamlined development and maintenance.** By providing integrated views of data in a layer separate from the applications themselves and separate from the original data sources, an EII approach makes it easier to maintain data integration logic over time as data locations, technologies, and other factors change. Applications do not have to be rewritten and core databases do not have to be restructured.
- **An architecture that can support growth and expansion.** As the company continues to grow, the data service layer will support more users, applications, and data sources.

A Flexible Foundation,
Now that the company has determined that an EII system can address its key requirements, the company's architects will expand the scope of the project to incorporate a variety of applications, including customer service applications, customer self-service portals, agency systems, and various operational reporting and dashboard applications.

Enterprise Spend Management (ESM)

Enterprise spend management is a term that defines the process of managing the trail of spending, and pay-through-procurement, across an enterprise Tracking the use of funds across an enterprise is a daunting task that typically falls on the shoulders of accounting and bookkeeping personnel. Yet people across business lines and departments are involved. If you consider all the minute payable entities that a corporation has, it quickly becomes overwhelming to answer questions, such as:

- What items were purchased?
- Who did the purchasing?
- Why was it purchased?
- Which vendor was used to purchase it?
- Was there any tax implication that was not addressed?
- Did the purchasing agent have proper authority?
- Was this an approved use of the funds?
- Was misuse or fraudulent activity involved in this purchase?
- Can the month end books be closed without issue?
- Are there unreconciled transactions that require payment to the bank?
- Or, more complex questions such as what items based on Merchant Category Codes (MCC) where purchased over time from which vendors?

Proper integration of purchase and payment information provides knowledge for strategic decision-making for managing an organization's spend, with a goal to reduce costs and optimize rebates and savings. The most basic possible outcome of not managing spend is that expenses may overtake revenue, and drive the company into bankruptcy. Today, for some public company CEOs and government officials, not being able to answer these questions could lead to jail time. Enterprise spend management is serious business and it's an information integration issue that is going to cost companies millions of dollars over the coming years, if not properly addressed.

Here are some additional factors that enter into understanding the complexity of ESM.

1. Level 3 data, the data that describes the line-item details of a purchase, is often lost in downstream processes. It could be captured by a point-of-sale system, or on the purchase order, but unless that data is correlated with the spending statements

from the bank, it is not going to be properly tracked in the accounting system. This is extremely difficult when employees provide just the credit card receipt with their expenses, but have two different expense entries that are associated with that expense, for example, lodging that includes meals and communications costs.

2. Banking is an extremely competitive business today; especially corporate banking. A revolution of customer empowerment is in the initial stages. Customers are gaining the upper hand over banks to define rates and rebates on spending. Basis point negotiation is becoming a hot spot for "shopping" or changing financial institutions. If the company cannot organize itself to provide a majority of its spending through one particular bank, it becomes much more difficult for them to negotiate these rates. Additionally, if a company is able to document and track spend patterns and data, they have the critical information required to be empowered. The information provided by ESM helps organizations direct and control this spending. Appropriately controlled growth in spending leads to greater cost savings via efficiencies ranging from strategic sourcing, to issuing bank rebates.

3. Sarbanes-Oxley Section 404 describes the need for companies to implement processes for identifying, tracking, removing, and reporting fraud. Any company without ESM is going to find it very difficult to fully comply with this requirement. Here are the four key controls that must be instituted by every public company after 11/15/04:

   - Controls over initiating, recording, processing and reconciling account balances, classes of transactions and disclosure and related assertions included in the financial statements.
   - Controls related to the initiation and processing of non-routine and non-systematic transactions.
   - Controls related to the selection and application of appropriate accounting policies.

- Controls related to the prevention, identification and detection of fraud.

4. For the US Government, the GAO now mandates very tight controls on spending. This originated out of a very famous scandal in which military personnel were using government credit cards in adult entertainment clubs. The inability to understand what these cards were used for, and by whom, led to a major changes in spend management in the government. The following is an excerpt from the July 23rd 2002 Salt Lake Tribune:

> "A General Accounting Office audit recently revealed that about 200 Army personnel have used government credit cards to get cash to spend on lap dances and other services offered at strip clubs near military bases. Its Army investigation also found that cards had been used for personal purchases of more than $100,000 in electronic equipment, $45,000 for cruises, and $7,373 for closing costs on a house."

The following case study from TakeCharge Technologies illustrates the use of ESM in state-based education.

State-based Education Systems (TakeCharge Technologies, LLC)

Managing Spending

State-based education systems, both universities and Kindergarten through 12th grade, have to be extremely cautious about their expenses. Their funds are limited, and any waste directly impacts the quality of learning for the students. Allowing schools to directly manage direct purchasing for themselves, while allowing the superintendent to manage and distribute funds as needed, is an especially daunting task.

Integration of Information from the Bank, Accounting, Purchasing and Fulfillment

---

Managing spending, end-to-end, is a difficult task. Information generated during the procurement cycle, such as line-item detail, is often lost when reconciling against bank statements, which show total amounts only. For education systems, most purchases are non-taxable, which means if tax was charged, the school needs to apply for refunds at the end of the year. Additionally, when different individuals within the school can procure outside of the traditional procurement systems up to a limited amount, those expenses must be identified and integrated into the whole process of reconciliation. Finally, for state-based education systems, this information needs to be made publicly available to those who live in the county. This means that the information must be accurate and audited. In order to accomplish this task, information must be correlated and integrated across different systems and processes. For example, one of the top 10 largest school systems in America uses a home grown procurement system, TERMS general ledger, banks with US Bank and TakeCharge's Pro/Charge application to glue it all together.

The Solution: Enterprise Spend Management (ESM)

ESM is a vertical market implementation of a specific EII problem. The requirement is to aggregate and correlate the Level 3 data (the line-item detail) created at the time of procurement, typically on the purchase order or receipt, the statements provided by the bank issuing the purchasing instruments (e.g. credit card, procurement card, etc.), the internal accounting systems with the possible addition of expenses reports and special procurement systems.(and payment data) In order to answer and understand key questions about how money is spent, who is spending it, which vendors are being used to supply goods and services, is money being allocated appropriately, and are the tax implications being handled in accordance with the law, this information must be joined together, typically by the accounting and bookkeeping staff. ESM software is special EII software that understands the touch points for spending within an enterprise and offers the ability to incorporate each endpoint into the aggregation and correlation process.

Post-Corporate M&A Systems Convergence

Many organizations that have undergone significant growth, especially through mergers and acquisition, face issues of increasing total costs of management due to managing multiple systems all serving the same purpose. However, moving all the data to one platform can take months, as it requires the IT staff to analyze the system being decommissioned, and the gap or mapping of data to the system that will handle this function going forward. EII fulfills both a short-term, and possibly a long-term, need to access this data across the silos as if it were a single system.

In the interim period following a merger or acquisition, organizations need a solution that will allow them to create a de-fragmented view of the data for the new organizational entity. This de-fragmentation includes identification and correlation of overlapping customers into a single record, in addition to, overlapping suppliers and MRO [10]orders. So, this de-fragmentation needs to be applied to both internal- and external-oriented operational data.

Consider the essence of an organizational data object, such as a customer or product. Parts of this object are distributed across multiple systems, some of which is possibly redundant, yet organized or keyed by different factors. For example, one system may represent the customer by a 5-digit customer number because this was how the original system represented customers, while a newer system may represent customer orders using a 10-digit customer number. Reconciling these two sets of data as a part of the whole customer requires an understanding of the similarities and differences of the various systems that contain related data.

Creating a de-fragmented view of the data requires special correlation processes within the aggregation layer, to allow users to define the characteristics for joining the data together, once it has been gathered from its individual locations. Here are some methods for dealing with data that is not correlated:

---

[10] Maintenance, Repair and Operations

Unified Keys

In order to correlate data across systems and data sets that have data identified by different names and keys, you can create a unified key table. A unified key table enables each system to transform their local key data into a consistent, organization-defined key. For example, if each system has a different identifier for customer, the unified key table can provide a transformation from the original identifier to the corporate customer identifier.

In cases where the organization doesn't want to maintain a separate table of unified keys, it is sometimes possible to join together other pieces of data from the record to generate dynamic keys.

Key Transformation

In many cases, the identifier is the same across systems, but, an older system uses less characters than a newer system. This happens because the newer system was developed to handle a greater number of customers than was needed at the time of the older system's development. In these cases, processes can be added that pre-pend additional characters onto the front of the older system's identifier.

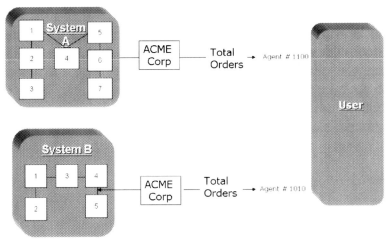

Figure 27: Fragmented Data Problem

Figure 27 above illustrates a typical data fragmentation problem. In this scenario, the user is attempting to identify the amount of total orders for ACME Corporation. However, due to the way systems developed over time, the sales orders are found in multiple systems, and identified by different Agent identifiers. Figure 28 below illustrates the role EII plays in de-fragmenting the data and providing the user with a common way to request the total orders for a single customer.

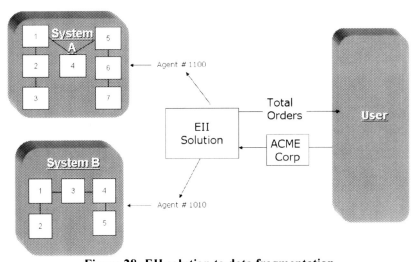

Figure 28: EII solution to data fragmentation

In contrast with up-to-the-minute CRM, the convergence of systems is consistent with a virtual data warehousing approach. The addition of caching, consolidation, matching, and cleansing, ensure that users are able to see related but distinct data captured across multiple systems in the organization.

Global Transportation Company (Software AG)

Enterprise Architecture is Key to Successful Mergers and Acquisitions

With a presence in over 175 countries, this company is a leader in moving and transportation solutions. This company has been growing through mergers and acquisitions, and also works with independent insurance agents and truckers. Rapidly integrating hundreds of data silos across the globe is critical to the success of the organization and the satisfaction of its customers.

The Challenge: Guaranteeing Sound Decision Making by Executives and Employees

With branches and partners in 175 nations, monitoring business activities and tracking shipments quickly becomes challenging. The organization has been using a patchwork of data integration approaches, such as ETL (Extract Transform Load), to manually build dozens of executive reports or gather customer information. In order to improve decision making and productivity, and decrease cost, the transportation company understood it couldn't afford costly and purely tactical projects but needed a strategic infrastructure to access real-time information around the globe.

The Requirements: Provide a System for Integration of Information Across Data Silos

In an effort to provide consistent reporting and analysis of customers, seasonal loads and to institute a more efficient billing process, this company required an information integration solution that was capable of aggregating data across silos and dynamically correlating inconsistently labeled data in each silo. Hence, the solution to this company's problem must meet the following attributes:

- Provide a strategic infrastructure to deliver real-time information to business users and client applications worldwide
- Ensure the infrastructure can support future projects such as mobile integration
- Guarantee the rapid integration of acquired companies in the future
- Liberate the company from vendor lock-in through reuse of existing systems and standards
- Build a flexible framework that can respond quickly and painlessly to business initiatives

The EII Solution

With data stored on the mainframe in two different database formats and across a wide array of proprietary and packaged applications, this EII solutions is extremely complex. Here are some of the steps take to deliver a complete information integration solution:

- Step 1: Bring data from two mainframe databases with inconsistently labeled data together into a single query. This required the development of a specialized query engine that executed the query across these two databases using their native protocols. In this case the data was stored in Software AG's ADABAS and IBM's DB2. Software AG's Natural application environment was capable of implementing a Web Service that could execute native queries on both of these database platforms.

- Step 2: Correlation. Once the routines were implemented for querying the data from the two databases, a separate application was developed that would correlate the information based on a scale of factors. Factors included: Name, billing address, billing zip, and procurement contact among others. Higher degrees of matches were merged together under a separate company identifier, while lower degrees of matches were kept as separate records.

- Step 3: Cache the data. The data from Step 2 was cached as to minimize direct hits against the production databases on an ongoing basis. Software was developed that synchronized future queries with the cache.

- Step 4: Develop the Service-Oriented Architecture (SOA). The SOA is the infrastructure for aggregation of data. Each service represents a subset of the enterprise data and will be used by downstream processes to access data in a consistent format using a consistent interface.

- Step 5: Develop the corporate vocabulary: The company developed a corporate vocabulary (semantics) that was captured in the metadata repository.

- Step 6: Link the vocabulary to its underlying representations. In this step, definitions of the semantics were provided for resolution.

Benefits: Operational Efficiency, Flexibility and More Business Value from IT

The benefits of the new architecture are beyond replacing tedious and error-prone ETL processes. By using a Service-Oriented Architecture (SOA) and XML-standards, the transportation company is able to:

- Improve operational efficiency – Executives, customer representatives and agents benefit from more sound decision making through real-time single views of information that are provided by a unique framework rather integration silos.

- Flexibility – By providing real-time information through business terms, the organization has decoupled information access from back-end delivery mechanisms. As such, access to critical information is not disrupted if data sources or Web services change— IT only has to link new services or data sources to business terms, or remove them.
- More Business Value from IT – In addition to reusing existing assets, the "Business Information Gateway" and Web services exposing data sources and business logic can be reused for future integration projects. For instance, Business Process Management (BPM) projects will be able to access data through business terms and without rewriting code. Enabling reuse and Enterprise Architecture through SOA also allows IT to focus on delivering business value rather than being unproductively occupied with maintaining "spaghetti' code and tightly-coupled integrated processes.

Self-Service Portals

Every technology needs that "killer" application that will launch it into ubiquity. For portals, that application seems to be self-service. Self-services portals deliver greater levels of service to the user, at a lower cost to the supplier. Indeed, self-service has been a driving force behind the growth of the commercial Internet, and increased productivity for businesses in general. The portal is an information-driven application, and, therefore, a candidate for implementation using EII.

Self-service portals initially benefited customers by providing greater access to their information at all hours of the day. However, contemporary applications of this technology are also being directed at employees, suppliers, and trading partners. The employee self-service portal is perhaps the most high-profile of these types. The goal of the employee self-service portal is to empower the employee, and to have all the data entry and data gathering initiated by the employee. This includes expense report capture, benefits management, tax and wage management, IT provisioning (passwords, access control, email, etc.) and pay slips. Some companies even provide the ability for the employee to manage their retirement accounts directly from within the portal. It is obvious from this description, that in most large organizations, this data is most likely shared across a number of systems.

In the early days of portals, when there were still stand-alone portal providers, these providers were divided up into two camps: integration and user interface. The user interfaces providers focused on delivering tools that would help developers deliver better-looking portal-based applications, faster. The portal integration providers focused on delivering tools that would assist the developers in linking to, and retrieving data from, disparate data sources for display in the portal. Many, if not most, of these integration tools were based on an EAI foundation, instead of an EII foundation, which resulted in very expensive early portal implementations that required significant amounts of coding.

Using EII for portal development allows developers to focus on the aggregation and delivery of data, instead of data access; cleansing, location, and format (see Figure 29). Additionally, the semantic abstraction allows developers to expose the available data directly to the portal users, providing them critical flexibility in the types of data available for viewing, and without requiring consistent intervention from the information technologists. EII solutions that use XML as the primary data representation simplify this process even further, by enabling simple XML transformation tools to prepare the data for display.

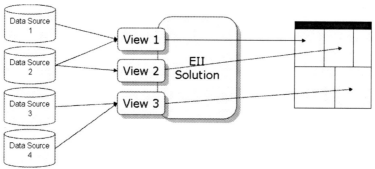

Figure 29: EII as a portal infrastructure

Metadata Reporting

As discussed in Chapter 4, EII relies heavily on the capture and use of metadata. The metadata provides the basis for accessing and retrieving various points of data from the multitude of data sources that exist. This large base of metadata also provides the basis for an excellent reference source for the technical staff that maintains and designs systems and applications within the organization.

General ad-hoc reporting of metadata helps increase reuse within the organization. However, most studies show that unless strict policies are enforced, data reuse is generally limited. That is, most engineers and data architects often find it problematic to use what exists due to poor documentation, limited access due to governance issues, and a general lack of understanding of how the data is modeled. The metadata repository can assist engineers by clarifying some of these issues, but it is unlikely to change this pattern dramatically, without a policy. Understanding the impact of changes to what's there, and how the data progressed to its current state, are two functions that can easily be leveraged by engineers, and helps significantly when planning new functionality or systems.

Thus, two key functions of the metadata repository, outside of general keyword-type queries, are the impact analysis and data lineage reporting. Impact analysis is only as good as the linkages or relationships defined between metadata. The more metadata relationships are established, the greater the chance that an impact analysis will identify mission-critical hits to existing systems, should the underlying structures or formats change. This means that a single component of data needs to be related to the tables that it is a part of, the business processes that use it, the transformations that use this data, and the systems that read and write to this particular field. It is only with this information that a change across any of these entities can generate an alert to the engineer, and signal a potential danger or requirement for upstream changes.

Data lineage provides us with an understanding of how data came into being. Think about all the data within your organization, all the ways that it is captured, all the locations that it is stored in, all the reports that use this it, etc. Unfortunately, data is not a stagnant element within our organizations. If it were, we would probably not invest the money required to store and capture it in the first place. The metadata repository can help the engineering staff understand where data enters the organization, and all the changes that it goes through as it transforms and takes on new life and new meaning in our organizations. For example, a contact, that starts as a name on a list purchased through marketing, becomes part of a marketing campaign, and then, hopefully, turns into a customer. As this data moves from system to system, it changes form, name, type, etc. It is critical that we maintain an understanding of this flow over time, and that we understand where data originates from.

Data linage also helps with the common organizational problem of data discrepancy. Have you ever had two different departments generate fairly similar reports off of what should be a consistent data set, only to find that the two reports aren't identical? For example, this happens a lot with financial budgeting where accounting's numbers don't match the department's numbers. After days of investigative research, it is realized that the department uses a formula that looks at budget minus actual - after commission, while accounting looks budget minus actual - before commission. Data lineage reports help us understand how the final value is computed on the report, in each of these scenarios, more quickly than a team of people who compare data until they hit upon the correct reason, by chance.

In addition to the support of EII as a means of retrieving and transforming data into information, the same principles used to accomplish this can also be used to help create a unified view of metadata across disparate metadata repositories. Throughout this book, we will see references to the use of a metadata repository. It would be great if that repository could be a single entity. However, the reality is that it may make sense to have metadata stay with the applications that create and manage that metadata. In these cases, an EII solution could be used to help create singular views of disparate metadata, and the taxonomy can be used to create linkages to processes to retrieve that metadata on-demand. This will still allow you to build a powerful ontology, based on existing metadata, without having to harvest it from its current source.

Additional Design-time Value of Metadata

As you have seen earlier in the book, there is a strong run-time connection between the business terms and business process metadata. However, the traditional use for metadata management is a design-time function. By capturing the core physical properties of our systems and data source, and relating them back to our logical layer, we produce a map that allows us to navigate between the logical and physical worlds.

The following examples illustrate the relationship between physical terms and business terms, and between physical terms and business process metadata:

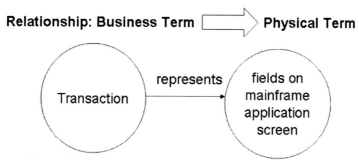

Figure 30: Business term relationship with physical term

This relationship links the *Transaction* business term with a set of fields on a mainframe application screen. For simplicity, we have used a descriptive term to encapsulate the real metadata that would be captured there. It includes navigation to the screen or screens where the data is located, the horizontal and vertical location of those fields on the screen and the length of each field.

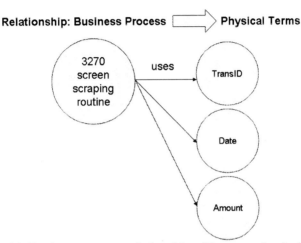

Figure 31: Business process relationship with many physical terms

The relationship identified in Figure 31 above shows the relationship between physical fields on the mainframe application and a particular business process.

When we take the information model as a whole, we have enough data to provide the following design-time capabilities:

- We can trace how the data evolves over time, and which business terms and business processes operate on distinct pieces of raw data
- We can determine where data is redundant in our current systems
- We can provide impact analyses that tell us what will be impacted by change across our systems and processes

- Process analyses to determine improvements in the systems, e.g. Six-Sigma
- Find places where data can be captured and integrated with other processes.

We should note that the activity outlined above was depicted to illustrate what capturing the relationships between different types will do for us. At the points where processes are linked to physical terms, we are not indicating that these processes have to directly access the data, but instead, they could communicate with a process that uses a data structure—for example a Web Service—and the relationship is with the fields of the data structure, and not the underlying physical store.

We will explore this aspect further in chapters 9 and 10. Suffice it to say, metadata can play a key role in simplifying integration. Indeed, it is a key component that provides us with the required supporting data needed in order to successfully integrate our data components together.

Analysis, Reporting & Executive Dashboards

Business intelligence tools provide useful and powerful ways to organize and look at data. However, their complexity of use means that only very sophisticated business analysts and those with programming skills can make efficient use of this power. Sometimes, non-technical or semi-technical users will develop models in spreadsheet applications or simple reporting packages, and need access to the data in a consolidated way to make a business decision. Sometimes, it is also necessary to access up-to-the-minute data rather than the aged data marts that most business intelligence tools require. In these cases, EII makes an excellent adjunct for reporting and analysis.

Here is a case in point. A major pharmaceutical company needed to provide their district managers with the ability to analyze sales representative performance, market share, budget and expenses, and target physicians, in order to better assist the sales force. In order to accomplish this task, the information technology department of this pharmaceutical company needed to provide dynamic views across five separate applications and data sources, in a way that was conducive for the district managers to review and update the data. In this particular case, the answer was to create an executive dashboard application for these district managers.

The executive dashboard is a tool that is used by executives to gain insight into the organization as a holistic entity. While this may sound simple, it is perhaps one of the most complex initiatives being undertaken in organizations around the world. More than ever, the viability and character of the organization is being questioned due to changing economic tides and new compliance requirements. How can the busy executive gain true insight when his team cannot even identify the authoritative sources of data that are needed to provide him with the accuracy required to manage his organization.

The dashboard uses the EII infrastructure to: a) provide the busy executive with an aggregate view of the organization in a graphic form that can quickly be analyzed and b) identify trusted, timely, accurate, valid, and authoritative sources of data from within the organization. The sidebar below entitled "Major Global Pharmaceutical Case" by Composite Software illustrates the requirements that drive the need for EII in this type of solution, and how they met the needs of a large global pharmaceutical company.

Global Pharmaceutical Company (Composite Software)

Information Integration: Evolution vs. Revolution.

With an employee base well over 50,000, this global pharmaceutical company has a large number of diverse business units and a dynamic employee environment. The company has been growing through both mergers and acquisitions and organically to build this base. It is not practical to force certain information integration requirements on a company of this side, and thus an evolutionary approach must be taken.

The Challenge: Employees Information Reside Across Many

Systems
With employees being hired and departing on a daily basis across both legacy areas of the organization as well as new ones, the challenge in the human resources department is considerable. The organization has been using manual processes to load employee data from various databases and applications to manually build dozens of corporate reports. In order to improve decision making and lower IT costs, the pharmaceutical company began to seek alternative approaches.

The Requirements: Provide a Single View of an Employee
In an effort to provide consistent reporting and analysis of employees, the company required an information integration solution that was capable of aggregating data across silos and dynamically relating employee data across each data source. Hence, the solution to the company's problem must meet the following attributes:

- Provide a strategic infrastructure to deliver real-time information and data from disparate sources to business users and client applications worldwide
- Guarantee the rapid integration of acquired companies in the future
- Liberate the company from vendor lock-in through reuse of existing systems and standards
- Provide report creators independence from the DBA team

The EII Solution

Here are some of the steps taken to deliver a complete information integration solution:

- Step 1: Extract the metadata from the appropriate source systems where employee data is resident today. This requires the designer with appropriate authorization to the underlying systems to be operating in a metadata capture and design environment.
- Step 2: A designer then develops aggregated views of the fragmented data using the metadata captured in Step 1. Workforce data is stored in a myriad of systems including

packaged applications such as PeopleSoft, homegrown HR systems, local databases, and spreadsheets. In this phase, users can apply transformations to the data or build complex relationships, such as inner joins. Due to complexity, additional design time should be given during this step to develop out an appropriate taxonomy for the resulting data.

- Step 3: The Composite EII software uses the metadata and the views to develop an efficient query plan. This is a critical requirement given that each data source could have various response times and abilities. The query plan identifies the lowest cost based on a number of criteria, including cardinality, ability to push down joins, expected results, and shape of data

- Step 4: Performance Tuning. Rarely is a view complete after one iteration. Once the right data is being selected and returned in the right structure, the hard work of incorporating it into business processes occurs. This requires that additional performance tuning in the form of caching of data for use in repetitive queries or tuning the underlying data management systems where possible.

Benefits: Operational Efficiency, Flexibility and More Business Value from IT

The benefits of the new architecture go beyond replacing expensive IT resources required to build custom SQL to generate load scripts and reports for executive users. Benefits also include:

- **Improve operational efficiency** – Executives and HR leaders benefit from getting accurate information to help them make better decisions related to the company's workforce.
- **Flexibility** – By providing real-time information via a Composite View, the business user does not need to understand the semantics in the remote system nor be aware of where the system resides. This information can be made available to validate that the correct data is being leveraged in the Composite View.
- **Evolution to SOA** – This deployment now provides a node in

Composite Software's Data Services Grid whereby HR data can be shared to other teams within the global company. This facilitates enterprise wide metadata management solutions. As other similar companies deploy their SOA, EII plays a critical role in the evolution of non-SOA systems into the SOA fabric by exposing Composite Views as services. At the same time, these views can be leveraged with existing business intelligence tools.

Traversing Structured & Unstructured Information

Perhaps you have heard of the game "Six-degrees of Kevin Bacon," in which people relate an actor back to Kevin Bacon through a series of actors who they've been in other movies with. The fun of the game is to try to trace the shortest path back to Kevin Bacon from the current actor. Success requires the individual to have a strong knowledge of the casts of many movies.

The concept behind this game is called inference, and it can be used as a tool in business as well as to create fun games like the one described above. When used as a business tool, the goal is to automate the determination of a particular path, using a knowledge base that includes the data and relationships within that data. Using this technique, we can locate and identify data across the knowledge base by knowing any starting point and ending point. In this scenario, the knowledge base may also incorporate both structured and unstructured data sources.

With inference we gain the ability to obtain an answer using the data that we already know, but which is not clearly identified, based on the raw data alone. For example, we know that a path exists from point A to point B, and that point exists from point B to point C. Then, we can infer that we can get to point C from point A. However, we only know that this path exists, if we understand the relationships between each of the points, and the rules for traversing points. This is the role that the ontology plays in developing an inference solution. The ontology defines the relationships between various pieces of metadata in such a way that we can navigate the data to glean answers that an aggregate data set alone does not provide.

The following real-world example illustrates the value of developing the ontology and then combining it with the aggregation capabilities of the EII solution. Health and Human Services departments often need to determine if someone is a well-suited guardian. The case worker in charge of the minor in question may want to ask simple questions, such as "Have any of Susan's guardians ever been arrested?" Given the sample aggregation below, there is an implied relationship between Tom Williams, Susan Moore and an arrest date.

```
<person name="Tom Williams">
    <is-guardian-of>Susan Moore</is-guardian-of>
    <was-arrested-on>12/1/96</was-arrested-on>
</person>
```

Given this set of information, in this way, an inference engine could provide the case worker with the answer she is looking for. However, it is the ontology that provides the aggregation engine with the metadata necessary to structure the result set in this way. The matching ontology for this might be represented as:

person is-guardian-of steward – where person and steward are terms
person was-arrested-on date – where person and date are terms

Knowing how the terms relate to each other and then capturing the instance of the terms, along with their known relationships, allows us to analyze and use the data in new and unique ways.

An EII solution can provide the means to generate properly structured information model instances that include both the data and metadata necessary to derive this outcome. Within EII, there are two primary methods of creating a combined result set that contains both the metadata and data. The first is a manual method which defines a mapping between the ontology and a particular result set. These three components—the result set, the map and the ontology—are then fed into a translation engine that produces a combined result set.

The second method is to query the data based on the ontology. This requires the query engine to understand a particular ontology definition language, such as the Resource Definition Framework (RDF) or the more comprehensive Web Ontology Language (OWL). It also requires the engine to understand how to locate and retrieve instance data from underlying data sources. To accomplish this, you can map the relationships identified in the ontology with data retrieval procedures. For example, the ontology Figure 32 would result in three procedures: find-children, find-siblings and find-descendants.

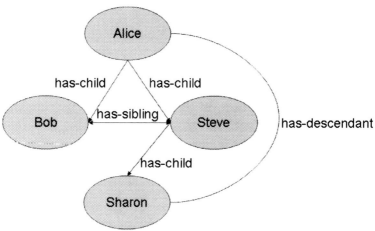

Figure 32: Sample ontology

The resulting data set might then resemble the following truncated XML structure, which can be supplied to an inference engine to help resolve answers from this knowledgebase. Notice that Alice, Bob, Steve and Sharon represent data in the structure below, and that the remainder is the metadata combined from the ontology that helps us understand how the data relate to each other.

```
<owl:ObjectProperty rdf:ID="has-child">
        <owl:inverseOf>
                <owl:ObjectProperty rdf:about="#has-parent"/>
        </owl:inverseOf>
```

```
</owl:ObjectProperty>

<rdf:Description rdf:about="Sharon"/>

<rdf:Description rdf:about="Bob"/>

<rdf:Description rdf:about="Steve"/>
      <has-child rdf:resource="Sharon"/>
</rdf:Description>

<rdf:Description rdf:about="Alice">
      <has-child rdf:resource="Steve"/>
      <has-child rdf:resource="Bob"/>
</rdf:Description>
```

Use of the inverseOf object property provides the means to understand that a request for has-parent is satisfied by any resource that has a has-child relationship with another resource.

Legacy Revitalization

It's the age old debate: Rip-n-replace or reuse? Rip-n-replace strategies allow companies to redesign older, less sophisticated applications to meet the demands of today's fast-moving business world, but at a very high monetary cost. The difficulty in this strategy is not as much the money as it is articulating a return-on-investment for spending this money. The return for these types of efforts may be intangible, such as being able to respond to new business process requirements faster or with less expense. Unfortunately, most executives still see this return as a nice-to-have versus a need-to-have. It takes a very visionary executive who makes the connection between the benefits of her information systems to her ability to execute, in order to spend in these circumstances; especially in harsh economic conditions.

The alternative approach to rip-n-replace is to revitalize existing legacy systems so that the current system can at least provide value to modern information architectures. While many legacy platform and application vendors have made great strides in providing the technology that allows legacy applications to participate in distributed architectures such as Web applications, Web Services, CORBA, Java, etc., sometimes, putting a new face on an old application just doesn't meet the needs of the business. For example, using screen scraping tools to transform legacy green-screen applications into modern Web applications works in about 80% of cases. However, these applications are often very fragile and can incur considerable latency.

One alternative is to use EII integration techniques to assist in the legacy revitalization process. Simply, EII can be used to help unlock the data trapped in proprietary data formats, such as VSAM, as well as simplify the process of combining data from multiple applications into a single view. While much of the EII best practice focuses on the integration of data across disparate systems, the concept applies to multiple applications running on the same machine that might not be directly integrated due to:

- Cost of changing existing source code
- Lack of knowledgeable skills about the existing source code base
- Time requirements to accomplish integration

Using EII to create a single portal for all the related legacy application data allows these applications to continue operating without change, but exposes their data to new processes.

Of course, straightforward access to the legacy data is not always a possibility, due to a host of reasons, such as:

- Cryptic codes used in place of full strings to save disk and memory space
- A known version of the source code matching the current disk structure may not exist
- The files are managed by a third-party library or application
- Potential for read/write conflict with the transactional environment

In these cases, possible options include:

- Rewrite portions of the application to support operating in an interactive manner
- Wrap third-party application interfaces with more modern Web Service-based interfaces
- Implement a replication solution and operate only off of the replicant database
- Wrap screen-scraping routines as interactive Web Services

Clearly, legacy revitalization is on the rise, as more and more information executives are seeking ways to operate effectively, under tightened budgets. A full EII lifecycle initiative will help the organization identify and integrate this critical data, while potentially allowing the company to continue running their existing applications and systems without changes, and, where change is necessary, to do so in the least intrusive manner possible.

Secure Data Access

One concept that has been consistent throughout this book is that the needs of the business often create or enforce a distributed data environment. This could be due to the need to have data highly available, which forces replication of existing data out of transactional systems. It could also be because the organization is really a group of independent operating units. Regardless of the reason, having data spread throughout the organization makes it very difficult to protect and maintain confidentiality; especially when the needs of the business force us to make the data available on a more liberal basis.

By implementing an EII solution, we provide our business users with the data they need, in the formats and structures they need to see the data, without having to fish around the organization or speak with multiple parties. This design also provides us with an excellent opportunity to also secure access to the data in a consistent manner, and provide the basis for ensuring privacy and confidentiality of all new data brought online, as part of new business initiatives.

EII has the capability to expose new access controls to the wealth of data being made available through this solution, based on our business vocabulary, rather than discrete fields and functions within our applications. Using an EII solution to provide secure data access is proving, for many customers, to be a significant upside benefit, albeit not the original intent. As part of the EII best practice, IT implementation specialists can associate roles and access controls with specific business terms that ease the maintenance burden on the back end systems.

Consider how much effort it would take to manage information integration across two or more data sources, each with its own access control and user policies. This effort is made all the more complex by legacy applications that have implemented security at the application level, potentially forcing changes to the source code, in order to support new security measures. By moving the access control into the information integration solution, IT can centralize their data access policy and role management, so that data is made available on a consistent basis.

Moving toward a centralized security management solution is not without its challenges. Using the EII solution to provide this type of access control management requires that the existing data sources establish trusted relationships with the information integration solution. This can be fraught with both political and technical barriers. For example, this process still requires analysis of what level of trust will be given for each system. Will full administrative access be given? Or, will a special user be created that only has access to a subset of the overall data available in the existing system?

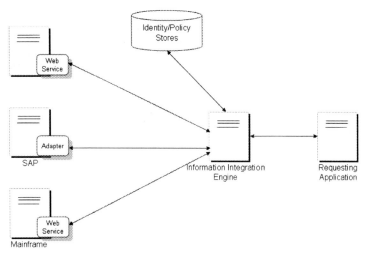

Figure 33: Secured data access architecture

Figure 33 illustrates a secure data architecture using the information integration solution. In this architecture, there are multiple levels of trust that must be granted. First, the Web Service, or adapter, must have a trusted relationship with the individual systems for which it is providing access for. This type of trust may be granted in two ways:

- IP-based trust specifies that only a machine with a specific IP address can make requests and all other requests are ignored. For added security, this type of trust can also be granted at the Ethernet MAC address layer—the address physically burned into the Ethernet card—which makes spoofing much more difficult. Most hacking attacks are performed by inside personnel, and because we're exposing confidential data in a generic fashion, locking the application down in this manner is often preferred.

- Role-based trust specifies that the Web Service, or adapter, presents itself as a client of the application and has all the rights of that particular client's access. Usually, in this type of trust, a special user is created and given access to the necessary data, protecting data that is not designed to be exposed.

163

It is not uncommon to find a combination of these techniques in use in highly secure operations.

Next, the information integration engine needs to be provided with a trusted relationship with the Web Services or adapters. Again, we can use the IP-based or role-based approaches to provide this trust. Finally, the requesting application needs to authenticate itself to the integration engine so that the proper levels of access controls can be applied to the information aggregation. With this authentication, the user will only be able to see the data for which they have read or write access.

Key Concepts

1. EII solutions can satisfy both a developer and end user audience. For the developer, the EII solution provides control and understanding of the systems and data structures in use. For the end user, EII hides the complexity of data being distributed across multiple systems.
2. EII provides the basis for compliance reporting, up-to-the-minute customer relationship management, metadata reporting, post-corporate M&A systems convergence, self-service portals, analysis, reporting, executive dashboards, legacy revitalization, inference, standard taxonomy management and semantic integration.
3. EII enables semantic integration by providing the means to develop and capture a common vocabulary that all other data can be mapped into, as well as, provide the means to associate the underlying data with its common representation.
4. EII provides the ability to secure access to information distributed throughout the organization through a centralized management facility.

"Plans are only good intentions unless they immediately degenerate into hard work."
– *Peter Drucker*

EII Components

An EII solution requires many different combinations of components to work in tandem. It unlikely that you will find a comprehensive set of these components provided by a single vendor, and therefore, already integrated into a single product. Since many of these components can operate as encapsulated entities, the integration between them does not have to be tight. Indeed, many of these components are now starting to implement standards that ease the burden of moving reusable data between them.

This chapter provides an overview of the various components that are part of implementing an Enterprise Information Integration solution. With each component comes the identification of properties for each component, followed by a discussion of its role in the overall solution.

Metadata Repository

The metadata repository is the central store for all the metadata that will be used in the EII solution. Metadata repositories exist on the market in many different forms, and offer various levels of functionality. Most of these repositories that support information integration requirements are components of integration suites and manage the metadata in a proprietary manner. Unfortunately, this locks the user into an integration approach that is prescribed by a single vendor, instead of offering openness and flexibility.

Of those metadata repositories that are represented as standalone, most do not support the full complement of metadata required for a complete EII solution without significant customization, and the parts they do support, may not provide adequate integration interfaces to other components of the EII solution. In fact, most packaged metadata repositories on the market today deal mainly with data structures and code, but have limited support for taxonomy or ontology.

In fairness to both types of metadata repositories, today's world generates new metadata types at such an incredible pace, that it is impossible for any vendor to provide adequate support. The pragmatic approach of having both an open metadata repository that can be used by many components of the EII solution simultaneously—even if they are provided by different vendors,—and a repository that can support an ever-growing base of metadata types, means limiting the management functionality within the repository. For example, using an enterprise content management system will allow storing, revisioning, sharing, and searching of different metadata content, regardless of their structure.

This approach implies that we will forgo having intimate knowledge of the metadata content. Additionally, this approach could limit our ability to relate metadata together at a fine-grained level. However, this approach can be balanced based upon the needs of the specific implementation. For instance, one customer chose to manage their database and transformation models at a fine-grained level, and all other metadata at a coarse-grained level. To accomplish this, the customer developed a specialized viewer and editor for these two types of metadata. This did not impact the way the users created or stored these models, but it did allow the rest of the organization to incorporate subsets of these models into the overall ontology at a fine-grained level.

The following list illustrates the overhead of developing a metadata repository that manages all metadata in a fine-grained manner. This list is just a subset of the most heavily used types of metadata used in EII solutions:

- XML Schema
- XML Stylesheets
- Relational Database Schema
- Data Transformations
- Online Analytical Processing Models
- Multidimensional Models
- Business Taxonomy
- Business Ontology
- Business Rules
- Business Processes
- Web Services Definitions (WSDL)
- Universal Definition, Discovery, and Integration (UDDI) Models
- Unified Modeling Language (UML) Models
- Directory Service Models (for location and security metadata)
- Security Policies

It was mentioned above that there are considerable downstream advantages for building out and using the metadata repository, if multiple components could all share the metadata. In the past, many information management tools managed their data in a proprietary manner, but, today, that approach has been replaced by a user requirement to share common efforts across tools. Hence, many vendors are now supporting an expanding base of standards to enable the exchange and sharing of metadata. Metadata repositories that support these standards natively gain the benefit of openness and can potentially support new metadata types more easily than their competitors, or even home-grown metadata repositories.

An example of these emerging standards is the Object Management Group's (OMG) Common Warehouse Metamodel (CWM). CWM is a framework for describing most of the key models that are developed as part of an overall information management strategy. These include, but are not limited to, entity relationship models, transformation models, online analytical processing (OLAP) models, business nomenclature, object models and even XML models. Moreover,

CWM defines an interchange format based on an XML representation of these models called the XML Metadata Interchange (XMI). Suffice it to say that anything that needs to be represented that is part of a robust data management strategy, can be defined in CWM and expressed in XMI. This offers tremendous potential for capture and use of this metadata. Chapter 10, by John Poole, covers the OMG's Model-Driven Architecture, of which CWM is just a single component, and it's relation to EII.

Nevertheless, in a complete distributed integration strategy, data is just one component. A complete integration strategy will also need to express business rules, business processes, workflows, configurations, etc. Unfortunately for implementers, CWM was not chosen as the way to define and express these types of metadata, which means that we need to rely on the adoption of other standards to simplify the capture and use of this type of metadata. To this end, one may look to the emerging Web Services standards since they use XML to define their structures and definitions.

In addition to the capture and management of metadata types, the metadata repository needs to support basic metadata management functions. These include revision control, versioning, impact analysis reporting, and data lineage reporting. Revision control and versioning provide the means for the organization to control the metadata that is deployed in various stages of development or production. Impact analysis reporting identifies the impacted dependencies of a change to any particular piece of metadata. Thus, if a relational database model needs to change its underlying structure, the repository should report on the adverse effect this will have on other systems in development or production. Finally, data lineage reporting illustrates the lifecycle of a piece of data over time. This includes how and where the data entered the organization, and the transformations that the data is a part of, as it moves between systems and applications within the organization.

These functions are pertinent to both the development processes around implementing EII, but also may be critical to the business user. For example, suppose the use for implementing EII project was the development of an executive dashboard, and on that dashboard was a number that represented total cost of development for a new product. Now, assume that the number on the executive dashboard is different than the number being presented by accounting. The aforementioned functions of the metadata repository can help us ensure the quality of data being produced by our EII solution, and in this case, trace the data back to its origin to isolate the reason for the discrepancy. At least in the case of two known users, the data being produced by the EII solution was more accurate than the numbers being produced through other means, and provided the basis for bringing those methods in alignment.

Likewise, some of the adverse effects noted when putting a new application into production, stem from a lack of understanding of the change on the existing environment. By harvesting and organizing metadata as part of an EII best practice into the metadata repository, your organization gains the downstream benefits of identifying these impacts in advance of deploying a change, and, thus, minimizes the costs associated with having to roll back to older and less capable versions.

The more types of metadata that can be captured within the metadata repository, the easier it is to relate the metadata together, thus creating a stronger ontology. In turn, a stronger ontology will eventually lead to better methods for turning data into information. Of note, we loosely defined "metadata repository" here, on purpose. We have defined the metadata repository as a facility that can capture and relate several types of metadata together. Thus, the metadata repository you select should offer the ability to customize the metadata types supported through user customizable mechanisms. More importantly, the user-defined metadata needs to be available for inclusion into the overall information model.

Another reason for loosely defining metadata repository is to avoid conflict with preconceived notions of what a metadata repository is, based on the existing tools on the market, such as Computer Associates' Advantage Repository. Due to the needs of Enterprise Information Integration, we see a growing need for the repository to provide traditional metadata repository capabilities, as well as function in a transactional manner. For example, Web Services metadata should be directly accessible through existing registry standards, such as UDDI, thus enabling the repository to provide operational support, in addition to its general metadata management functions.

The inescapable fact is that the metadata repository is a key, if not the most important component of any EII solution.

Information Modeling Tools

An information model is a template that defines the structures and relationships between data. There may be multiple modeling tools that are used to define the metadata that is captured as part of our EII solution, such as transformation modeling, relational database modeling and process modeling. However, the modeling tool that is critical to your EII solution is the ontology or taxonomy modeling tool. It is this component that provides us with the abstraction upon which all other metadata are mapped.

As discussed in Chapter 4, EII solutions start with a focus on the business vocabulary. Ontology or taxonomy modeling tools (called information modeling tools from here on in) enable both line-of-business and information technology workers a common facility to define this vocabulary. However, experience shows that overly complex modeling tools may more easily be adopted by the line-of-business workers than by information technologists. In these cases, the complexity may need to be disguised behind a basic forms-based entry system, or similarly simple interface.

Line-of-business workers will use the information modeling tools to define the terms that the business uses on a daily basis, group terms together into a classification scheme or taxonomy, and define the relationships between terms to form a business ontology. The information technology worker will use the information modeling tools to establish the relationships between the physical metadata, such as database schemas, transformations, business rules, business processes, and Web Services, with the established business vocabulary. These relationships will become critical for translating requests for data from the logical or business layer into requests for corresponding physical data.

Information modeling tools can take many forms and may not always be graphical. For example, line-of-business workers will often feel more comfortable entering their data into a spreadsheet since this is a tool that they commonly use. The spreadsheet is an excellent way for line-of-business workers to capture basic terms and simple relationships between terms. However, they can sometimes introduce significant challenges for capturing in a metadata repository, as they don't always follow a consistent design format. In these cases, it may be necessary to rely on their ability to produce output in many different formats, such as XML and comma separated values, which are more easily imported into by a metadata management tool. Figure 34 illustrates how a spreadsheet can provide basic modeling.

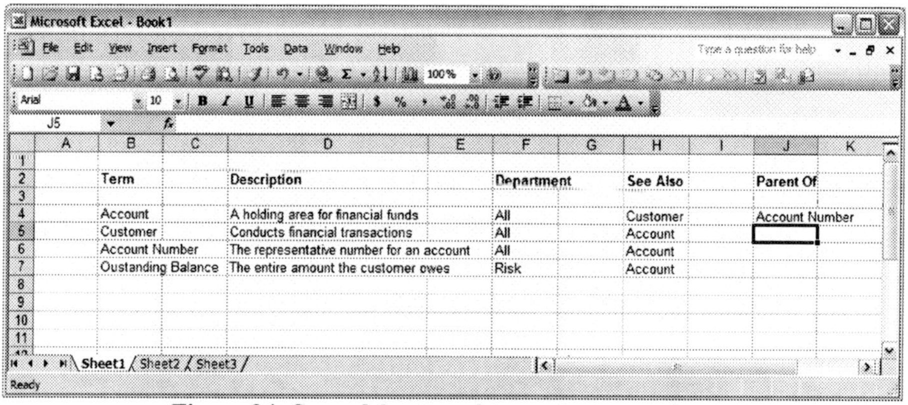

Term	Description	Department	See Also	Parent Of
Account	A holding area for financial funds	All	Customer	Account Number
Customer	Conducts financial transactions	All	Account	
Account Number	The representative number for an account	All	Account	
Oustanding Balance	The entire amount the customer owes	Risk	Account	

Figure 34: Spreadsheet used to capture metadata

Since information models tend to increase in complexity quickly, once relationships are formulated, a graphical representation can often assist the modeler to visualize the model as an entire entity, and drill down on subsections of the model, as needed. Figure 35 illustrates a visual information modeling tool based on the Resource Definition Framework (RDF). (See Appendix A for a detailed discussion of RDF. These types of information modeling tools tend to incorporate symbols that represent the modeling nomenclature, and, thus, increase the complexity of their use as the user must now learn this symbolic nomenclature, in order to define their model. Furthermore, in the early period of learning this new nomenclature, it is possible that a modeler may inadvertently mislabel a relationship, or the direction of a relationship. Therefore, the use of these information modeling tools may require some quality assurance processes.

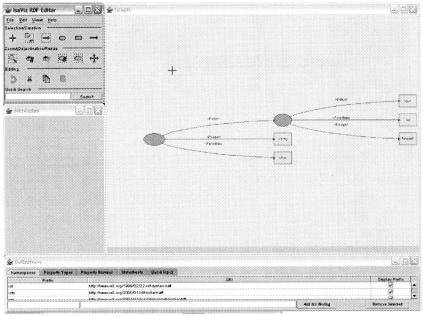

Figure 35: Graphical modeling tool

A robust EII solution should provide the means for expressing an information model to multiple audiences. For example, developers often desire to see the information model in ways that are immediately consumable and understandable by them, such as the Unified Modeling Language (UML). UML was created by combining the modeling techniques and nomenclatures of three leading modeling methodologies: Booch, Rumbaugh and Jacobson. The body of this work has since transitioned into the Object Management Group and is therefore being fostered by an independent standards organization.

UML is typically used by software engineers for specifying and modeling software applications. UML offers a robust framework for expressing ideas visually; especially business entities and the relationships between them. Due to the complexity of learning UML, it is unlikely that business workers will embrace UML modeling tools for the purposes of defining the business taxonomy—this does preclude them from embracing UML for other purposes, such as process modeling—but, UML tools can provide an excellent means of presenting the business taxonomy to development, so that they may further extend the resolution of those terms into the back office.

The Resource Definition Framework and its corresponding ontology development language the Web Ontology Language (OWL) are another way to express an information model in a meaningful way to both business and development. For the business users, RDF/OWL offers a substantial capability to identify the means for information classification and to combine instance data with its classification scheme. For developers, this classification scheme provides the focal point for additive metadata that is directly related to how data is transformed into information for use by the business worker.

Metadata Extraction

Given that EII is a solution that operates on multiple, disparate data sources and applications, we can surmise that these data sources and applications already exist, and have embedded in them, critical metadata that is required to enable our EII solution. Therefore, we need a set of tools that can analyze these existing data sources and applications, and extract the metadata into known, usable formats. This process is also sometimes called metadata harvesting.

These extraction tools are very specialized, but you can usually find a tool that supports your environment, regardless of the technologies employed. Examples of sources that extraction tools analyze are programming source code, databases, unstructured documents, as well as other metadata repositories.

Harvesting tools come in many forms, but the most common one is the scanner. The scanner is a piece of software that has intimate knowledge of specific metadata types. For instance, a COBOL copybook scanner will identify the data structures within a COBOL program. Most often, scanners operate in tandem with existing metadata repositories, so that the output of a scanning operation will populate the repository automatically.

Program source code, such as COBOL, happens to be among the most complex sources to extract metadata from. The reason for this is that as long as the program meets with the compiler requirements, the program will execute. However, the structure does not always meet with a well-ascribed design. Therefore, these types of scanners need some additional configuration, in the form of rules, which help the it identify the types of data that are of interest. In addition, the scanner is required to understand some of the program's logical flow in order to better identify when, and where, structures are applied. For example, a developer may define an internal data structure to store data temporarily during processing. If the data is not stored to a persistent medium, it's most likely not very useful to our EII implementation.

Another complex source to extract metadata from is packaged applications, such as SAP and Peoplesoft. These packaged applications introduce additional complexity because the data models they use are managed by the applications. This means that harvesting an underlying relational database model in use by a packaged application will yield the underlying physical layout of the data, without any clear understanding of how to organize that data into an intelligible structure. Therefore, harvesting metadata, and data for that matter, from these packaged applications requires the use of programming interfaces supplied by the packaged application vendor, or a third-party supplier that has extensive experience customizing and working with that specific packaged application.

Not all metadata is so complex to extract. In the case of relational databases and Web Services, extracting the metadata is relatively straightforward. Most relational database management systems provide interfaces for querying the structure of databases and tables, the Open Database Connectivity (ODBC), and Java Database Connectivity (JDBC) standards provide standardized interfaces for retrieval of that metadata. Additionally, in the case of Web Services, the XML schemas and Web Services Definition Language that comprise a Web Services implementation are simply XML documents that can be parsed by any off-the-shelf XML parser.

For many organizations, harvesting requires a mix of software tools to catalog the diverse mix of systems and applications that are in production. This often requires that those organizations rely on tools from multiple vendors in order to achieve a high-degree of automation around the harvesting process.

Data Cleansing

Components may be required as part of an EII solution for data cleansing (AKA data scrubbing), if the data quality of the systems of record have duplicated or inconsistent identifiers. The process of bringing together correlated data from disparate data sources is hindered by poor data quality. Thus, data cleansing tools may have to be applied directly to the systems of record, or on an interim view of aggregated data. In these cases, traditional data cleansing tools can be used. However, there are times when the data is owned by external parties and these tools cannot be applied directly to it. In these cases, the data cleansing process requires additional rules and processes to assist in the correlation process.

Performing data cleansing in real-time can be a very difficult process, and is made more difficult by having different identifiers across data sources. In these cases, record-matching algorithms may need to be custom-developed. Take, for example, one that is in use in a state government. This state government is broken up into multiple agencies, and each agency has its own systems and data. However, a health and human services case worker may need to see the interactions of a particular person with each state agency, in order to make a decision about child custody or welfare entitlement. For example, in the case of child custody, the case worker may want to verify that the person, who is being evaluated as a foster parent, does not have a criminal record (justice systems), and that they've held a job for the past five years (tax systems). In this case, one state government came up with a five-point system to identify correlated records. In this system, a record is said to represent a person if five pieces of data, such as social security number, first name, etc. within those records all match. Three matches indicate a high probability of a match and less than three points matching usually is rejected as a match.

Dynamic Data Aggregation

The dynamic data aggregation engine is the component of the EII solution that brings the solution to life. The general goal of the aggregation engine is to convert a collection of business terms into an instance of corresponding data. Accomplishing this conversion requires the engine to understand the structure of the information model in the metadata repository, and how to resolve a business term. The latter task is often the most difficult part of an EII solution, as there are many complexities associated with data access; especially across disparate platforms and applications. Hence, the aggregation engine relies on a strong adapter strategy, which is covered later in this chapter.

Some EII solutions provide the aggregation engine as a service that can be called through programmatic means. Others provide a user interface into the engine that facilitates queries by non-technical end-users. A third category of engines generate the underlying code for the aggregation engine at design-time. The service-based approach provides easier deployment and maintenance, while the code generation model provides the means for developers to introduce additional logic more easily, such as transformation or de-referencing. An EII solution that offers all three interfaces would provide the most comprehensive support options.

The final aspect of the aggregation engine is the result provided by running a set of terms through the engine. While the actual physical representation of this instance of data is dependent upon the specific implementation, all engines should ensure that the resulting data set is a combination of the metadata and the data combined; even if the metadata only represents the names of the business terms. Examples of results that can emerge from the engine include the following:

- Table-based – the aggregation results in a relational table view of the data that is comprised of rows and columns typically interfaced through a standard data access capability, such as Open Database Connectivity or Java Database Connectivity.
- XML – the aggregation results in an XML document that matches a proposed XML Schema. This includes XHTML, which can be displayed in a common Web browser.
- Flat-file – the aggregation results in the creation of a file that uses tab or comma delimited formatting.

Business Rules and Business Process Management

A business rule engine is a specialized version of a virtual machine—a software version of a machine code instruction processor, like Java—that is designed to optimize and execute business rules. These rules are usually written in a special rules language that is very high-level, and allows developers to express business rules in a reusable manner. These rules can then be executed directly from applications, as needed, but the key benefit is that the rules are no longer trapped in a particular programming language or hardware platform.

Rules engines are event-oriented facilities, which means that they manage a set of rules to be executed under a given condition. The input to a rules engine is typically an event, and some supporting data that is generated at the time of the event. A common example is the change in date at midnight. The event is identified as a date change, and the supporting data is the new date. When the rules engine detects the date change event, it triggers all events associated with that occurrence. Since this same rule can be associated with the triggering of multiple events, this facility provides tremendous reusability of rules; hence the reason why a business rules engine must first optimize the sequence for triggering before executing.

Assume, for this example, that a bank has a single update account rule that takes an amount and a source. This same rule can be triggered by either a deposit event, or an interest event. Of course, this is just another methodology for developing modular software, but, in contrast to binary modules, rules engines usually have rules languages that evaluate at runtime and, therefore, can be implemented on multiple hardware and operating system platforms.

However, just because rules engines provide a multi-platform runtime environment, this does not immediately translate into the ability to use cross-platform virtual machines, such as .NET and Java, as a rules engine. The key difference between rules engines and.NET or Java, is the ability of the rules engines to understand the dependencies across rules, and ensure that execution occurs in a manner that will not introduce a conflict.

The rules engine can play a significant role in the development of an Event-Driven Architecture (EDA). Unlike traditional procedure-based processing environments, which tend to be static and reactive, EDAs are configurable and proactive. EDA is a powerful infrastructure to use for the development of an EII solution. Instead of having to directly target each data source, the data source itself can be event-enabled, so that multiple instances of these targets can respond to a single data request. For example, the "getAllTransactions" event could be associated with two or more transaction-based systems, so that upon receipt of this event, it would generate a list of its internal transaction, and meet some criteria supplied with the event, such as time or account identifier.

Likewise, the EDA also provides a powerful infrastructure to support publishing data back to the systems of origin. In this way, the ontology or business terms can be associated with underlying systems and update procedures for each type of data. Upon receipt of an "update" event, the rules engine can take a single structure and update multiple data sources simultaneously. Moreover, each of those updated data sources can leverage the EDA to trigger further downstream processing, in a cascading effect, which, in turn, can result in additional updates (see Figure 36). For example, a change in

179

the price of an underlying security in a financial brokerage system could yield a complete re-calculation of the portfolio.

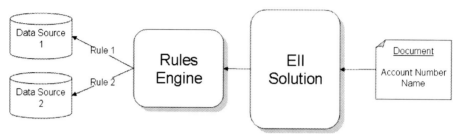

Figure 36: EDA applied to data source updates

Within the context of EII, business rules can also be used to define the business terms in the ontology. When used in this manner, a request for the resolution of a business term represents an event that the rules engine will respond to, where the data provided to the event is the input required to retrieve the data that is desired. Approaching the development of the aggregation engine in this manner will have direct impact on the design of the EII solution, since the definitions of the business terms will now be delegated to the rules engine. Therefore, additional attention needs to be paid to how the rule metadata is linked to the business term.

While EDA and business rules engines are very powerful tools, they are also very complex to control. As the base of rules within the engine begins to grow, it becomes more and more difficult for a single individual to know what the impact of a single event will produce. As chains of dependencies increase and overlap between rules occur, it's very possible for inexperienced (and sometimes even very sophisticated) users to create never-ending loops, data collisions, dead-locks and other generally negative side-effects. Constant vigilance must be paid to keeping the rules table pruned, and understanding the outcome of each event.

Adjunct, or orthogonal to business rules, is the concept of Business Process Management (BPM). BPM seemingly encompasses both workflow and process orchestration; thus the asynchronous and synchronous execution of logic, respectively. Workflow, the asynchronous process, whereby an external event causes a change in the state of the system, forcing some action to be taken until an end-state is reached, introduces the ability to operate in a consistent manner, over time boundaries. Orchestration, the synchronous cousin to workflow, organizes sequential steps together to bring about the routine output of some automated task. Together, they represent the Ying and Yang of distributed computing, facilitating the dance of data across systems as effortlessly as if it were contained in a single machine.

Business processes represent the entire sequence of events that lead to the completion of a business-oriented task. For example, order management in manufacturing, which includes (in simplified form) the acceptance of the order, the acknowledgement of the order, the manufacturing of the ordered goods and the packaging and shipping of the goods. Throughout the entire lifetime of this order, there are a number of tasks that are accomplished, with the goal of delivering product to the customer. Additionally, this business process has its own set of semantics that are associated with its delivery, such as "Bill of Lading" and "Purchase Order", both of which are types of documents associated with the ordering and shipping of goods.

BPM and EII share a very uncommon relationship, in that it is not always clear which technology benefits the most from the relationship. BPM can be used, like business rules, to assist in the resolution of business terms as part of an aggregation, or it can be used to support publishing data back to the underlying data sources. However, EII offers BPM the ability to represent, and associate, the semantics of a business process with its underlying implementation, thus providing a way to organize and categorize discrete processes for later inclusion into an aggregate business process.

Taken together, business rules and business process management provide a configurable infrastructure for developing a powerful EII solution.

Transformation Tools

Transformation tools are a primary component for all distributed, data-based solutions. The primary reason for this is that data from System A has a different structure from the data in System B. If the structures weren't different, there would be little need for an integration solution in the first place, since the homogeneity would make data sharing and exchange across system boundaries a snap.

However, all transformation tools are not created equal, nor do they provide the same capabilities. Some transformation tools focus on the physical bits and bytes of the data, to convert and combine them as needed. Sometimes this is through a formula, and other times, data values are simply copied from one moniker to another. For example, ETL tools can take multiple data sources as input, and map pieces of each into a new structure. The rules that define how data moves into the new structure is not always straightforward or one-to-one, but can go through many stages where it is evaluated and manipulated before being passed onto the next stage of transformation.

Other transformation tools focus on the structures themselves, such as XML Stylesheet Transformation Language (XSLT). XSLT provides the ability to transform one XML vocabulary into another. There is less focus on changing the data as part of this transformation, and more focus on labeling the data or deriving new XML vocabularies, based on the original content.

Transformation tools also differ in how they approach transformation. Take, for example, ETL and XSLT. ETL transformations are usually sequential processes that have a well-defined path that the data will take. That is, it is easy to trace the route that a single instance of data will take though an ETL transformation. Alternatively, XSLT is rules based, which means that each XML element will fire up a different rule to produce an unlimited number of paths that can be executed, depending upon the XML document that is used as input, to the stylesheet. Indeed, a single stylesheet is capable of handling the transformation of more than one XML schema. This style of transformation makes it more difficult to create and troubleshoot, than ETL-style transformations.

Service-Oriented Architecture

In Chapter 5, we discussed SOA from the perspective of XML and Web Services standards. However, for the purpose of our discussion of EII components, we will adjust the definition slightly to represent a set of software that supports the distribution of computing, across a group of disparate machines in a loosely-coupled manner. Of course, XML and Web Services have demonstrated themselves to be a very strong set of technologies for the implementation of this type of infrastructure. However, for the purposes of implementing EII, other technologies, such as CORBA, RMI, RPC, DCOM, etc. will provide the following capabilities that are critical to the success of an EII implementation:

- Locality of access. Data access mechanisms are better suited co-located with the data source, rather than connected from a single controlling entity.
- Transparency. Access to the underlying data is hidden from the applications and users requesting that data.
- Balance of computing. The basic operations of transformation, filtering, cleansing, validation, aggregation and consolidation occur where best suited within the distributed architecture. That is, not all processes need to be consolidated on a single machine as this could bottleneck or reduce performance.
- Security. EII needs a way to ensure controlled access to data in a scalable, but fine-grained manner.

Query Engine

Some EII solutions incorporate a query engine that implements the ability to aggregate data dynamically, based on constraints, examples, and other search criteria, such as phonetics. Such query engines can be a very powerful component of the EII solution, as they help hone in on the real data being requested, and limit the overhead to the application, or and reduces the need for the requesting individual to apply additional resources to qualify the resulting data.

The requirements of an EII query engine are slightly different than that of a relational database query engine, such as SQL, because it may have to operate over many different sources of data, some of which may not be available, or have longer accessing delays. The first thing these query engines must do is analyze the data being requested, and then figure out a plan for obtaining the data. This means that the engine is heavily reliant upon the metadata repository, in order to understand where a specific piece of data resides, the structure it is currently in, any required keys for retrieving it, and the methods it can use to request that data. Once all the data is analyzed, the query engine can then develop a query plan that it will use to extract the data.

A simple EII query engine could provide this minimal set of functionality, but the results would most likely exhibit poor performance, since the same data source or application may need to be queried multiple times. In some cases, this may not even be possible, if the query changes the state of the data, or its content. Therefore, a robust EII query engine should provide some optimization of the query, so that only one query is issued to each source, where that source provides multiple pieces of data that belongs to the same request. For example, if one Web Service can provide both the account information and current balance, then only query should be made to that Web Service instead of two (see Figure 37).

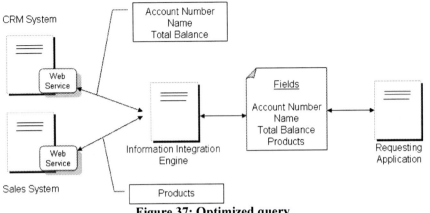

Figure 37: Optimized query

The final element of a query engine is how it supports access from applications and users. Most EII users will look for familiar integration capabilities from a query engine, such as the one described here. For example, they may desire to have either an Open Database Connectivity (ODBC), or Java Database Connectivity (JDBC) interface. These are programmatic interfaces that allow application developers to interact with them in a consistent manner. They typically return the results of the query to the application as an array called a result set that can be navigated using program logic.

XML Query (XQuery) engines provide an additional benefit over simple ODBC/JDBC interfaces, since it structures the data as an XML document, which makes the data even more understandable and usable by the requester. An XQuery engine uses a specific XML vocabulary to issue requests. This XML document defines the XML document structure that the requester would like the data format returned in. The following example shows an XML Query and its corresponding results.

Query:
for $t in document("books.xml")//title return <books>$t</books>

Result:
<books>   <title>EAI with XML and Java</title>   <title>Manager's Guide to Distributed Environments</title> </books>

Data Cache

In some cases, there may be a need to cache the data as part of a data aggregation scenario. The cache acts as a temporary home for the data, until it is ready to be used. In some situations, the EII solution may either generate a very large result set that cannot possibly be contained in memory, and, therefore, needs to be cached until it is retrieved, or delivered to the requesting entity. Alternatively, some EII solutions may be limited by time-based constraints, such as a system that takes longer to respond than other components that are part of the same aggregation. In these cases, it may be desirable to store the results that have been aggregated, prior to the completion of the slower components, so that those resources can be returned to the aggregation engine. Additionally, the cache also represents a facility that can be used to store the results of an aggregation that is going to be transformed or cleansed.

The data cache should not enforce a particular data model, or require advanced modeling techniques to be used, in order to store data in the cache. In this way, you can view the cache as a semi-structured data store. The cache should also institute automated garbage collection by instituting expiration dates on each different type of data stored within the cache. This will lower the need for administration and maintenance, and make the cache less of a burden on the overall EII solution.

186

Publishing Engine

The publishing engine is less of a requirement and more of a supportive feature of EII. The publishing engine leverages the same metadata that is used for aggregation to update the original sources, effectively making the EII solution bi-directional. However, if the aggregation engine is complex, the publishing engine is daunting. After all, aggregation is to reading what publishing is to writing, at least in digital form, whereas a write takes three times the amount of effort of a read, because a write must guarantee success.

In the publishing engine, we begin to see the impact of the three-legged stool of integration. The publishing engine could be developed specifically for the EII solution; however, it would be redundant with many existing EAI toolsets. It is better to leverage the EAI tools to support the transactional needs of writing data back to the original data sources, and expose those tools as services to be leveraged by the EII implementation.

Adapters

Typically, there is a wide variety of data that one might want to make available through an EII implementation. Each of the data sources, in turn, contains both data and metadata that will need to be accessed in order to incorporate the data into the EII solution. Unfortunately, however, many data sources were developed without forethought of integration, and, may therefore provide limited-to-indirect access through the data. Where access is provided, it may only happen through proprietary means, versus open standards. To overcome this hurdle, companies have specialized in the development of adapters which have intimate knowledge of the data and metadata of those systems.

Adapters come in many forms. If made available from the company that produced the application or data source, the adapter interface could be exposed as an export mechanism from within the application, or through an application programming interface. Sometimes, adapters are provided by third party companies that offer more robust access mechanisms, such as distributed computing interfaces, application programming interfaces and, now, more importantly, Web Services.

The important thing to keep in mind, when selecting an adapter, is the level of capabilities that it offers with regard to EII. For example, an EII solution may be involved in performing highly selective queries against the data, or filtering, based on access control mechanisms. It is important that the adapter extend these facilities outward from the application or data source, or it will impact the amount of effort needed to make the data usable within the overall solution. For example, some adapters can directly access the data models of packaged applications. Because they have an intimate understanding of the underlying model, they can get at all the data, but because they are accessing the data at such a low level, they sometimes bypass the security mechanisms that were implemented by the packaged application, thus possibly compromising security and privacy. While, in many cases and as will be shown in the next section on security management, it is natural to extend all data to the EII solution in a trusted manner, and let the EII implementation handle access control, there may be cases where it is a requirement to emulate the capabilities of a particular client of the underlying system. In these cases, the adapter needs to extend the source of origin's security facilities.

Key Concepts

1. Understand the types of components that will be used to implement an EII solution and the role that each component plays
2. EII requires an understanding of data modeling
3. The more diverse metadata, that the metadata repository supports, will provide a stronger foundation for ontology development and impact analysis
4. Rules engines respond to events and manage dependencies in a very sophisticated manner
5. Business process management engines provide orchestration across a set of tasks
6. Query engines provide well-known interfaces to data as well as optimize the retrieval of data

> *"An apprentice carpenter may want only a hammer and saw, but a master craftsman employs many precision tools. Computer programming likewise requires sophisticated tools to cope with the complexity of real applications, and only practice with these tools will build skill in their use."*
> – *Robert L. Kruse,*
> *Data Structures and Program Design*

EII Implementation Details

This chapter covers many of the real-world issues associated with EII implementations. Since EII can satisfy a wide diversity of needs and be applied to many problem domains, it is possible that you will run into a wide array of issues, hurdles and dilemmas as part of your implementation. EII provides a good foundation for moving to an up-to-the-minute view of data within your organization, but the realities of legacy environments will continue to get in the way of this for some time to come. Additionally, there are always going to be trade-offs that you need to make between performance, data quality and timeliness of the data.

Metadata Lifecycle Management

All EII solutions start with metadata lifecycle management. This may include any or all of the following: metadata extraction, modeling, capture, and ontology development. In some EII implementations, the metadata lifecycle may consist of a single, one-time, synchronization against the current production environment. This means that the production environment is the gold standard for metadata, and all changes will only be enacted on this environment. This approach to metadata lifecycle management requires that each change to the production environment invoke an eventual update with the EII solution. Due to the nature of the change, it may not be necessary to perform this update immediately, and, possibly, may never be required until the underlying change actually impacts the user.

An alternative approach to metadata lifecycle management is to leverage the EII solution as a revision control system for all production metadata. In this scenario, an initial synchronization is performed to load the necessary production metadata into the EII metadata repository. From this point forward, all changes that impact metadata in the EII solution are first checked out of the repository. Then, the change is implemented and tested, and then checked back into the repository, while incrementing the revision for that piece of metadata.

Ultimately, we would like the metadata lifecycle management tool (the metadata repository) to manage all metadata at a very fine-grained level, so that each component of metadata can be versioned separately. In lieu of a fine-grained solution, it may be possible to revision at the source level, which means that all the metadata contained in a particular source is grouped together. For example, if a change is made to a field in a database, then the metadata represented by the schema for that database is versioned as a whole.

Metadata can also be grouped together to form libraries that represented dependent modules. For example, if you have two database schemas, two XML schemas and three business processes comprise the self-service portal for customers to check their account balance. It would be useful to group these seven components together as a single unit, so that a change to any piece of metadata in any of these components will force a revision of the entire library. Therefore, it is hoped that after the change, a quality check will reveal that all the modules still work properly in the production environment, and if not, that the change can be rolled back in a single action..

Managing the lifecycle of typical data asset metadata, such as database schemas and ETL transformation models, is a well-documented and mature area. However, the addition of ontology development causes some changes to the typical lifecycle management process. With the addition of this effort, the ontology itself must be created and maintained over time. This includes optimizing, pruning and expanding the ontology as the business begins to represent itself digitally in new ways. Moreover, this process usually requires the input of non-IT personnel, whereas the rest of the metadata lifecycle management can be maintained solely by IT. In addition, the relationships between metadata that enable the EII solution to operate, such as the linkages between the ontology and the underlying services and data sources, add yet another layer of complexity to the metadata lifecycle management process.

An EII Example Architecture

Chapter 7—EII Components—covered the individual components that are part of an EII implementation. Figure 38 depicts a possible configuration of some of those components. Each implementation will deploy some subset of these components, as part of its task of creating information. The following sections will explore multiple approaches to solving this complex problem, details and issues regarding deploying EII solutions, and the types of applications that rely on this type of infrastructure.

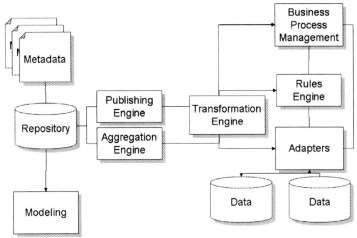

Figure 38: EII component architecture

Example architectures, such as the one depicted in Figure 38, help us understand how the individual components can be organized to provide an end-to-end solution. However, what's not directly stated here, but is critical to understanding the architecture, is how the data flows across the components.

The analysis below describes the data flows across each component:

- **Metadata/Repository.** This connection represents the interface on the repository for management of the metadata lifecycle. Typically, this interface should support some version control, Web-based accessibility for upload and downloading of metadata and impact analysis and data lineage reporting.
- **Modeling/Repository.** This connection is similar to the Metadata/Repository interface. It is called out separately in this architecture to represent the different processes that create each set of metadata. The modeling interface represents the process of ontology and taxonomy development versus modeling and metadata created external to the EII solution, such as a database schema.
- **Aggregation Engine (AE)/Repository or Publishing Engine (PE)/Repository.** These connections represent the interface on

the repository that the engines use to navigate the metadata, which, in turn, is used to perform data aggregation or publishing. These engines will leverage the Web Services Definition Language (WSDL), database schemas and business processes to determine the best way to retrieve data or update the data at the source.

- **Transformation Engine (TE)/AE or TE/PE.** These connections represent a change in the data's structure as it passes onto other components, or as it is processed from other components. In this architecture, the Transformation Engine is actually layered over other connections, and is optionally applied.

- **AE/Business Process Management (BPM) or AE/Rules Engine (RE).** These connections represent a bi-directional data flow. First, the AE can use the BPM to execute a complex business process that will result in the formation of information that will be part of the aggregation. Likewise, the AE can generate events that the RE will respond to. Alternatively, the BPM or RE can use the AE as a tool to aggregate data from disparate sources that is required as part of a complex business process, or in the handling of an event, respectively.

- **PE/BPM or AE/RE.** These connections represent a bi-directional data flow. First, the PE can use the BPM to execute a complex business process that will result in updating data sources. Likewise, the PE can generate events that the RE will respond to. Alternatively, the BPM, or RE, can use the PE as a tool to aggregate data from disparate sources that is required as part of a complex business process or in the handling of an event, respectively.

- **BPM/Adapters, RE/Adapters, AE/Adapters or PE/Adapters.** All of these connections represent communications with existing data sources through a well-defined interface. In this architecture, the Adapters component can also represent Web Services that may be providing access to the underlying data sources.

Design Considerations

The reason for differentiating EII practices from EII tools is apparent when viewed in light of implementation. The EII practice provides us with a roadmap of how we will design an EII solution. But, this is akin to saying that a building has four sides and stands two stories tall. There are many different ways to satisfy the EII best practice, and this section discusses design considerations that will impact the overall EII tools selection process to include:

Response Time

Creating information from disparate raw data sources incurs overhead. Determining the response time requirements is one of the guiding requirements for your EII implementation. Consider the fact that simple aggregate structures take less time to build and return than complex or transformed structures. Therefore, where the work is completed will impact overall response time. For example, using a front end application to analyze, transform, and display a simple aggregate structure may provide better response time than allowing a server-based implementation to provide these functions and return a complete result. As a rule, response time will be impacted by all other choices and limitations. Therefore, you should know the acceptable minimum response time for your application.

User Interface

The user interface for your EII solution will center on three areas: administration, reporting, and modeling. Options here include Web-based or fat-client. Web-based interfaces push more work onto the server, reduce overall system response time, and require much greater scalability. Fat-clients provide users with more interactivity and better responsiveness. The Web-based client is usually satisfactory for an administration interface, and this includes report creation. However, Web-based clients are only moderately useful for report execution, and are usually problematic for modeling.

Data Volumes

In contrast to many solutions that can be designed around median support requirements, EII solutions must be designed around the size of the maximum results set. Improper planning in this area can result in a detriment to the performance of the overall solution in production, and even potential crashes due to overwhelming data volumes. Depending upon the maturity of the ontology and intelligence of the aggregation engine, it is possible that the result set could be boundless. For this reason, the solution must take into account maximum data volumes, as well as provide a way to place limits on the result set creation.

The problem of the boundless result set may require an interim cache as a solution. In this case, the cache is an interim data store that is not optimized for a particular data structure, but has the ability to manage the storage and update of very large, and growing, data structures. These caches must offer highly responsive loading of data (write operations), and be able to handle extremely large volumes. Solutions that support the creation of scalable terabyte data management, using affordable approaches such as Linux-based database clusters, can satisfy this caching requirement.

Data Marts/Warehouses

A question that emerges frequently during the design phase of an EII project is, "Do we still need a data mart/warehouse?" If the question is predicated on the fact that you needed a data mart/warehouse before initiating your EII project, then chances are you most likely will continue to need it, even after the EII solution is implemented.

EII and virtual data warehousing are often confused. The data warehouse offers very specific capabilities for highly-normalized queries that support operational efforts, such as marketing and risk-management. Virtual data warehousing requires the same quality assurance and data cleansing as traditional data warehousing approaches, but does not necessarily house the clean and condensed data in a single facility.

The data mart/warehouse can be a part ofan EII solution by acting as a data source. However, most recent implementations of EII have been used to supplement the data mart/warehouse due to the aging of the data in these facilities. This is due, primarily, to the processes required to cleanse and load this data. Instead, the EII solution often comprises more up-to-the-minute data that may not have gone through data quality checks, and is accessed directly from the systems of record.

Data Consolidation

Sometimes it is necessary to summarize a group of data in order to satisfy a query. For example, in order to determine the top 25 salespersons, based on total sales for the quarter, one would have to first summarize the sales for all sales people, and then rank them. This is even more complex when the sales data does not exist in a single sales database (see Figure 39).

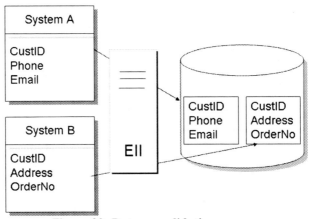

Figure 39: Data consolidation

This is different than caching. With caching, we simply replicate the data on a temporary basis, but will not necessarily change the content. With consolidation, we examine and group the contents of the temporary data set. This temporary data set then becomes the data source that the EII solution will leverage as the underlying representation for data.

The main purpose of using data consolidation in an EII implementation is speed and responsiveness. Attempting to use EII alone, to satisfy the 'top 25 salesperson' requirements, may require that hundreds, possibly thousands, of records need to be retrieved and then filtered. Sometimes, it makes sense to leverage the existing query facilities of the existing data management systems to link a view of the data to a particular type of query, and let the data management system generate that consolidated view of the data.

Query Complexity

When dealing with distributed data, queries cannot always be satisfied by a single level request. Here is a list of issues that can impact query complexity:

- Cascading queries – in order to successfully obtain the desired data, the results from other queries are first required as input into the final query. If any of these queries fail, of course, the entire query fails. Additionally, these queries may not all be directed at the same data source. Related to cascading queries are recursive queries, which require that prior results be maintained, until the next recursive query completes. With deep recursion, this can force the requirement to maintain a high-volume of data until the query completes.

- Interim caching – sometimes the final result set can only be obtained by first creating an aggregate result set out of prior queries, and storing that result set in a temporary cache. Since this is a very complex requirement, it is unlikely that this will be a functionality that is available out-of-the-box from a vendor. This means that it must be designed into the solution.

- Security – managing access to disparate data may require multiple levels of security clearance. The EII solution must be capable of authenticating itself into each data source, as required, as part of a complex query.

Legacy Systems

Where your data is currently stored, and the format that is stored in, will also impact the design of the overall solution; this includes accessibility to the data. The following is a set of characteristics of legacy systems that must be taken into account when designing your EII solution:

- Interface – Does the legacy application offer a programmatic interface to the data, or force direct access to the data in its stored format? Also, does the interface support ad-hoc queries, or, are the queries fixed and new ones need to be developed before the data can be accessed?

- Speed – How quickly can the legacy system respond to requests? Screen scraped applications and high-volume transactional systems can take longer to respond.

Best-of-Breed Applications

Companies that use a best-of-breed approach to applications selection may have the greatest need for an EII solution. They may also have the greatest difficulty in implementing such a solution. This is because the best-of-breed solutions often incur overlap of data. For example, a best-of-breed approach to CRM and ERP may require overlap of customer data. When this occurs, companies will have difficulties selecting the "gold" standard for their data given that both systems act as systems of record in their selected capacities.

Overcoming this hurdle is usually done by first integrating the best-of-breed packages using an EAI strategy, and identifying one of the systems as the system of record. For instance, in our CRM and ERP example, the company may select the ERP package as the primary system and replicate changes from that system, to the CRM application.

This is not a serious consequence, but, as we've stated, it will require that additional, and sometimes expensive, application integration occur before EII can be implemented successfully.

Transience

When designing and EII system, you may come across data that exists only between systems and is not physically stored in that form, except during a short period of time, when it is being transferred between systems. Consider the case where an insurance application computes and applies risk ratings upon processing an application. That data is then used to help the new applicant application assign policy pricing in a downstream application, but throws the original risk rating away, in favor of a new risk rating that is computed using different business logic. If you want to capture the risk rating as it was computed by the original application processing system, you will have to intercept the message in transit.

This approach can leverage the data caching solution that we discussed earlier in this book. In this case, the cache is used to capture the transient data for use in information integration solutions, becomes another source of data that is represented by the business vocabulary, and has a greater life span than other types of data that may reside in the cache.

Data Quality

The importance of data quality in an EII solution cannot be stressed enough; it will have a significant impact on the overall success of the EII solution. That is, it is a simple chore to implement a solution that aggregates data from multiple SQL databases together into a new structure, but if that data is "dirty," then the value of that data to the creation of information is minimal.

The following example illustrates just how important data quality is.

> One transportation customer implemented EII to gain insight into combined sales for customers. The data for this effort was captured in different systems, due to recent acquisitions, and each system represented the customer by different identifiers and names, such as their sub-division name.
>
> The first report generated amounts that were very different than the hand-generated versions of the reports. Both systems, the hand-generation and EII process, then underwent a series of analyses and tracing. The result yielded that the difference in the amounts was due to a discrepancy in the representation of a single sub-division of a large corporation, as a single independent entity.

Unfortunately, poor data quality is often an overlooked problem, or organizations apply "band-aid" solutions to them, in order to overcome the hurdles they introduce. In fact, data quality is most often the culprit for increased front- and mid-office costs, because it takes additional resources to help cleanse and organize the data into a format that they cannot obtain from the sources of origin. Indeed, many requirements for business process management are nothing more than an attempt to minimize human resource costs, as part of this poor data quality problem. This is an instance of the forest and trees problem, because organizations see the need to automate the cleansing process (the tree) instead of the data quality problem, causing the cleansing overhead (the forest).

EII, often times provides users with a view of the data that is unfamiliar to them, because their prior interaction with a particular data set may have been indirectly accessed through business logic, or manually-derived reports. When users see the "real" data for the first time, it may not match up with existing views of that data in existence in the organization. For example, the actual marketing dollars spent on a particular activity may differ from the actual amount represented in the accounting system.

Quality control is about understanding the cause for these differences, and getting to the most accurate version. The reasons for these discrepancies can vary. For example, the new EII process may include time worked or indirectly-related expenses that exist in the human resource timesheet system.

Quality control in an EII solution often requires traditional debugging or reverse-engineering skills. The lineage of the data must be traceable all the way back to it's inception into the system, and the solution must help the user see where the data that is being aggregated comes from, and why it might be different than other sources that are supposedly providing similar data.

Data Governance

In many organizations, data is one of the areas that delineate organizational boundaries. The governor of the data may see controlling access to the data as a defining aspect of their role. The thought of opening that access to the world at large can be extremely threatening to these individuals. The best technical solutions in the world are not always an indicator of future success, as the entire solution can fall apart due to a simple data gatekeeper that will not cooperate.

Overcoming this hurdle often requires senior executive support for the project, and all stakeholders must be willing to cooperate in sharing their data and implementing the required data access interfaces.

Organizational Skills

Your EII solution relies upon the skills and knowledge of the individuals that you have, or can hire, to implement the solution. The most important skills are defining and building access to legacy applications that do not offer modern interfaces. For example, mainframe developers who used Software AG's Natural application environment often combined the user interface and business logic into the same modules, because, at the time, modularity was expensive. Today, without Natural programmers who know how to modularize that code, in order to separate the business logic from the user interface, you will be forced to use screen scraping technologies to retrieve the data, instead of being able to access it directly, as a remotely callable module.

A Balanced Approach to Integration

When deciding if EII is the right approach to a project, you must consider the goals of the project and then evaluate the hurdles, just like those listed above. However, the outcome of this analysis will be different, depending upon who does the analysis. Most developers we have worked with on this type of approach quickly debate the merits of all the overhead, instead, proposing that the same solution can be provided much more quickly using a pure coding effort. In their defense, if this is a "one-off" project—that is, the solution is isolated to a single problem and the results of the effort cannot be leveraged elsewhere—then a pure coding effort would be the best choice for implementing this type of integration.

When the analysis is completed by an architect or a project manager who has a wider view of other problems that exist, or that are currently being solved, there is a greater appreciation for the up-front design requirements, because these individuals can see how that work will be applied elsewhere on other projects.

Additionally, if we consider a scale for the initiation of integration development projects that are represented on the low-end, with no up-front design, and with pure coding, and a high-end by pure modeling with no code, then the approach to EII falls somewhere in the middle. Certainly, it is true that the metadata lifecycle involves some level of effort that yields only modest rewards on the first project(s). However, if you developed Web Services for purposes of unlocking your data, then these services are immediately usable, even as part of a pure-coding effort.

Perhaps this is more of a side-effect than a strategy, but this approach to integration has been shown to yield both tactical results quickly through the development of a services-oriented architecture, while positioning the company to implement a more strategic approach to overall integration, through a semantic layer.

EII Implementation Strategies

The following are different EII implementation strategies to that have been used either by vendors through their tools, or in custom implementations. They represent various ways that EII can be exposed as a set of functionality to users.

Distributed Query

Distributed query is a popular approach to developing an EII solution. It is typically used by application developers since it provides a lower-level interface to the data, and the results must then be processed for use by the application, versus providing an interface that can be used directly by end users. The distributed query approach provides for ad-hoc reporting, since the query facility does not limit the types or elements of data that can be requested.

The goal of the distributed query approach is to provide a single query interface that can parallelize that query across a group of disparate data sources, where each of those data sources may support varying means of applying that query. This query interface is then responsible for gathering the responses from each query handler, and creating a single, usable result set.

There are two methods of implementing the distributed query: ordered and parallel. The ordered method requires the facilities of a controller that understands:

- which data sources need to be accessed
- the query parameters to retrieve the required data
- how to map the results sets

Using these three key pieces of information, the controller then issues the query to each corresponding data source and handles the response.

In parallel distributed queries, the data sources or adapters interfacing on behalf of a data source receive the query, and handle the translation of both the query and the results set. An aggregation facility then organizes the results sets into a single result set that is returned to the calling application. Figure 40 below illustrates the architecture for a parallel query.

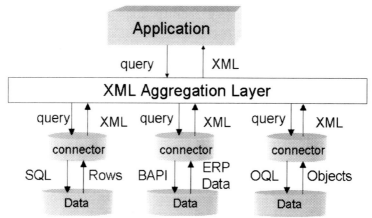

Figure 40: Parallel query architecture

This approach works well when all the data sources have consistent query semantics. For example, in Figure 40, each data source can translate between the common query syntax and its own query facilities. This may not always be possible, especially when one of the data sources is represented by a Web Service or other programming interface.

Virtual Modeling

Virtual modeling is a technique that combines traditional data modeling techniques, with integration, to create logical models that have connections to physical counterparts, which are distributed across many different data sources. Each virtual model can represent a combination of different physical architectures, such as databases, documents, and application interfaces, with each model also mapping to a particular format for production, such as XML or a database table.

Creating the virtual model requires an understanding of the existing data sources structures and elements. The metadata must be harvested from these existing sources and made available to the designer of the virtual model. Similarly, there must be a process capable of resolving a logical entity into its physical counterpart, in order to create instances of the virtual model from those existing sources. Here, you may actually combine solution strategies and employ the distributed query facility to manage query and data retrieval on behalf of the virtual model.

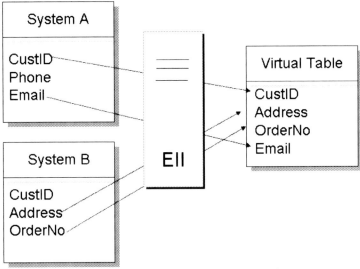

Figure 41: Example of virtual modeling

Virtual modeling offers applications greater control over the data being requested and used by an application, but increases the rigidity by limiting what data can be selected. That is, once a virtual model is created, it requires human intervention for modifications. This does not serve very well the need for serving up dynamic data structures.

Ontology-based Modeling

The ontology-based modeling approach to EII combines aspects of both the distributed query and virtual modeling approaches. Ontology-based modeling uses an information model as the basis for integration. In this model, the ontology represents the new structure for the presentation of information. This is where the similarity with the virtual modeling approach is apparent. However, the ontology model is much more robust than a simple virtual table.

The ontology also represents the relationships between terms within the model. These relationships can then be used to enhance either the aggregation, or filtering of data. In aggregation, the set of relationships can be used to navigate through a space of terms that are related to automatically derive a new structure, based on the information model. For example, if the model represents a family, and the family includes a mother, father, children, aunts, uncles, etc., then the aggregation logic can automatically infer which data sources need to be queried and what those queries are, in order to retrieve the family structure. Likewise, the ontology information can be used to automatically filter a large data set. In this way, the relationships identify only the data that should be returned.

The ontology-based model is similar to the distributed query model because a single ontological structure can incur cascading queries that need to be resolved. Again, in the case of retrieving a family model, multiple queries may have to be issued and satisfied, in order to retrieve all the components of a group of related individuals.

Key Concepts

1. When deploying an EII solution, it is critical to take into account the multitude of design requirements, such as response time, user interface, data volumes, query complexity, legacy systems, transience, data governance and organizational skills.
2. There are multiple methods to achieve the integration of information, such as distributed query or virtual modeling. Distributed query abstracts disparate data sources through a query facility, while the virtual model creates a logical abstraction of multiple data sources, by modeling the data into a new structure. The former provides the opportunity for more ad-hoc reporting with less control, while the latter provides greater control with more rigidity.
3. Distributed query implementation strategy works well when all the data sources are capable of handling query syntax.
4. Virtual modeling provides greater control over the data made available through EII, but limits dynamic queries.
5. Ontological modeling provides a good balance of modeling, without limiting the ability to dynamically request new data structures on demand.

"Knowledge is of two kinds. We know a subject ourselves, or we know where we can find information upon it."
    – *Samuel Johnson*

The EII Practice: A Macro View

If, thirty years ago, you knew what we know now about information technology, would you have designed your systems differently? Most likely, the answer is yes! However, thirty years ago, the minicomputer was state-of-the-art in information technology, and automating the back office was a major advancement over the paper-based systems of the time. This resulted in silos of applications that paralleled the single-task mindset of the time.

Need to automate accounting? Develop an accounting system? Need to manage inventory? Develop an inventory management system. Little thought was given by developers to the fact that inventory impacted both accounts payable and accounts receivable; this was the purview of the systems analysts charged with capturing the requirements. In lieu of a robust business process methodology toward systems development, a network of paper shuffling filled the void. That is, reports were generated from the inventory system and sent to the accounting department for re-entry. Problem solved! It wasn't until mounting data entry errors and inconsistencies forced companies to re-evaluate this approach and realize that systems design is not an isolated task, it must be done within the scope of a larger ecosystem—an enterprise architecture.

It is unfortunate that our automation practices did not keep pace with the rapid advancement in computing's increased performance, at lower cost structures. Thus, we continued to developed systems in isolation, even though our ability to network these tasks together had advanced to the point where parts of tasks could be reused across the organization. Ignoring this capability has caused data quality problems such as: the lack of authoritative data sources, redundant definitions for the same data, incompatible definitions that share the same name, and general errata caused by manually re-keyed information between systems.

As a result, data quality problems have impacted front- and mid-office productivity by adding overhead, such as requiring manual massaging of the data. This limits our ability to integrate existing data and systems at a reasonable cost, and limits our ability to quickly develop new applications that leverage our existing data assets.

The EII best practice is a reusable configuration of a group of non-integrated components. When integrated in a particular configuration, this best practice emerges to help overcome the self-imposed design limitations of our legacy systems, and free our data and business rules from the static worlds in which they are trapped. This pattern can also help overcome the existing data quality problems, and make data more readily accessible to the organization as a whole.

The Enterprise Information Integration Practice

Based on the experience gathered over the past ten years, had we known the impact of our prior decisions, we would probably have designed our applications using an architecture similar to the one depicted in Figure 42 below. This figure illustrates state-of-the-art information system design where data exists in a high-quality, normalized form. Business rules are discrete and reusable. New applications can quickly be developed by joining the discrete rules together in a general workflow, and all of the metadata underlying this design is captured in a central repository where it can provide the basis for future work.

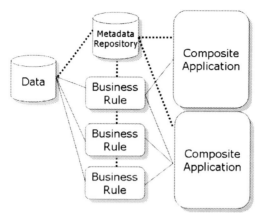

Figure 42: Best practice for application design

This architecture does not limit you from being focused on delivery of application silos, it just enables the internals of those applications to be reused either in similar applications, or for integration purposes. Moreover, this architecture should not be seen as an indicator that data must exist once, and only once, in a single store. There are times where, when managed appropriately through process, it may make sense to replicate data.

Yet, in both of these circumstances, it is important to separate out the needs of the application from the underlying architecture. For instance, a composite application should focus narrowly on solving one problem or a related set of problems for end users, such as inventory management. But, the rules for managing inventory data and the underlying data models to support this function do not need to be developed with this one and only scope in mind. Thus, a part of the practice is to formulate an extensible data management architecture that can drive the development of well-scoped applications.

Likewise, it is unreasonable to expect that you will develop all data to only be defined only once in one repository. Transactional performance, privacy and confidentiality, high-availability and general accessibility, all are good reasons to introduce redundant data sources, and have data defined in multiple data sources. An example of this is when users are geographically dispersed and access will be faster and more reliable when staged locally. However, this requirement does not yield to the practice of defining authoritative sources. The underlying data management architecture should support prioritization of data sources, such that general inquiries are first satisfied by the authoritative source. Moreover, non-authoritative sources should only be replicated from authoritative sources, and there need to be explicit policies about when data flows in the reverse direction.

Fortunately, we have the knowledge to make existing information systems assets adhere to this best practice today. Accomplishing this feat requires us to follow a formal methodology that will lead us to understand how our existing systems are designed, extract their metadata, and use that metadata to assist us in providing a modular and reusable architecture for integrating our data.

It's been stated that integration is a practice and not a technology, for the better part of this book now. This chapter drills down into the best practice behind implementing an Enterprise Information Integration solution. Accomplishing this feat first requires reviewing a high-level approach to these types of solutions, and then drilling down into each part of the best practice, to provide needed insight and implementation details.

The best practice laid out here is based on an abstraction of techniques used on several successful projects, and focuses on three key steps: unlocking your data, aligning it with the needs of the business, and enabling users to interact with the data.

As indicated in Chapter 2—Integration: The Three-legged Stool—EAI is best at ensuring that transactional integrity is maintained across disparate applications, and ETL tools are best at stripping data down to its basic elements and recombining it in new ways for downstream processing. Neither one of these approaches directly addresses the volatile, unpredictable, and rapidly changing needs of users with regard to the data. Indeed, EAI and ETL tools work best when operating in a well-defined environment with few changes.

EII has emerged to respond to users' need to access their data in unique and original ways without imposing the development and maintenance overhead associated with other integration techniques. But, the important aspect of the EII best practice is that it provides the business users with a sense of control over the data they need to operate the business, without requiring the data administrators to give up control and governance. Effectively, this is a win-win situation for any organization.

Figure 43, below, represents the goals for implementing EII. In this diagram we have three disparate data sources, one being an application while the others represent physical data assets. These disparate data sources are then mapped into a business taxonomy that represents the vernacular of the business. The business terms are represented within the business process management modeling environment so that business analysts are totally abstracted from the underlying implementation of the data and its location. Finally, the business taxonomy can be leveraged by front office applications to access the data assets in a consistent manner.

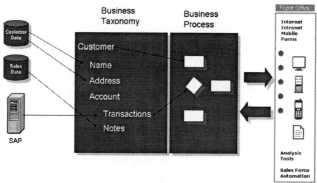

Figure 43: Vision for EII

Figure 44 below illustrates the architecture that underlies the vision in Figure 43. If we overlay Figure 44 with Figure 43, the union of these two diagrams depicts the following:

- Capturing and understanding the metadata, stored in our physical data assets and inside of our applications, is critical to achieving our goal of delivering information to the front office

- Metadata must be classified and organized in a way that is presentable for easy incorporation into front office applications
- Applications will use this logical view to access data from the disparate sources as well as publish data back into the underlying systems

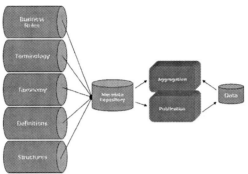

Figure 44: Physical model of EII solution

Granted, there are many different approaches to implementing these requirements; some of which we will explore shortly. But, ultimately, at least in a macro sense, they all adhere to the following steps: Unlock, Align and Integrate.

The Macro View

At a macro level, an EII practice follows three simple steps: Unlock, Align and Integrate (see Figure 45). An overview of the goals of each of these steps is provided below. As you read the overviews below, keep in mind there are vast numbers of complexities in achieving each of these goals. Indeed, each goal may result in hundreds of additional tasks, depending upon the scale on which this practice is applied.

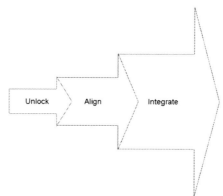

Figure 45: Steps for delivering EII

Unlock

Enterprise Information Integration strategies all recognize data as an asset of the organization that is, often times, trapped by its ancestry and lineage. Exposing this data can be an expensive process, often requiring significant manpower and custom software development. Early integration strategies also focused exclusively on the connectivity and data flows between systems that participated in those processes. In some of these cases, data that was locked away "shook loose" and was accidentally made available for other uses. In most cases, however, integration was handled on a case-by-case basis, and data was replicated and formatted for the task at hand.

Historically, integration strategies do not focus on "unlocking" the data for the purposes of general query and broad accessibility throughout the organization. Instead, they focus on accessing the data required to complete the integration task. Indeed, for most organizations, the thought of allowing large-scale generic access to the data would be akin to letting people put money in and take money out of the bank, at will, without the assistance of a teller (automated or human). However, clear and open access, when associated with the appropriate security mechanisms to ensure continued confidentiality and privacy, allows those with the appropriate access to select, filter, and order information, as they deem necessary, to complete their jobs without having to rely on information technologists or rogue technological solutions.

Still, further problems hinder the ability of the organization to provide clear and open access to data. In an effort to minimize resource consumption in the early days of computing, many early business systems didn't store verbose data, as we often do today. Instead, these systems stored just the core essential data needed to enable the application to process and present the data when needed. For example, early application developers, with minimal memory and storage resources, combined multiple fields into a single byte, such as using one bit to represent Boolean values. The result of following this approach is that it renders the data virtually unusable, without knowing the role of each bit or set of bits, which is typically only available as part of the application source code.

Since most of the early systems were developed on mainframes, before the advent of PC computing, where each user accessed data only through terminal applications, assumptions about data structures were fine. However, once distributed systems started being developed, access to this data from outside the mainframe became a complex task that was only made more complex by the fact that the systems that created these data sets were still in operation. Thus, the choices for accessing data from mainframe applications are often limited to changing the existing code, terminal emulation screen scraping, or application porting.

Unlocking data means neutralizing the physical hurdles to accessing the data. These hurdles include data format, data structures, proprietary interfaces, access controls and machine byte orientation. In the best case scenario, we would want to have one single approach for accessing all the data in our organization. In many cases this will not be possible, due to the limitations of the operating system, application design, or data models. Additionally, unlocking can, and may include, any or all of the following: adapters, migration, replication, consolidation and wrapping.

Unlocking also means capturing the metadata that describes our existing data assets. This metadata will become an important issue for us during the business alignment phase of the practice. In many cases, unlocking the data and the metadata are not discrete steps, but, instead, are intimately tied together as the metadata tells us the structure and format of the underlying physical data assets we are beginning to expose. Unlocking the metadata is also known as "harvesting."

Unlocking is also about working with partners and peer organizations to neutralize the problems of accessing data outside of our organizations. There is a basic understanding among organizations that the Internet provides the basis for sharing and exchange of data for the purposes of increased productivity, higher data quality (due to lack of re-keying data) and business process automation. As more organizations begin to share their data electronically, it will pave the way for us to incorporate that data more seamlessly into our own applications and processes.

Align

The Align phase of the practice focuses on organizing data and processes so that they meet with the needs of the business. The goal of this phase is to overcome the impact of developing silos of systems and data that result in related data being trapped in a disconnected manner, and to deliver the information required by the front office or line-of-business user, in a way that relates to the role they perform. By capturing, organizing, and understanding the metadata underlying the data and processes, you can formulate new ways of combining and delivering critical information, leveraging the work of the Unlock phase and providing higher quality of data.

Alignment of data with the needs of the business can be accomplished by developing an information model that includes a business taxonomy to classify our data, and express how one piece of data relates to another, in the context of our business. As indicated in Chapter 4—The Role of Metadata in EII—this information model has many components. The more of these components are bound into the model, the more comprehensive our understanding of our information assets.

Hence, the Align phase captures the most identifiably unique component of our business—industry semantics. This is one of the greatest differentiators between EII and other integration techniques or best practices. By capturing this, metadata business users and information technologists have a common ground on which to discuss data capture and information management.

Historically, information technologists represented data in a manner that was most identifiable to them; usually with arcane names that indicated the role of the data, relative to a particular information system. For instance, a systems developer may identify sales order data by common sales terms such as "ship to" and "bill to", whereas the sales representative may refer to these pieces of data as "recipient" and "payer" respectively. Although it may seem simple for a human to translate a request for payer information into a request for the "bill to" data, this represents the knowledge that a worker must have in order to interact with the organization's data. It also introduces a need for unnecessary knowledge that must now be incorporated into the training of a new employee. Data alignment removes this need by allowing the business users to query and review information in terms they use, in order to conduct their business without the potential errors that can occur due to a misunderstanding of semantics.

An additional need for alignment arises when organizations have not identified authoritative sources for data. The alignment phase of the EII best practice requires that we select authoritative sources for resolving the meaning of business terms within the organization. Therefore, alignment addresses some of the issues relating to data quality, relieving the front office from the burden of ensuring that the data used, as part of operations, is correct.

Case in point, one major retirement fund management company recently mailed a statement to their investors with incorrect information on the statement. When the problem was discovered, an assessment of how this error occurred was traced directly to ambiguity in the field names within the information system where the data was stored, and due to the lack of an authoritative source for where this data was stored. As a result, the data provided for the mailing came from a system that was designed to capture data when an account is opened, and which ignored modifications made by the user via the Website that was stored in a secondary system. Ultimately, the newer Web-based data was then copied into incorrect fields in the older system. Thus, the older and incorrect data was used for the mailing.

This problem is not an uncommon one in many organizations around the World. With the rapid rise of the World Wide Web and the need to satisfy customer's demand for Web-based access to their information, many organization established newer applications to provide Web-based interfaces because their existing systems were not capable, or it was too expensive to modify them to provide this interface directly. Because many of these companies have not aligned their systems and data with the business, they too suffer from these data quality issues.

As more applications are added to the organization's portfolio, the level of complexity for managing the data behind the overall portfolio increases. The net result of this impact is increased costs across the organization, as the burden shifts between those who govern the data and those who use it as part of their daily operations. Aligning the data with the business minimizes the impact of adding new applications to the overall portfolio, by providing facilities for managing this complexity.

Integrate

The final phase of our EII practice provides the means for any organizational employee to leverage the work of the previous two phases to access information versus basic data. Data alone provides little value, unless the recipient of the data has the skills to understand and process that data. If you speak only English and receive a document in French, it would provide little value, without the capability to have it translated. Thus, you would require the assistance of a person with specialized knowledge in translating French into

English; an unnecessary cost if you could have received the document in English to being with.

In the world of data, translation of data into information requires the skills of technologists who have specialized skills in understanding data and transforming it into a form usable by operational workers. This group not only includes software programmers, but also business analysts who develop complex spreadsheet models, or clerical workers skilled in using word processing and presentation tools who must also understand how to first gain access to, and extract the data required to complete their tasks. Ultimately, these translation issues result in higher costs of doing business.

By exposing data through an aligned information model that is ultimately tied to high quality authoritative sources, the business analysts and clerical workers can focus on their individual tasks, without the overhead associated with transforming, massaging and cajoling the data into a form that is ready to use. Instead, this group can leverage the business taxonomy to identify and request the right data, relative to the task at hand. This means that the user has to be able to navigate, select, and incorporate data and processes, using common front office applications.

Integration is achieved by formulating collections of business terms that are defined in the business taxonomy. Each collection equates to a logical view of the organizational data, relative to a particular task. For instance, a customer service representative who wishes to send a letter to a customer, detailing their past orders and communications with customer service, may be required to aggregate data from multiple systems, in order to complete this task. In this instance, the customer service representative would formulate a collection based on the information they would like to provide to the customer, and request resolution of that collection for insertion in to the letter. We will explore the concept of resolution of a collection further in the next section.

Alternate Approaches

This section illustrates alternatives within the EII practice. The approach described above is a bottom-up approach that delivers immediate feedback by providing immediate access to data through the unlocking mechanisms. This approach often leads to exposing more data than may be required by downstream processes. Once the data is made available using approaches we will review shortly, other applications can readily incorporate that data into existing processes. This is also known as the "Quick Win" approach and is very useful in demonstrating the value of continued investment to organizational executives, and should be used when access to data is a major hurdle to front office productivity.

One alternative, is to use a top-down approach (see Figure 46 below), which serves organizations that have identified the value of the business taxonomy to their business and want to focus their efforts on unlocking data through that taxonomy. This approach requires more investment in capture and modeling of the business taxonomy up front, but can minimize the unlock efforts by focusing on unlocking only the required data. The benefit of this approach is to establish common meaning for the business terms across the organization, resulting in higher productivity due to better overall communication.

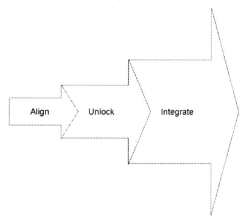

Figure 46: Alternate steps toward delivering EII

Another alternative approach is depicted in Figure 47 and it illustrates a combination of a bottom-up and top-down approach being performed in parallel. Using this approach, the business users will work to define the business taxonomy, while information technologists work to expose the data. The value of this approach is that the business will gain the immediate benefit of establishing the common meaning, while incrementally gaining access to the data as it becomes available. The cost of this approach is that business and information technologists must work closely to prioritize the effort. Otherwise, the overall value of the work could be diminished by a failure to deliver the necessary data in a timely fashion.

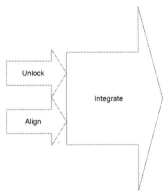

Figure 47: Alternate steps for delivery of EII solution

In the next section, we will drill deeper into the concepts identified in this chapter. We will specifically examine explicit tasks that occur during each phase of the practice, as identified in this chapter.

Key Concepts

1. The primary phases of the EII best practice are Unlock, Align and Integrate
2. During the Unlock phase we neutralize the physical hurdles to accessing data, and harvest critical metadata that is used to understand the existing environment
3. At the end of the Unlock phase, a specific and authoritative subset of data should be available for inclusion and delivery to other applications
4. During the Align phase, we develop the information model that classifies data relative to its role in business and defines how the information model relates to the physical model, and identifies the authoritative sources of data for the organization
5. During the Integrate phase we allow users to access the organizational data in a way that is meaningful to them and without the need for custom programming through common desktop applications
6. Aggregation provides the means of dynamically generating new data structures from existing data
7. Publication provides a general capability for updating the authoritative sources directly without additional programming
8. The information model created as part of employing the EII methodology provides the ability to turn raw data into information

"Our mind is capable of passing beyond the dividing line we have drawn for it. Beyond the pairs of opposites of which the world consists, other, new insights begin."
    – *Hermann Hesse*

The EII Practice: A Micro View

In the last chapter a macro view was provided of the Enterprise Information Integration practice. This chapter drills down one level deeper, and takes a look at some of the activities and properties that underlie this practice.

As we move along in implementing an EII practice, a question arises quickly and noticeably concerning where certain tasks will be performed. The question will take a similar form to this:

> The human resources information system represents the start date as the string "1/10/04", and the payroll system represents the start date as a long integer. Where does this incompatible data representation get addressed?

> One system identifies a customer by the identifier "CustNum" and another system identifies customer by the identifier "CustID". Where do we handle issues of labeling dissonance such as this?

These issues will be addressed as a result of the work of either the Align phase or the Unlock phase. Applying data type standardization through the business taxonomy during the Align phase, such as defining "Start Date" to be a string formatted as "month/day/year", ensures that all downstream applications using this metadata will be in agreement. Likewise, defining "Account Number" as the business term that is always used to identify a customer also provides a similar level of standardization through the metadata.

However, the impact of approaching standardization through metadata during the Align phase adds a requirement to implement software that transforms data from its current format into a format defined by the business taxonomy. That is, by allowing the business taxonomy, alone, to define the canonical format, all transformations are held off until the time of resolution, where resolution is the process of obtaining the data from existing data sources and systems

Data type standardization can also be accomplished during the Unlock phase, by requiring all services responsible for providing data access and query functions to transform the data into the standard format at the time of delivery. For example, all dates can be specified to be returned in "Month/Day/Year" format, and the customer identifier is always identified by the moniker "Account Number." This simply shifts the burden of transformation onto software that is already required to provide access to the data.

The impact of this approach is a requirement that all tools and developers building data access services, as part of the Unlock phase, follow this specification. Since most services are always going to be more intimate with the underlying system than the business taxonomy, this is often the best choice for handling transformation issues.

In the former approach, automated capabilities assist with the transformation process, but these transformational mappings will need to be maintained over time. That is, as additional variations of a particular data type are uncovered, there will be a need to add appropriate logic and mapping to support them. The latter approach relies on humans to follow the rules and implement the organizational standard as specified. Neither of these is a perfect scenario. However, experience shows that developing for canonical form in the Unlock phase seems to provide the greater odds for success. The reason behind this is that even if humans fail to follow the specification, the source of the problem is quickly realized downstream, and easily corrected. Whereas the requirement to trace and debug failed transformations is considerably more difficult, it takes longer to complete, and leads to greater chances for systematic failure in downstream processing.

Ultimately, the division of work is an architectural decision that will need to be made by individual implementers. The following sections provide a more detailed presentation of the three phases of the EII practice.

Unlock

The process of unlocking the data from existing data sources and systems is probably the most expensive and complex task of any integration methodology. This process requires humans to analyze the metadata from these sources and apply the correct technology for extracting the data. Achieving the desired result requires a mix of skill sets, such as the ability to read programs written in a variety of programming languages, manipulate database management systems at the administrator level, and/or develop complex data transformations. Beyond the ability to directly understand the physical layout associated with the storage of the data is a requirement for secure access to and the ability query of that data.

One best practice emerging in the data management space is the use of the Service-Oriented Architecture (SOA) for developing a consistent method for applications to access and query. The SOA is widely-touted as a major innovation in software, because it allows applications to access software as a set of services using common and inexpensive technologies: XML and Web Services; a discussion of their impact on the Unlock phase follows.

XML has emerged as a ubiquitous way to format and structure data. It supports the capability to encapsulate metadata and data together in the same structure, providing greater context around the content. Web Services uses XML as the language for defining how a service accepts input, provides output, and represents itself to other software. The value these two technologies provide to the Unlock phase is that they overcome the hurdles of accessing data in proprietary systems, arcane systems security, hardware byte-orientation issues, undocumented data formats and inconsistent data typing.

Cause	Effect
All data is formatted in XML	Applications have a common way to read and exchange data
Wraps existing applications and data sources with common data types	Normalizes the way similarly typed fields are represented across various data sources and systems
Wraps existing applications and data sources with well-defined communications interfaces	Replaces non-existent or complex access and query mechanisms with common facilities
Allows development of trust relationships between Service and back end and new ways to secure Web Services.	Wrappers can be secured in a standard way using ubiquitous security tools, such as LDAP[11], and the Web Service can communicate with the existing system using a trusted communications pathway (see Figure 48 below)

Table 3: Role of XML and Web Services in the Unlock phase

[11] Lightweight Directory Access Protocol

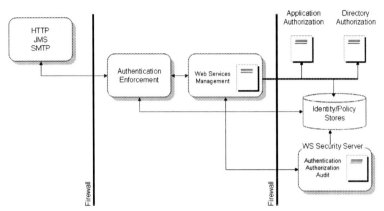

Figure 48: Secure Web Service architecture

Additional methods for unlocking data include:

- The development of data marts, where data can be normalized using traditional database management technology (see Figure 49).

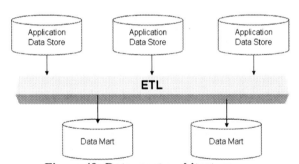

Figure 49: Data mart architecture

- Adapters, which provide programmatic interfaces other than Web Services, are intimate with the software and systems that they interface on behalf of the requesting application

229

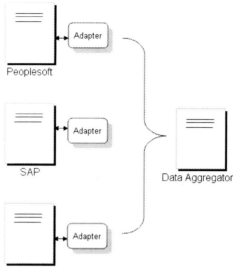

Figure 50: Adapter architecture

- Extract, Transform & Load tools can help turn complex formatted data, such as EDI and comma-delimited, into more accessible formats
- 3270, 5250, and VT100 screen scraping software can capture data from existing terminal-based applications while preserving the business logic
- Application programming interfaces (API) allow applications to request data directly from applications, without bypassing the business rules
- Business process management provides access to data that has undergone some form of evaluation, either by a human or a machine
- Migration, consolidation, and replication can be used to move the data from an inaccessible data store to one that has greater accessibility and common programming interfaces, such as SQL and Web Services.

Each of the above methods can be used directly, or can be used in combination with XML and Web Services. The latter approach of combining technologies simplifies the process of connecting the results of the Unlock and Align phases.

Due to the fact that unlocking data is dependent upon the availability of the metadata that describes that data, it is necessary to also capture and harvest metadata, during this phase of the practice. In many cases, the technologies used to unlock data, as described above, can also be used to harvest metadata. For instance, terminal emulation programs can be used to read the field names from applications screens, and relational database technologies have interfaces for retrieving database structures. However, harvesting metadata also introduces the need for new technologies, such as code analyzers, which can harvest both business rules and data structures.

Harvesting is one half of the equation. The other half is the storage and management of this metadata, once it is harvested. Here, XML is central to describing the metadata in a way that is non-proprietary, and, therefore, usable by many applications. Although it is not a requirement, the use of XML for describing metadata is clearly a best practice, and the document-oriented nature of XML provides ample options for storage and management. Indeed, by using XML as the format to represent the captured metadata, it is possible that a generic content management system may suffice for some organizations as a metadata repository. It is important to note that, while a generic content management system provides the means to organize and search the metadata, it may not offer some metadata-specific functionality of the kind that will be reviewed here shortly. That requires a more intimate understanding of the metadata.

Already, there is a number of standards that exist for the representation of metadata in XML. The Object Management Group (OMG) is a leading force in this effort, with the definition of the Common Warehouse Metamodel (CWM). CWM uses XML to describe different data management metadata models, such as entity-relationships, online analytical processing, transformations, object models, business nomenclature and multidimensional metamodels. The XML vocabulary that CWM uses to represent this metadata is called XML Metadata Interchange or XMI. This consistent and descriptive format makes it simpler to develop a repository to store this metadata, in both native XML repositories, and relational database management systems.

Of course, with so many diverse sets of metadata, CWM does not cover some other very important types of metadata, such as the business rules that are captured in source code, or the references to physical data assets in that source code, Web Services metadata, or screen definition for terminal applications. Moreover, the ability to relate concepts together, using the CWM business taxonomy model, is limited.

With regard to Web Services metadata, OASIS[12] has fostered a standard called Universal Description, Discovery and Integration or UDDI. This standard describes how to build a directory of Web Services metadata, inclusive of programming interfaces for management, query, migration, replication and notification of changes. Other than UDDI, the aforementioned shortfalls for CWM require proprietary models.

Finally, the World Wide Web Consortium (W3C) has put forth a separate XML-based recommendation for the capture and representation of metadata; it is called the Resource Description Framework (RDF). RDF is already heavily leveraged in metadata-rich environments, such as government intelligence and library management. RDF also forms the foundation of a set of additional standards, such as the Web Ontology Language (OWL), that add the capability to classify data. In Chapter 4, the concepts behind ontology and taxonomy were introduced. OWL and RDF provide the means to physically describe these abstract representations.

For more information see Appendix A, which provides in-depth overviews of the technologies discussed in this section. However, it is critical to introduce them here to illustrate what types of tools, technologies and standards will be required to implement the Unlock phase of the practice.

---

[12] Organization for the Advancement of Structured Information Standards

Capturing the metadata is only one small part of the overall effort; analysis of the captured metadata is equally important. However, once the metadata is available in the repository, the process of identifying the following environmental characteristics is possible:

- Redundant definitions of physical assets and their data type declarations
- The origin of data, the transformations applied to that data and the targets of the transformation (also known as the data lineage)
- The impact change has on dependencies within the environment
- Potential targets for authoritative sources
- The data types for the data
- Dependencies between processes and data

At the end of the Unlock phase, a specific and authoritative subset of data should be available for inclusion and delivery to front-office applications. The manner in which this data is accessed and delivered is provided by the work of the Align and Integrate phases of the practice.

Align

Alignment is a strategic approach to ensuring that business is the focal point for the creation, storage, and maintenance of data. Most information systems developed over the past thirty years focused on automation, which resulted in massive increases in productivity. The automation of manufacturing was accomplished through the use of robotics, while the front office was automated through word processing and spreadsheet applications, and the collaborative work environment has been enabled through the use of workflow. Each incremental step of automation contributes to the whole of the organization, making it faster and more effective, but unfortunately, not to the whole of a data management strategy.

Why should we care about a data management strategy if such phenomenal increases in productivity can be obtained with straight automation? There is a ceiling to the return in productivity that automation provides. This ceiling is due to the lack of available data to fully understand the impact of automation on the organization, and/or the data is available, but not accessible to applications that can make use of it. An enterprise data management strategy provides the foundation for being able to overcome this ceiling, by ensuring the availability of high-quality, authoritative data that can be used to identify appropriate targets for automation, or optimize existing ones.

The Align phase of the EII practice provides a basis for categorizing data, based on the role of the data within the organization. In turn, this categorization provides the visibility of business entities, as it is represented by data inside of existing data sources and applications. This means that commonly recognized business terms provide the ability to interface with existing data.

Using the concept of a dictionary often helps in explaining the alignment process. Organizations that follow disciplined data management strategies maintain a data dictionary, in addition to the other types of metadata they capture about their application environment. Hence, this is not a new approach, what is new is that this discipline is rarely applied to a distributed application environment. The dictionary maintains definitions of the data and has typically been a static supporting environment that acts to provide documentation to the development community within an organization. Additionally, the terms in this type of dictionary often reference cryptic names that represent entities within an application structure. However, because this information has had such limited use, it is likely that the dictionary is out-of-date or abandoned completely.

In EII, the role of the dictionary is expanded to provide actionable references to existing data, and capture the business terminology rather than the names of the physical data assets. Moreover, in the same way that a common spoken language dictionary term has definitions, the business term's definition describes how to resolve a business term into a related instance of data. Table 4 illustrates the difference between these three types of definitions:

Definition	Description
Spoken language definition of the word *customer*	One that purchases a commodity or service
Physical definition of the term *customer* in a CRM system	Represents the basic fields of the customer contact information • First Name, String(15) • Last Name, String(25) • Account Number, String(10)
Aggregate business definition of the term *Customer* of a software company	Description: One that purchases product Data Type: Aggregate Definition: • Name • Address • Product Licenses • Outstanding Balance • Account Executive • Last Visit • Last Logged Call to Customer Service
Atomic business definition of the term *Last Visit* of a *Customer* software company	Description: Date of last visit for by an account executive Data Type: Date Definition: SalesDataService:GetLastVisit(account number)

Table 4: Differences in definition types

As you can see from this table, there are some similarities in that each definition supplies a human readable representation of customer, but the spoken language stops there while the physical definition supplies data types and size. The business term goes one step further to define customer by the related business terms that aggregate to define customer across the organization. Additionally, the individual entities that make up the aggregate can be further defined to provide a reference to a means of retrieving the data from the underlying infrastructure. The method used to define this data will be discussed shortly.

A business term can have different contexts for each of its definitions, just like a spoken language dictionary. For example, in a spoken language dictionary, the word late has both an adjective context, such as "a late date", or it can have an adverb context, such as "got to work late". In the business dictionary, the context may be defined by the role the data plays within a certain department or business unit. The business term "customer," used within the context of a single business unit, may yield an aggregate structure, as shown in the table above. However, the term "customer," in the context of the parent organization, may be an aggregate of customer data across all business units. The context defines how the underlying data will eventually be resolved.

Similarly, business terms have different meaning depending upon how they are used within an organization. For example, a customer used in the context of sales represents someone who purchased a good or service, while a customer in context of marketing represents an entity in a target market. It is important, when deriving the semantics of your organization, that these contexts are captured in addition to the business terms themselves.

The act of providing a means to resolve a business term into an instance of data is what makes the metadata actionable. This is known as the business term's definition. These definitions can resolve to single pieces of data, or entire data structures. The following are three examples of types of definitions:

- **Explicit definition** – these are definitions that are statically defined with the business term. For example, the business term "Rate of Change" can be statically defined as 0.5.

- **Implicit definition** – these are definitions that point indirectly to data, such as through a database query or a Web Service.

- **Derived definition** – these are definitions that are computed at time of resolution. For example, the term "Credit Rating" requires the invocation of a business process that evaluates many pieces of data, and may even involve a human underwriter to resolve the term to its underlying value.

The data extraction methods developed as part of the Unlock phase of the EII practice enable both the implicit and derived definitions, hence, establishing the relationship between these two phases of the practice. Developing business term/definition maps, such as the one in Figure 51 below, helps to formulate and visualize these relationships.

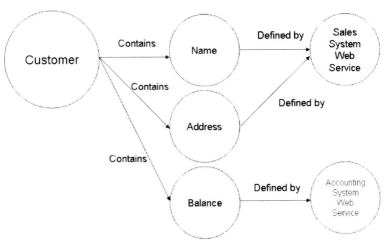

Figure 51: Business term / definition map

In addition to the fact that each term can have a definition, that definition can be different for each context in which the business term appears. In this case, the structure of Customer would be consistent across the organization, but how the data is resolved changes. This is depicted in Figure 52 below.

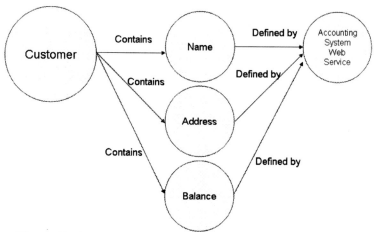

Figure 52: Customer defined within the context of Accounting

Enabling a business term to be self-resolving in this manner will greatly increase the overall benefit to the organization for developing and maintaining the business taxonomy. Business taxonomies can provide further value when the relationship between terms becomes part of the overall information model.

Relationships provide additional context to a business term, which directly impacts its meaning. They are analogous to the parts of a sentence, in that they provide the structure needed to understand the context of the term. For example, the role of the word "hit" in the sentence "That was a good hit," is that of a noun, while its role in the sentence "He hit the ball," is a verb. In these sentences, there are implied relationships between the words that are identified by their relativity to other words in the sentence, and these relationships, in turn, further define the role the word is playing in the sentence.

Ultimately, the relationships that are defined between two business terms will allow non-technical users to interact with the data in a common way, such as asking questions, like where they live, and how much they owe. Figure 53 below depicts the relationship between "Name", "Address" and "Balance" as business terms.

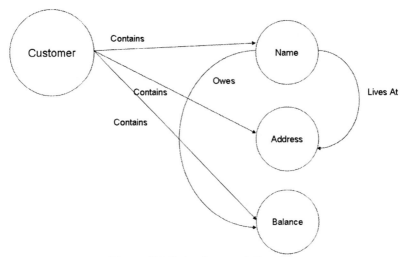

Figure 53: Inter-term relationships

There are two basic classes of relationships that can be defined by the information model: structural and referenceable. Structural relationships indicate a classification binding between the two business terms, such as "has a", "is a" and "is like". That is, one business term uses another business term to help define itself. Referenceable relationships allow business terms to have orthogonal relationships to other business terms, such that the complete set of terms can be navigated to infer knowledge about the data represented by the set of terms.

The image depicted above illustrates three different relationships between business terms. These relationships are indicated by the labels on the arcs. For example, "Customer" contains "Name". The "contains" relationship indicates that there is a structural relationship between these two terms, such that "Name" is element of "Customer". However, the "Lives At" and "Owes" are referenceable relationships. They provide information about how "Name" relates to other business terms, but they do not change the meaning of "Name".

Thus, it is the combination of business terms and the relationships between them that formulate the basis for a complete information model. This information model is informative during both development and downstream processing. The use of relationships will be explored further immediately following this.

Integrate

The Integrate phase of the EII practice combines the efforts of the Unlock and Align phases to present non-technical users with a simple way to access organizational data, in dynamic ways. A key requirement for EII solutions is the need to access real-time data that is spread across multiple systems and data stores in unique and dynamic ways.

Real-time has ambiguous meaning and can be misinterpreted, but in relation to EII, real-time means data that represents the last known value. This is very different from many data warehouses, where the data can be hours, days or even weeks old and the actual value can differ. EII solves the requirement for accessing data in a time-sensitive fashion. Take, for example, the need for a bank representative to be able to see the last transaction performed on an account when handling a lost ATM card. If the card is being used by an unauthorized party, data that is delayed even a minute could result in a loss.

EII also provides the ability for non-technical users to select and combine data in ways that makes sense to them. If the goal of integration is to provide a consistent view of the data that all people will use, it would probably be more cost-effective to develop a one-time custom software solution, rather than spend the time and money necessary to implement this practice. A key benefit of implementing an EII solution is to handle the complexity associated with providing users with a mechanism for delivering disparate data in combinations that are unknown, at the time of development.

Two key activities that factor into the Integrate phase are aggregation and publication. Both of these activities leverage the information model to provide direction. Aggregation and publication are defined in more detail below:

<u>Aggregation</u>

An aggregation facility resolves a collection of business terms into a single structure. To accomplish this task, the aggregation facility needs to have an intimate relationship with the information model. It needs to understand the taxonomic structure and be able to resolve business terms, inclusive of all of its sub-terms. These collections are sometimes referred to as "views," and relate directly to the logical view concepts outlined earlier in the book. Figure 54 illustrates a typical aggregation process that might be used to deliver complete transaction detail to a customer service representative.

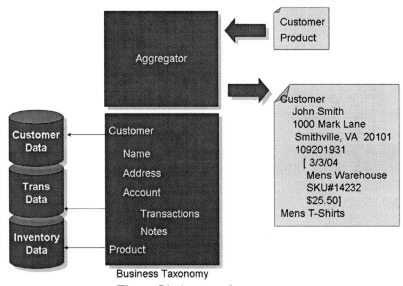

Figure 54: Aggregation

<u>Publication</u>

Publication is the inverse of aggregation. It provides the basis for updating the originating source of data, based on providing that data in the context of a particular business term. Given the example provided for aggregation, publication may be used to handle a return and "undo" the transaction. Figure 55 below illustrates the publishing process.

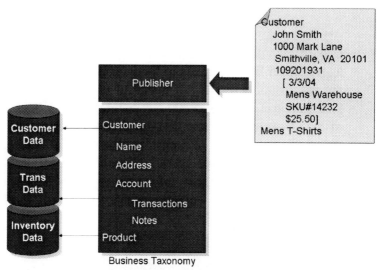

Figure 55: Publishing

In the cases of aggregation and publishing, the role of the business taxonomy provides the details, through its definition of how to either resolve the term, or update the source of the data. The act of selecting and submitting a collection of business terms to the aggregator or a set of data to the publisher is in the domain of the implementation. Examples of how each of these components is employed will be discussed more in depth in the chapter on the applications of EII.

The topic of leveraging the relationships between business terms was introduced in the section on alignment. Here, in the Integrate phase, the metadata generated by specifying the relationships between business terms can be incorporated into the aggregation process, so that the resulting data set provides a more informative view of the data. For example, the aggregate data set returned by the aggregation process may provide an account balance, but it would be up to an application or human to specify the meaning of that account balance relative to the task at hand, such as generating an invoice. By combining the relationships with the instance data, however, more informative queries can be created, such as "How much does Acme Trucking owe?" Since the metadata defines the relationship between "Name" and "Account Balance" to be "Owes" it is possible to infer that the user is requesting the balance, as referenced by the business term "Name".

It is important to note that there exist many alternatives for general information integration. The approach outlined in this chapter leverages the well-defined business information model as the source that drives the integration. Indeed, the systems metadata itself can also act as the source to assist in the integration, as is the case with Extract, Transform and Load. What differentiates EII from these alternatives is the derived benefit that comes from building, and later, referencing the entire information model.

Securing Your EII Solution

As is the case with any information solution, security is a theme that runs throughout EII. And, because EII is a distributed solution, securing the data end to end is a major theme. Coverage of security, as a component of an EII solution, provides a means to discuss security as a single concentration, rather than looking at it only within the context of where it is being applied. The following illustration (Figure 56) depicts the majority of the security picture.

Enterprise Information Integration: A Pragmatic Approach

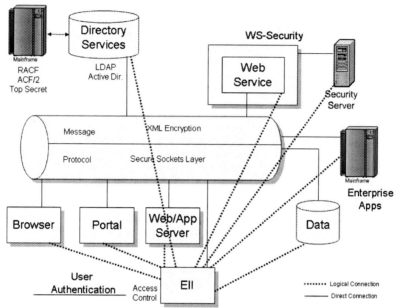

Figure 56: EII data security architecture

Security is broken down into 5 key methods:

- Authentication – the process of ensuring the user is who they say they are
- Authorization – the process of allowing users to access systems resources
- Access control – the ability to control individual paths a user may follow within a system
- Privacy and confidentiality – ensuring only the user that has authorization to see the data
- Authenticity – the ability to ensure that the data has not been compromised

The following section explores each of these areas deeper with respect to the three phases of our EII methodology.

Security in the Unlock Phase

The Unlock phase deals with making data and metadata accessible, and normalizing the data types. This means that a new component will be introduced between the data sources and the components that want to access those data sources (see Figure 57). Thus, security must be addressed on both sides of the component. For the sake of clarity, this component will be called the data service.

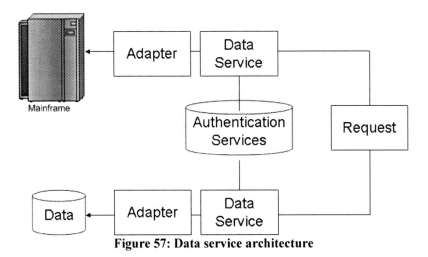

Figure 57: Data service architecture

Looking at the data service from the perspective of the source being accessed, the data service has to be able to directly authenticate itself to the adapter, repository, or application. This may be as complicated as having to emulate a mainframe or UNIX terminal session, or as simple as making a call to an application programming interface.

The data service, when examined from the perspective of an application that wishes to request data, must also provide authentication of the user. There are multiple solutions for implementing this level of authentication. For instance, the data service could directly extend any authentication implemented by the underlying data source, and simple pass username and password data across. The data service could also integrate with existing security mechanisms, such as RACF[13], LDAP[14], Netegrity Siteminder, and Microsoft Active Directory, to provide centralized user authentication. Finally, the data service could implement its own authentication policy.

Introduction of the data service also introduces the opportunity for security breaches by intercepting communications between the data service and the data source, or the data service and the requesting client applications. Therefore, to maintain the privacy and confidentiality of data, the data service should implement some level of encryption, either at the message passing level, or at the communications protocol level.

Finally, because data is being handled and accessed by a third party component, it may be desirable to ensure that data has not been touched or changed since it was retrieved from the source of origin. One way to provide this level of assurance to the recipient is for the data service to digitally sign the response. Digital signatures encompass information about both the data and the sender in such a way that any changes invalidate the signature.

Security in the Align Phase

The Align phase has more security administration requirements than the Unlock or Integrate phases, due to the requirements to enforce policies about accessing both the data and metadata. The first encounter with security in this phase is on the metadata repository, which will require that the user must first be authenticated and then authorized to see and manage metadata.

However, in addition to the basic authentication and authorization policies, the repository should support the added ability to control access on each individual piece of metadata, separately. This means that basic authorization provides conditional access to repository

---

[13] Resource Access Control Facility (RACF) is a mainframe security system
[14] Lightweight Access Directory Protocol (LDAP) is a standard interface for interacting with directory services

objects at a coarse-grained level. For example, basic authorization may control whether a user can read a particular type of metadata. Assuming that the user does have access to see all the relational database metadata that is in the repository, then the next level of access control provides limits on what a user is allowed to see or do on individual fields, keys, tables, etc., within that metadata type.

All of this security management can be burdensome and should be delegated when possible. For example, the system administrator can create a new user in the repository and provide rights to manage a subset of data within the repository. It would then be up to that user to manage access control for the metadata that they govern. For example, a business user can be given rights to create and manage the business taxonomy. However, when a business user creates a new business term, it becomes their responsibility to define what other roles and users in the system can read, update, delete or resolve that business term.

Security in the Integrate Phase

Based on Figure 57, all that is left is to create a view of the enterprise data using the business taxonomy, and then execute that view. Accomplishing this task requires that the user is authorized to create views within the metadata repository. The security policies that have been implemented during the Align phase ensure that a user can only create a view of business terms that they have the access to see. Even if they execute a view that someone else with greater access rights created, the system should still ensure that only the terms they have access to actually get resolved.

Using this architecture provides the organization with a powerful facility for rectifying some of the more difficult data access problems that have emerged, due to the incompatible security policies and mechanisms for each individual system. For example, many early mainframe applications were developed under different parts of the operating system, requiring users to authenticate themselves as many as five or six different times, to retrieve one set of data. This was only exaggerated by the introduction of client/server applications, without a corresponding centralized security management policy.

Forcing all data to be retrieved through the EII interface allows the organization to once again centralize the policies for data access. The Unlock and Align phases provide a strong security infrastructure that minimizes the opportunity for hacking into, and snooping of the enterprise data, while enabling the logical layer to maintain the confidentiality and privacy of the data, based on its role within the organization.

Key Concepts

1. The Align and Unlock phases of the practice can provide both data type standardization, and consistent naming of business terms
2. A service-oriented architecture simplifies the infrastructure for implementing an EII methodology
3. Metadata is critical to successfully implementing the Unlock phase of the EII methodology
4. A comprehensive dictionary is developed as part of the Align phase of the EII methodology
5. Business terms can be defined explicitly, implicitly, or they can be derived through a sequence of steps
6. Security must be provided at all levels of the solution, from the protocol up through the application

"Whenever we make up 'ideal languages', it is not in order to replace our ordinary language by them; but just to remove some trouble caused in someone's mind by thinking that he has got hold of the exact use of a common word."
— *Ludwig Wittgenstein, The Blue Book*

Model-Driven Architecture and EII

(by John Poole)

This chapter presents a comprehensive overview of Model-Driven Architecture (MDA), an initiative by the Object Management Group (OMG) to standardize the application of formal modeling techniques to problems in systems architectural design, integration, and interoperability. MDA can play a key role in EII by providing for the seamless, model-based integration of disparate applications and legacy systems. The core components of MDA are discussed, along with how MDA supports systems integration in general. We also describe novel approaches to MDA, as well as the relationship of MDA to two technological areas in particular, that promise to enable MDA to support systems capable of dynamic operation and semi-automated reasoning. That is, the incorporation of both domain patterns and Semantic Web techniques within the current MDA technology stack.

Introduction to Model-Driven Architecture

In recent times, the Object Management Group (OMG) introduced the Model-Driven Architecture (MDA) initiative as an approach to system-specification and interoperability, based on the use of formal models [7, 12, 15]. In MDA, a *Platform-Independent Model* (PIM) of the application is initially defined in some platform-neutral modeling language, such as the OMG's Unified Modeling Language (UML) [13]. The PIM serves as a formal specification of the system, and is independent of any particular implementation. However, to ensure that the implementation is ultimately consistent with its specification, a PIM is subsequently translated into a *Platform-Specific Model* (PSM) by translating the PIM to some target implementation or platform language, such as Java or XML, using formal mapping rules. The PSM is adorned with enough target-specific information to enable it to be used as the basis for the automated generation of large parts of the target software system (for example, automatic generation of Java interfaces and implementation classes).

Thus, the crux of MDA is raising the level of abstraction of system specification to the level of visual models, usually formulated in UML. In this case, the formal UML model serves as more than just documentation, and is put directly to work in either the construction or operation of a software tool or application. For example, consider the example shown in Figure 58 of a very simple relational database design, expressed in UML notation. It is easy to envision the graphical notation being automatically translated into *Structured Query Language* (SQL) *Data Definition Language* (DDL) statements that, when supplied to a relational database engine, create the physical database schema. It is also equally easy to imagine the model being translated into XML, perhaps for communication or publishing via the Web, or visualizing it from a browser, using some specialized stylesheets. The OMG would refer to such database construction, data communication, and visualization as *model-driven* processes.

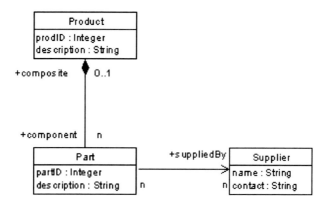

Figure 58: Simple relational database model in UML

What is profound about this simple example is the fact that the small UML model shown in Figure 58 is ultimately the metadata that defines the SQL database. Furthermore, it is a PIM—as expressed in the platform-neutral UML language—that is translated to an equivalent PSM (the SQL DDL), which enables it to be used for the purposes of populating the *Relational Database Management System*(RDBMS) catalog.

Furthermore, one might initially view this process largely as the use of static models to construct relatively static structures. That is, the relational tables, once constructed, are relatively static in nature. However, if you consider the fact that the relational catalog contains information used by the RDBMS in carrying out its runtime operations, you realize that, in some cases, the PSM might be used for the one-off generation of certain objects, but in other cases, it can serve a much broader role as a run-time model that is interpreted directly by dynamic processes.

This "static" or "constructional" nature of MDA is often emphasized in much of the current literature. For example, the use of UML models to automatically generate corresponding XML message structures, Java interfaces and implementation classes, which are subsequently embellished with additional, hand-written code. However, MDA also lends itself (in many ways, even much more effectively) to the creation of dynamic models that can be interpreted at run-time. It is this sort of application of MDA that will provide the greatest value to future systems, and it is this viewpoint that is emphasized and elaborated upon throughout this chapter.

So, to summarize: The basic premise of MDA is, rather than designing applications and data resources in relatively low-level, platform-dependent languages (like Java, XML, or SQL), developers should instead focus on the creation of formal visual models that are more readily understood by relatively non-technical human users, while relying on automated tools to translate these visual models directly into appropriate low-level languages and models that are better suited for machine execution. Thus, a large portion of MDA is also concerned with the concepts of model transformation or translation. That is, the ability to translate back-and-forth between equivalent representations of the same information, where each representation is targeted at some different consumer. Naturally, as models become very large and complex, the need for automated tools is almost a given.

As an OMG process, MDA represents an evolutionary step in the way the OMG approaches interoperability standards. In the past, OMG interoperability had been based largely on CORBA standards and services [9]. Heterogeneous software systems interoperated at the level of standard component interfaces. MDA, on the other hand, places formal, technology-independent system models at the core of interoperability solutions. The most significant aspect of this approach is the relative independence and separation of system specification from the implementation technology or platform. The system definition exists independently of any implementation model, and may, therefore, have any number of formal mappings to possible platform infrastructures (for example, Java, XML, C#, SOAP, J2EE, .NET, etc.).

Varying Perspectives on MDA

MDA has significant implications for software system design and specification, as well as metamodeling and metadata interchange. Metamodeling is the primary activity in the specification or modeling of metadata. In fact, the true definition of metadata is that of a formal description or model of some application or information schema of interest. Simply calling metadata "data about data" completely misses the point – metadata and formal system design are essentially the same thing: What we call metadata is very much the use of formal designs, or models in implementing, or controlling deployed software systems. Interoperability in heterogeneous environments is almost always ultimately predicated on the use of shared metadata, and the overall strategy for sharing and understanding metadata consists of the automated development, publishing, management, and interpretation of *models*[15].

Furthermore, once effective metadata sharing is achieved, having totally dynamic system behavior based on the run-time interpretation of shared models is not that far off. Such architectures, which don't exist commercially at the time of this writing, but are being developed, arc highly interoperable, easily extended at run-time, and completely dynamic in terms of their overall behavioral specifications – their range of behavior is not bound by hard-coded logic [16, 17]. We will have more to say on this topic throughout this chapter.

The diagram in Figure 59 provides something of a "spectral" or "magic quadrant" –style perspective on model-driven architecture, in general. This includes, but is not limited to, what the OMG considers to be "model-driven architecture".

---

[15] We use the terms *model* and *metadata* interchangeably, although *model* would seem to have a more general connotation.

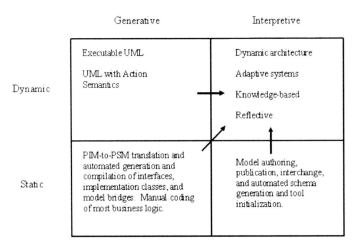

Figure 59: Varying perspectives on the application of MDA

Different authors have widely varying opinions on what MDA is, or perhaps what it should be. We can view the upper right-hand quadrant as stating the ideal for what we generally call MDA, while the lower left-hand quadrant is an expression of the predominant viewpoint of MDA within the OMG (at the time of this writing). These activities occur within the other quadrants as being necessary evolutionary paths toward the upper right-hand quadrant, not as ends in themselves. Of the four categories, the upper right-hand quadrant is the most difficult to achieve, but clearly provides the greatest value to end-user organizations. We will delve into this concept in greater detail throughout this chapter. But first, we will take a look at some of the more well-known foundation technologies comprising OMG's concept of MDA.

Foundation Technologies of MDA

The following lists the main OMG interoperability and modeling technologies that most people tend to group under the general umbrella of OMG MDA (the version numbers are rather significant and represent the latest generations of these technologies at the time of this writing):

- Unified Modeling Language (UML) 2.0
- UML 2.0 Profiles
- Meta Object Facility (MOF) 2.0
- MOF 2.0 Query, Views, and Transformations (QVT)
- Object Constraint Language (OCL) 2.0
- XML Metadata Interchange (XMI) 2.0
- Common Warehouse Metamodel (CWM) 1.x
- CWM Metadata Interchange Patterns (MIP) 1.0

In addition to these specific OMG standards, there are a number of non-normative technologies or usages of the OMG standards. Although not necessarily ratified by OMG as standard technologies, they are, nonetheless, very important to MDA and worth discussing. These include:

- Executable UML
- Model Interchange Patterns
- Archetype Patterns
- Model Transformation based on OCL

The interested reader is referred to the following authoritative sources for additional information on three of the above cited non-normative technologies: Executable UML [14], Archetype Patterns [1], and Model Transformations based on OCL [7]. Of the non-normative technologies, only the concept of a Model Interchange Pattern is discussed at length in this chapter. Although the concept of a Model Interchange Pattern is non-normative, it is very closely related to (in fact, is a generalization of) the OMG normative standard for CWM Metadata Interchange Patterns [10]. For our purposes, these two technologies can be viewed as essentially the same thing, the only difference being that CWM Metadata Interchange Patterns are wedded to the CWM metamodel.

The following sub-sections summarize, in very general terms, the key points of the normative OMG standards that serve as foundations of MDA. Note that we will not discuss the difference between the 2.0

generation technologies and earlier versions; suffice it to say that the 2.0 versions attempt to provided more commonality and unification of infrastructure of the various separate standards.

UML

The *Unified Modeling Language* (UML) is the OMG's standard language for modeling discrete systems [13]. Although primarily used as a visual modeling language for object-oriented software systems, UML is also the notational basis for many other OMG standard languages, such as MOF and CWM. In fact, the UML metamodel generally serves as the base metamodel for MOF and CWM.

Within MDA, UML is the OMG's language of choice for formulating PIMs. UML is independent of any particular software technology or computing platform. Furthermore, the use of visual modeling is the preferred method for formulating these models, since visual models of complex systems tend to be more easily managed and comprehended by human beings, than other notations, for example, textual representations. On the other hand, since the UML language has a precise definition (via the formally defined UML metamodel), visual UML models lend themselves to automated translation into other formally defined languages, such as Java and XML.

This facilitates the translation of UML PIMs into PSMs in some other target, implementation language, as well as the use of UML in the interchange of information and models in a tool- or platform-independent format, such as that provided by XMI. For example, CWM extends the UML metamodel with data warehousing and business intelligence domain concepts. CWM models have a standard mapping to XMI, so tool metadata represented in the CWM language (which is essentially an extension to UML), can readily be interchanged between software tools via XMI (which is just a way of using XML).

MOF

The *Meta Object Facility* (MOF) is an OMG standard language for defining a common, abstract language for the specification of metamodels [11]. MOF is sometimes referred to as a *meta-metamodel*, or *model of the metamodel*.

MOF has an unfortunate reputation of being rather difficult to understand. But MOF is actually quite simple in concept. It is merely another formal model that defines the common characteristics of object-oriented languages like CWM and UML. The relationship between MOF and object-oriented languages is very much like the relationship between Latin and the various Romance Languages. If you understand Latin, you can easily determine the meanings of many similar French and Italian words that have their roots in Latin, without necessarily being conversant in either language.

It is basically the same with MOF. Elements of the MOF model provide common definitions for similar constructs across the broad spectrum of object-oriented languages, such as classes, properties, and associations. Each element of a language like UML or CWM is an instance of some element of the MOF model. Software tools that understand the MOF model are ultimately capable of understanding languages like CWM and UML, because they are directly derived from MOF.

The MOF model is very small and abstract, which means that it is relatively easy to define rules relating MOF elements to constructs of more concrete languages, such as Java and XML. This is important, because after you have established how a particular MOF element translates to, say, XML, you have established how all instances of that MOF element (for example, CWM or UML classes) are to be translated into XML. And this is a key aspect of building truly interoperable software systems using the model-driven approach.

XMI

XML Metadata Interchange (XMI) is an OMG standard that maps the MOF to the W3C's eXtensible Markup Language (XML) [9]. XMI defines how XML tags are used to represent serialized, MOF-compliant models in XML. Essentially, MOF-based metamodels are translated into XML Document Type Definitions (DTDs) or XML Schema Definitions (XSDs), and instances of those metamodels are translated into XML documents that are consistent with their corresponding DTDs or XML Schemas. So XMI is really nothing more than a set of rules for prescribing how MOF model elements (and hence, MOF-derived languages, such as CWM and UML) map to XML.

XMI solves many of the difficult problems encountered when trying to use a tag-based language to represent an instance of some formal model. The fact that XMI is based on XML means that both the metadata and the data it describes can be packaged together in the same, self-describing document. In fact, a particularly interesting consequence of this is that XMI can also be used to encode the definition of any MOF language (such as UML or CWM). A software tool that understands MOF should be capable of consuming the contents of an XMI representation of the derived language, and be able to put it to some sort of use, without necessarily understanding the derived language itself. Thus, both formal modeling languages, and the designs they are used to create, have the same uniform representation, and should be capable of being understood by the same tools.

CWM

The Common Warehouse Metamodel (CWM) is a metamodel of both the business and technical metadata that's most often found in the data warehousing and business intelligence domains. It is used as a basis for interchanging metadata between heterogeneous, multi-vendor software tools and applications [8, 11, 18, 19, 20].

CWM is essentially a generic model of a data warehouse, expressed in UML notation and derived from the MOF. It is comprised of a number of packages (or sub-models) representing different aspects of a typical data warehouse or information supply chain: Relational database, OLAP, data transformations and mappings, reporting, visualization, data warehouse management, etc. As a platform-independent, domain modeling language, CWM is used in the same manner that, say, an entity-relationship (ER) language is used to design relational databases, or UML is used to design object-oriented (OO) software systems. Models based on CWM are readily interchanged between software tools via XMI, and can be persisted in repositories or model stores that support the MOF.

We will delve into CWM in much more detail in subsequent sections of this chapter, as an example of a particular aspect of model-driven architecture.

MDA Case Study: Model-Driven Data Warehousing

This section provides a case study of the application of MDA, in the domain of data warehousing and business intelligence. In particular, we are concerned here with examining the interchange of shared metadata. In the detailed use case described here, CWM is used as the basis for constructing MDA PIMs, XMI is leveraged as the primary interchange medium, and the Java programming language plays the roles of the target PSM. In particular, formal transformations from the CWM PIMS to Java PSMs are defined in terms of the Java Metadata Interchange (JMI) specification published by the Java Community Process (JCP). JMI is essentially a formal mapping of the MOF (and subsequently any MOF-derived language, such as UML or CWM) to the Java programming language. We will not describe JMI in detail; the interested reader is referred to the JMI home page on the JCP web site [5].

An Overview of CWM

As we described earlier in this chapter, metadata sharing is a key prerequisite to integrating heterogeneous software tools, products, and applications. Effective metadata sharing requires both an agreed-upon language for describing metadata, and a standard interchange format or interface for representing shared models. In recent times, the use of formal modeling languages, such as the Unified Modeling Language (UML) and Common Warehouse Metamodel (CWM), and their mappings to various implementation technologies, such as XML Metadata Interchange (XMI) and Java™ Metadata Interface (JMI), have been proposed as solutions for model interchange.

CWM [8, 11, 18, 19, 20] is a generic domain model of data warehousing and business intelligence concepts that serves as a common model of metadata (a *metamodel*) for the various software tools, products, and applications comprising a data warehouse, information supply chain, corporate information factory, or other similar approaches to realizing business intelligence solutions. Instances of CWM (*models*) represent shared metadata, and may be interchanged between tools and repositories via XML documents that conform to the XMI standard.

Figure 60 illustrates the layered architecture of CWM, which, as alluded to earlier, is comprised of a number of sub-metamodels (or *packages*) representing different aspects of a typical data warehouse: relational database, online analytical processing (OLAP), data transformations, data warehouse management activities, and so on.

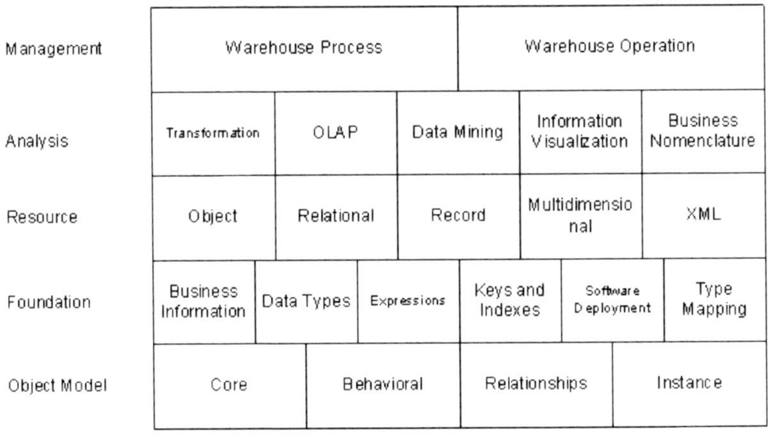

Management	Warehouse Process			Warehouse Operation	
Analysis	Transformation	OLAP	Data Mining	Information Visualization	Business Nomenclature
Resource	Object	Relational	Record	Multidimensional	XML
Foundation	Business Information	Data Types	Expressions	Keys and Indexes	Software Deployment	Type Mapping
Object Model	Core	Behavioral	Relationships	Instance

Figure 60: CWM layered architecture

A data warehouse architect can design a complete data warehouse by piecing together those CWM modeling elements that are relevant to various modeling sub-problems. For example, to design the extract, transformation, and load (ETL) process that builds the data warehouse, the architect might use CWM's Relational and Record packages to specify the raw data sources and operational data store (ODS), the Relational and OLAP packages to design the dimensional analysis store, and the Transformation package to design source-to-target data mappings and conversions. The complete model of the ETL process is a combination of modeling elements from each of these packages[16].Figure 61, for example, illustrates a CWM instance representing a high-level model of an ETL process.

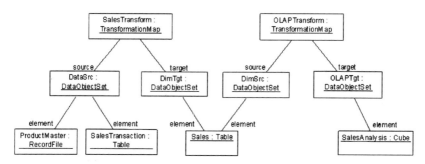

Figure 61: High-level CWM model of an ETL process

A data warehouse architect might construct such a model using a CWM-aware visual modeling tool, or perhaps a graphical modeling tool with a more user-friendly symbolic notation that is, nonetheless, back-ended by a CWM-aware export utility or model repository. The CWM instance is exported in the form of an XMI document that is subsequently consumed by a CWM-aware ETL tool. The ETL tool might use the model to initialize its internal metadata, or, alternatively, traverse the model in an interpretive manner, as part of the process of

---

[16] Any CWM model can be thought of in terms of a trajectory through some subset of the packages comprising the layered architecture of Figure 3.

managing its operations[17]. But regardless of how the model is actually used by the consumer, the key point here is that the ETL process has been defined in terms of a technology-independent representation that is external to any particular software process or tool. The ETL process model is readily usable by any CWM-aware tool requiring it.

CWM is sufficiently replete with both data warehousing and business intelligence concepts to represent any conceivable information supply chain. For example, in Figure 62, the previous, high-level model of the ETL process is further refined to include detailed descriptions of the attributes of the data resources, along with their associated source-target transformations. Here, we include an additional data source model, that of the dimensional store of the data warehouse, which is the primary target of the transformations. We will see subsequently that this model is that of a traditional relational star-schema database from classical data warehousing and business intelligence [6]. In fact, it is the same star schema model developed subsequently in this chapter and shown in Figure 67.

---

[17] A software tool that uses MOF directly as its implementation model is capable of understanding languages like CWM and UML, without necessarily having to be coded to do so. A software tool designed to interpret shared models directly (whether MOF-based or not) is fundamentally capable of totally dynamic operation and evolution over time. [16, 17]. This is, of course, the overall emphasis of this chapter; that greatest value of MDA will come from the eventual evolution of MDA toward greater degrees of automation.

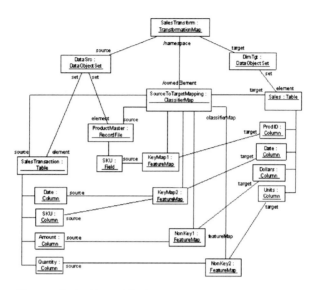

Figure 62: Refined CWM model of the ETL process

The key point here is that, since CWM is a formally specified language with precise syntax and semantics, it is possible to translate this graphical model of the ETL process into some other formally specified and software-consumable format, such as an XML document, or perhaps a collection of statements in some textual scripting language. In this case, the very same visual model used by human developers could also be used to directly generate the metadata required by the software components implementing the ETL process. For example, recall the UML description of the relational tables from Figure 58 that could be translated into SQL DDL statements, which in turn are used to build the tables within a relational database server. A result of this process is that the relational catalog gets populated with metadata describing those very same tables. So, the content of the relational catalog can be viewed as just another rendering of part of the original CWM model, but one that is used directly by operational processes.

This scenario illustrates a specific application of model-driven architecture, in the realm of metadata –based tool interoperability. Metadata is specified using formal models that are fundamentally

264

platform-independent. These models are then used (either through translation or interpretation) as the basis for creating platform-specific, operational metadata. Platform-independent models may persist outside of any particular software product or tool, and may readily be shared by any tools capable of understanding them. Multi-vendor software tools with a common notion of metadata should be capable of readily sharing data, and in many cases, are reasonably well suited for general interoperability. CWM, therefore, is a language for model-driven architecture, with a specific orientation toward data warehousing and business analytics. CWM provides data warehouse architects with the means to specify a complete data warehouse solution in a platform-neutral manner, based on a generic, data warehousing domain model, rather than on the implementation models of specific software tools.

Operational Scenario

Now that we have some notion of how both MDA and CWM (as a special case of MDA) are used in a real system, let's take a look at a detailed usage scenario, with particular emphasis on the degree to which the model-driven approach facilitates both inter-operability and the overall automation of typical metadata management tasks. The first step consists of the data warehouse administrator initializing a JMI service for use as a central metadata store. The administrator connects to the JMI service through an administrative console, and invokes the XmiReader interface of JMI service, supplying it with the URL of the CWM definition on the OMG Web site. The JMI service downloads this XMI file from the Web and uses it to build a CWM-specific metadata store automatically. Figure 63 illustrates this process.

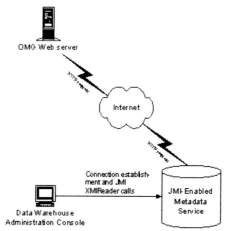

Figure 63: JMI metadata service initialization

After the CWM model definition is downloaded, the administrator instructs the JMI service to generate an implementation of the model automatically; that is, Java interfaces and a corresponding implementation class library. This is the basis for the persistent store and management services for CWM metadata.

Next, the data warehouse architect uses a visual modeling tool that is CWM / JMI—aware to build the ETL model presented in Figure 62. The modeling tool connects to the JMI service and specifies the CWM store as its default repository. As the architect draws the ETL model, the internal logic of the modeling tool constructs the corresponding objects by invoking CWM-specific JMI method calls. This process illustrated in.Figure 64.

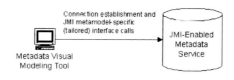

Figure 64: CWM model construction

Now that the ETL process has been completely defined in terms of a centrally stored CWM model, the next step is to initialize the various CWM / JMI –enabled software tools that will be used to implement the ETL process physically. The data warehouse administrator uses the administration console client application to open a connection to the JMI service. The administrator also opens a connection on each of the ETL tools, subsequently launching an XmiReader on each tool connection. The client application then launches an XmiWriter on its own connection to the JMI service, supplying it with a temporary output stream. The client then exports the entire ETL model to the output XMI stream. It invokes each XmiReader method on each tool-specific connection, supplying the temporary stream as a parameter. This has the effect of each data warehouse tool importing the entire ETL model. Each tool uses only those portions of the ETL model that are relevant to its operations.

For example, the relational database engine will use the relational table descriptions to build its relational tables. The OLAP server will use the OLAP model to build its own internal, multidimensional schema and to define its data links to the relational fact table. But the ETL tool, which is responsible for end-to-end data movement, loading, and conversion, will most likely consume the entire ETL model and use it to initialize its complete, internal, operational metadata store.Figure 65 illustrates this step.

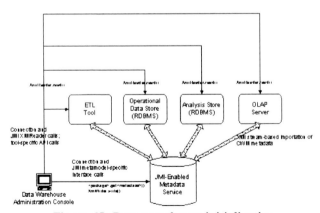

Figure 65: Data warehouse initialization

As a final example of tool interoperability, assume that now that the data warehouse is completely operational, the administrator would like to bring a new analysis tool into the environment. This tool is an advanced, multidimensional visualization and reporting tool that is based on a metamodel other than CWM. However, the new tool still has a reasonably straightforward mapping to the MOF, and its manufacturer has provided MOF rendering of the tool's internal data model. The data warehouse architect uses the visualization tool's setup screen first to initialize the tool's internal schema. The architect then constructs a programmatic script, written in Java, that connects to the JMI service and uses JMI reflective programming to find equivalent elements in the CWM OLAP model. This script is loaded into the tool as part of an interoperability plug-in architecture provided by the tool's vendor. In this manner, the visualization tool is still driven by its own internal metadata, but can dynamically map its own concept of an OLAP model element to the CWM OLAP model elements that are to be rendered.Figure 66 illustrates this process.

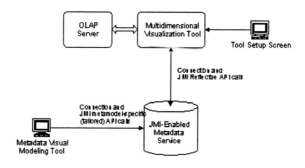

Figure 66: Model-driven tool interoperability

MDA and Patterns

We had suggested earlier in this chapter that the application of patterns, within MDA, provided a much needed means of elevating the overall precision of metadata and model interchange between dissimilar software components, tools, and applications. This is one of the deficiencies impeded in the development of model-driven architectures, as envisioned in the upper right-hand quadrant of Figure 59.

The overall strategy involves the application of more traditional "pattern techniques" to the problem of metadata sharing and interchange, when using generic modeling languages, such as OMG's UML and CWM to specify models and metadata. The ultimate objective is the development of pattern-driven and pattern-aware software tools based on the concept of a Model Interchange Pattern (as discussed earlier in this chapter), a specific example of which is the OMG's CWM MIP specification [10]. This subsection takes a more detailed look at both the problem and the proposed solution, within the specific context of metadata interchange based on CWM.

Metadata Driven Interoperability

As we've described previously, metadata sharing is key to integrating dissimilar software components, products, tools, and applications. Furthermore, metadata sharing is primarily facilitated by a common definition of metadata; it is often approached in terms of *formal modeling* and *formal modeling languages* (e.g., ER, UML, XML Schema). Effective metadata sharing also requires a common interface or interchange format (e.g., Java API or XML documents).

Open standards and consortia-based approaches like MDA are preferable to closed solutions, because they ensure equitable vendor representation, and relative vendor-independence of delivered solutions, and a very good example of an MDA approach to domain-specific metadata sharing is, of course, CWM. CWM essentially extends the core UML to include Data Warehousing and Business Intelligence (DW/BI) concepts, and, therefore, provides a formal modeling language for describing metadata in the DW/BI domain. Indirectly (by virtue of MOF and XMI), CWM also provides an XML-based interchange format for shared DW/BI metadata. Furthermore, as an MDA technology, potentially, CWM has a wide variety of mappings to other representations or implementation models, such as Java and J2EE APIs, C#, and .NET. One particularly notable PSM that is useful for repository-based CWM metadata stores, is the Java™ Metadata Interface, or JMI specification [4].

Formal modeling languages like CWM and UML are fully capable of describing domain-specific metadata for purposes of interchange. They are highly expressive and extremely flexible modeling languages. However, neither CWM nor UML (nor any other formal language, for that matter), provides a means of expressing the *intent* (or *meaning,* or *semantic context*, or *intended effect,* or *intended use*) of any particular model or interchange event. Furthermore, there is a (potentially) unbounded degree of variation in syntactically-valid models, which means that some models will be better suited than others, when it comes to achieving some specific purpose.

As an example of what we mean by this, consider the high-level ETL process model presented earlier in Figure 61. A refined version of the same model is also shown in Figure 62. This model contains more detail than the higher level model, as it defines source-to-target mappings between the data resources participating in the ETL process. Which model is better? Well, there's no right or wrong answer here. Both ETL process models (high-level and detailed) are equally valid (from a purely syntactic standpoint). But which one is "better" really just depends on what the intended use of the model is.

The phenomenon of syntactic variation is further complicated in the case of a collaborative environment consisting of heterogeneous, largely autonomous tools: potentially, many metadata publishers and consumers exist in such an environment. Whether a particular model is *useful* or *meaningful* (from an information perspective) really depends on what some consuming software process expects or requires

So, we have identified three (closely related) issues with regard to metadata interchange:

- Potential for unbounded variation in model structure/content
- Automated processes need to deal with model variation

- Human modelers must be able to *describe* model variation in a manner intelligible to *both* humans and automated processes

The early validation of CWM, by the CWM specification team within the OMG, made these points quite obvious. The CWM developers quickly discovered that the best way to deal with model variation was to agree on useful, general forms of model structure and composition. It was discovered that, as long as the interchanged models conformed to these general forms, a wide variety of models could easily be understood by different software tools – more specifically, import and export adapters were coded to handle these general forms, rather than any particular models.

What the CWM developers were dealing with, of course, were *patterns* for shared metadata. By "pattern", in this particular case, we mean an agreed-upon, general form (or perhaps *idiom*, or *idiomatic usage)* of the CWM language, that was intended to suit some particular purpose. What was also apparent, to many of the CWM developers, was that this problem had been solved before, in a somewhat different setting: that is, the famous "gang-of-four"-style *software design patterns* [2, 3]. The CWM team reasoned that they could co-opt, and effectively apply some of the established software design pattern machinery to the problems of unbounded variation and meaning in the case of highly generalized model interchange.

[SIDEBAR]
"A pattern is a description of communicating objects and classes that are customized to solve a general design problem within a particular context"
– Gamma, et al [3]

As a concrete example of what we mean by model patterns, consider the famous Relational Star Schema, which forms the basis for much of data warehousing and business intelligence solutions. The Star Schema is essentially an organizational pattern for relational database tables. Ralph Kimball's seminal *Data Warehouse Toolkit*, for example, is essentially a collection of Star Schema metadata patterns [6]. But as anyone familiar with this book can attest, there is tremendous variation across the various Star Schema developed by Kimball. So how would someone concerned with the ability to effectively interchange Star Schema metadata go about devising a single description of all possible Star Schemas?

Consider the Star Schema example shown in Figure 67.

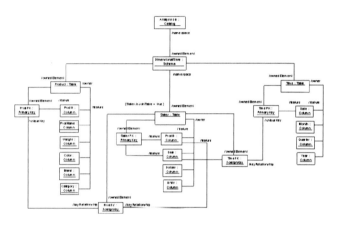

Figure 67: Simple star schema

A slightly more complex version of the previous Star Schema model (representing a *multi-cube*) is shown in Figure 68.

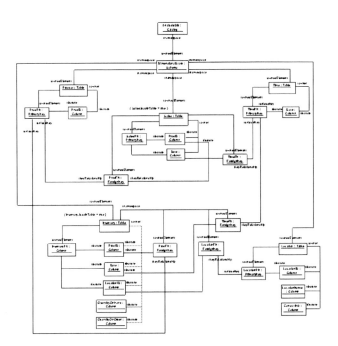

Figure 68: "Multi-cube" star schema design

So, we need to able to describe a single general form, or pattern, that could be used to classify either of the preceding examples as what one would call a "relational star schema". We can begin to address this challenge by asking ourselves three basic questions regarding the structure and content of any interchanged model:

- What portion of the underlying CWM or UML metamodel is required to represent the basic structure of any Star Schema database?

- What restrictions on instances of model classes are reasonable to expect in a Star Schema design (one fact table or multiple fact tables)?

- Is there generally some particular class that constitutes a "root element" or "entry point" of any Star Schema design (the fact

273

table, or perhaps an "outer-most" schema element containing the rest of the model)?

Assuming CWM, reasonable answers to the previous three questions might consist of the following:

- What portion of the underlying metamodel is required to represent the basic structure of any Star Schema database?
  Answer: The CWM modeling classes of Catalog, Schema, Table, Column, Primary Key, Foreign Key and all related associations.

- What restrictions on instances of model classes are reasonable to expect in a Star Schema design?
  Answer: At most, one instance of Catalog, at most, one instance of Schema, and at least three instances of Table. One Table instance in particular has a join relation (primary key / foreign key) to the other Table instances.

- Is there generally some particular class that constitutes the "root element" or "entry point" of the Star Schema design (e.g., the fact table, or perhaps a schema element containing the rest of the model)?
  Answer: Any of Catalog, Schema, or Table.

Assuming that all metadata producers and consumers agree on the preceding questions and answers as a description of the general form of any Star Schema database model, then a wide variety of Star Schema models can be interchanged and readily understood by any of the consumers. The fact that there is an unlimited amount of potential variation in Star Schema design has not prevented us from formulating a simple, finite description of all Star Schema models, based on a reasonable, idiomatic use of our modeling language.

It should be obvious that what we have just defined informally is a *Metadata Interchange Pattern (MIP)*.

Now, let's provide some more formal definitions of these concepts.

Definition. A *Projection* is some portion (sub-graph or cut-set) of the metamodel definition that is relevant to some particular model interchange event or scenario.

A projection has the effect of limiting the domain of discourse to some very specific subset of the underlying metamodel. For example, in the case of CWM and the Star Schema pattern, the CWM projection consists of the following subgraph of the CWM UML definition. This subgraph is shown in Figure 69.

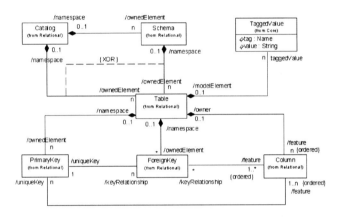

Figure 69: Projection of CWM relational metamodel

Definition. A *Restriction* is a set of constraints that is imposed on the extent of the metamodel projection, relative to some particular model interchange event or scenario.

Restrictions have the effect of limiting the number of instances, types, or subclasses, of metamodel classes that may participate in an interchange event. Collectively, a Projection and a set of one or more Restrictions have the effect of constraining the structure of any model conforming to them to a precisely specified form. All aspects of the model are free to vary, as long as the overall structural form of the model is maintained.

Definition. An *Anchor Element* is some metamodel class of the projection whose instances may be used as starting points for the inspection or traversal of a model.

The designation of anchor elements simplifies the processing of a model. The software consumer knows where to "start" in its traversal or inspection of what could be a large or very complex model. An anchor element should be regarded as a heuristic or optimization; it is not strictly a necessary part of the pattern description, but is still a very useful thing to have.

Definition. A *Metadata Interchange Pattern (MIP)* is an identified (named) projection of a metamodel, optionally with one or more restrictions on that projection, and optionally with one or more specified anchor elements.

Note that a MIP is always formulated in terms of some metamodel expressed in some formal language (e.g., UML, CWM, Java, XML Schema, etc.), although the MIP concepts of projection, restriction, and anchor element are completely independent of any particular metamodel or modeling language.

So, we now have a means of specifying the general form of any class of models based on our common metamodel. This means that the intended semantics of any interchange event can now be precisely specified, in terms of these general forms. Furthermore, shared metadata can also be described in terms that non-technical domain experts are familiar with (since these forms are usually based on concepts that have meaning to domain experts).

In terms of software interoperability, the construction of pattern-aware consumers is greatly simplified, because the pattern definition provides a precise strategy for processing the content of an imported model. This has the effect of increasing the reliability of interchange, as well as lowering the costs of software construction and integration (which means enhanced ROI for the information supply chain). Likewise, pattern-aware producers have guidelines for constructing models for export: lowers software construction and integration costs (again, enhancing ROI).

Documenting and Publishing Metadata Patterns

Now that we've defined metadata patterns, the rationale behind them, and know (more-or-less) how to formulate them, how do we go about describing them and publishing those descriptions to potential end-users? There are two possibilities:

- Human-readable pattern specifications
- Software-consumable pattern specifications

Human-readable metadata interchange pattern specifications facilitate pattern communication between humans (domain experts, programmers, software architects), while software-consumable (or machine-readable) metadata interchange facilitates pattern communication between automated processes. This is particularly significant, because having a pattern specification that is readily consumable by an automated process is the first step toward building *pattern-aware, metadata-driven software.*

Human-readable metadata pattern specifications are based on the use of a standard *pattern template* that borrows largely from GOF-style, other software design patterns, and community practices for describing software patterns. Proposed templates leverage a number of existing pattern specification techniques, but also define a number of specification artifacts that are particular to metadata and model interchange. Additional emphasis is also placed on Web-based publication and search, with the intent of establishing (or rather facilitating the establishment of) Internet-based *pattern catalogs* and *pattern repositories.* Part of the motivation for this comes from the desire that metadata patterns be created largely by their end-user communities: contributors should be domain experts, rather than technologists.

A number of metadata pattern templates have been proposed by different sources, but their overall content usually consists of the following:

- Name and Version
- Intent
- Universal Resource Identifier (URI)
- Contributor
- Problem / Forces / Solution
- Classification: *Domain, Macro, Micro*
- Category: *Interchange, Mapping, Generation*, etc.
- Projection / Restriction / Parameters
- Related Patterns
- Example

An actual online MIP catalog would feature a collection of useful MIP specifications, segmented or organized by application domain. An entry in such a catalog consists of a completed MIP templates submitted to the catalog by some contributor. End-users can search catalogs over the Web according to criteria such a problem statement, problem classification, or problem category.

As a case study of an actual MIP catalog, the reader is invited to peruse the Hyperion MIP Catalog published on the Hyperion Developer Network [4]. There, the read will find a standard MIP Template, several sample MIPs, and some coding examples.

Metadata Interchange Pattern Model (CWM MIP)

To better facilitate the automated publishing of an interchange of metadata interchange patterns based on CWM, the OMG recently developed a new MDA technology specification, which is essentially a formal metamodel that is capable of modeling formal metadata patterns. Called the CWM Metadata Interchange Pattern (CWM MIP) specification, the CWM MIP model is a non-intrusive parallel metamodel to CWM, that allows for the creation of formal descriptions of metadata interchange patterns, where CWM is the base metamodel [10]. In fact, the CWM MIP model can be viewed as an automated representation of the human-readable MIP specification templates we described previously.

Using the CWM MIP model, pattern definitions can be formulated in terms of the CWM MIP model, serialized to XMI documents, stored in online pattern repositories, and interchanged between pattern-aware software tools and applications. The CWM MIP model also allows for pattern definitions to be linked to instances of the actual CWM metadata conforming the pattern, and the two can be interchanged together in the same XMI document. Having such a standard, XML-based interchange model for describing metadata patterns, is a first step toward the future development of next generation visual modeling tools, definition of MIPs, as well as next generation pattern-aware and pattern-driven tools and applications, in general.

Figure 70 illustrates the high-level classes and associations of the CWM MIP model, while Figure 71 shows its associated "type model". Both are expressed in UML notation.

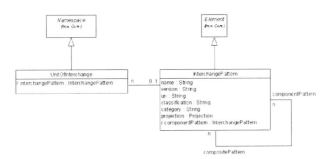

Figure 70: CWM MIP Model (high-level)

To get a better idea of how the model is used, let's first delve into the meanings of each of its major classes, and then describe a typical usage scenario.

The *Unit Of Interchange* class of the CWM MIP Model is essentially the logical container" for shared metadata that is being interchanged, while *Interchange Pattern* models the major MIP components as would be described in a MIP specification template. An instance of Interchange Pattern essentially describes the content of one or more related instances of Unit of Interchange. Please note that structuring the model in this manner makes it possible to interchange and persist MIP instances and MIP definitions independently of each other, or together (as we described previously). Finally, the component pattern – composite pattern reflexive association on the Interchange Pattern class makes it possible to arbitrarily model complex patterns, through pattern composition and reuse.

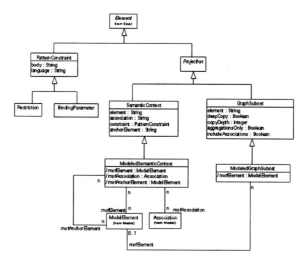

Figure 71: CWM MIP (type model)

The *Projection* class of the "type model" models the MIP concept of "projection" (that is, some metamodel subgraph that forms the basis for the overall pattern description), while the *Pattern Constraint* class models the MIP concepts of "restriction" and "parameters" (as described previously). *Semantic Context* is a specialization of Projection that defines the projection in terms of an enumeration of the logical names of the model element comprising the projections, while *Graph Subset* is an alternative means of describing the projection based on a physical sub-graph expression. Finally, the "modeled" projection subclasses allow for explicitly modeled projections based on MOF instances.

MIP Usage Scenarios

A typical usage scenario for the CWM MIP model might consist of the following sequence of activities:

1. A *pattern authoring tool* creates an Interchange Pattern object and defines the MIP by assigning relevant values to the object attributes.
2. The authoring tool stores an Interchange Pattern object in a pattern repository or serializes it to an XMI document. In this case, note that the MIP has been defined independently of any potentially associated metadata.
3. A *pattern-aware client application* locates and imports the MIP object, the pattern repository, or XMI document.
4. The client then uses the MIP as the basis for automatically expanding its own metadata import capabilities, as it has "learned" a new pattern.
5. The client is now capable of consuming and making intelligent use of metadata conforming to the MIP.

Note that the application client described above, is an example of a dynamic, *pattern-driven* tool.

As another example scenario, consider the following:

1. A *pattern-aware producer* constructs an Interchange Pattern object defining a MIP.
2. The producer then constructs three different application models (metadata instances), each represented by its own Unit Of Interchange object.
3. The producer relates each application model to the common descriptive MIP by creating links based on the Unit Of Interchange – Interchange Pattern association.
4. Finally, the producer serializes the entire object structure to a single XMI document and then stores it in a *pattern-oriented metadata repository*.

MIP Construction Case Study

Finally, as a case study in the programmatic construction of a MIP and associated metadata, the reader is invited to download an example of programmatic code that creates both the Star Schema pattern described earlier in this chapter, as well as associated metadata, from the Hyperion MIP Catalog [4]. In this Java code sample application, the Star Schema MIP and an instance of a Star Schema relational database structure described in terms of CWM both are created and serialized to an XMI document, as well as persisted in a pattern-oriented metadata store. The code sample is freely available from the Hyperion Developer Network [4].

Let's now walk though the construction of the MIP and its associated metadata, in terms of modeling diagrams. Note: Reviewing the code simultaneously with the diagrams should greatly enhance your overall understanding.

In the first step, the Java client creates the "Star Schema" Interchange Pattern object, and assigns appropriate values to its attributes. The resulting object is shown in Figure 72, as a UML instance diagram.

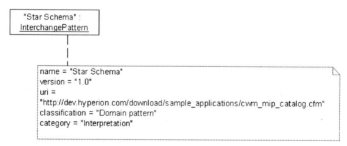

Figure 72: "Star Schema" Interchange Pattern object

Next, the Java client creates Semantic Context objects, and initializes the *element, association,* and *anchor element* arrays with the appropriate logical names of the various CWM model elements comprising the Star Schema projection (note that this corresponds to the CWM subgraph illustrated in Figure 69). The resulting Semantic Context is illustrated in Figure 73.

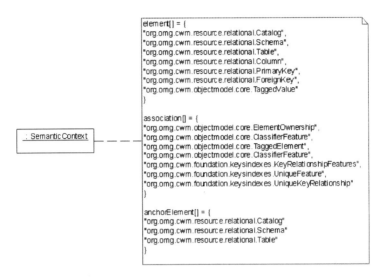

Figure 73: "Star Schema" Semantic Context

The next step is to define the Restriction objects (note that we show only one of them here for conciseness– there are actually four). The Restrictions are expressed in the Object Constraint Language (OCL) [21], which is a part of the UML. The resulting Restriction object is shown in Figure 74.

```
: Restriction

language = "OCL"
body =
"-- At least one Table in the model is a join table:
Table.allInstances->select( t | t.oclAsType(ModelElement).taggedValue->exists( p |
    p.tag = "isJoinTable" and p.value = "true" ) )->size > 0"
```

Figure 74: "Star Schema" Restrictions (partial)

The Java program then completes the MIP model by linking the various model components created in the previous steps together. The object diagram shown in Figure 75 illustrates the completed CWM MIP model.

283

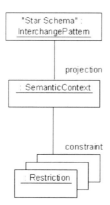

Figure 75: "Star Schema" MIP model

Now, the Java program needs to create the actual metadata. This is comprised of an instance of the CWM Relational Metamodel representing the Star Schema design presented earlier in Figure 68. (A partial rendering of this object diagram is shown here in Figure 76, for convenience).

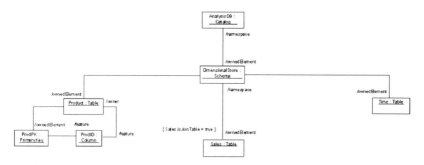

Figure 76: CWM "Star Schema" instance (partial diagram showing root classes only)

Finally, the Java client completes the entire information model by linking the "Star Schema" MIP definition with the "Star Schema" metadata. Figure 77 illustrates the result.

284

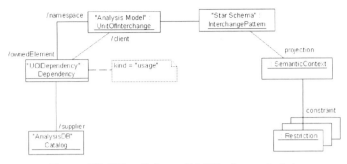

Figure 77: "Star Schema" MIP plus metadata

MIP Summary

Here are the key points that summarize our discussion of metadata interchange patterns:

- Metadata interchange is a pre-requisite for integration of most heterogeneous software systems, products, tools and applications.
- Metadata interchange requires a common language (metamodel) and interchange format or interface.
- Having a common language and interchange format is necessary, but not sufficient, for truly reliable metadata interchange, especially in highly collaborative environments featuring many metadata producers and consumers with diverse requirements.
- Reliable and precise metadata interchange requires some means of establishing *bounded variation* on model structure and content.
- By "bounded variation", we mean that models must somehow conform to fairly general, predictable structures, or general forms.
- Within the boundaries of these general forms, model composition is allowed to vary without restriction.
- Bounded variation is best described in terms of idiomatic usages of the underlying, formal language.
- A Metadata Interchange Pattern (MIP) is simply a formally described idiom (or composition of idioms).

- The use of MIPs simplifies software construction and facilitates the development of pattern-based, model-driven systems.
- Such model-driven systems based on the use of model patterns can exhibit a very high degree of operational autonomy and flexibility.
- MIPs are specified using *templates* largely based on the software design patterns community concept of a template.
- MIPs may be organized and published in terms of pattern catalogs.
- An approach to automating the process of MIP publishing and communication involves the use of a machine-readable model of a MIP.
- Such a machine-readable MIP model has been recently formulated as an OMG standard: The CWM Metadata Interchange Pattern (CWM MIP) Specification.
- CWM MIP enables CWM models and their corresponding descriptive MIPs to be persisted together in *pattern-based metadata repositories* (based on MOF) and serialized together in XMI documents.

Some avenues for future research and development of the CWM MIP concept include the following:

- Alignment of CWM MIP with the OMG's forthcoming "2.0-generation" modeling standards, such as UML 2.0, MOF 2.0, and MOF 2.0 QVT.
- Integration of CWM MIP with several, model-based, open-source Java™ IDEs: Eclipse 3.0 + Eclipse Modeling Framework (EMF), and Sun's NetBeans IDE.
- Ongoing collection, codification, and publishing of useful MIPs, in various online pattern catalogs.
- Ongoing development and experimentation with pattern-based and pattern-driven tools (e.g., possible extensions to MDA modeling tools).

Semantic Web and MDA

The next technological area of promise for enhancing MDA and enabling us to evolve MDA further in the direction of that upper right-hand quadrant, involves the integration of much of the MDA technology stack with the Semantic Web and its associated domain-specific technologies. We view this as being crucial to the development of future model-driven systems that can leverage vast stores of published domain knowledge, and are capable of automated or, perhaps, semi-automated reasoning.

Ontologies

The Semantic Web concept centers on providing far more intelligence and automation into the Web, by providing standard ways in which domain-specific semantics can readily be modeled, captured, and made available to both human users and software clients or agents. The World Wide Web infrastructure itself, has already provided us awith a number of important technologies in this direction. For example, XML was provided as a means of having a common syntactical representation for information, and URIs as means of locating any object on the Web. But the problem of providing standard ways of capturing, structuring, and publishing semantic knowledge, in general, is largely unaddressed.

In recent times, the use of *ontologies* has been proposed as a means of solving the semantic knowledge problem. An ontology is a formal information model that captures the key entities, relationships, and behaviors normally associated with some domain of inquiry. For example, a bioinformatics ontology would consist of a model of fundamental concepts regarding genetic structure, DNA sequencing, encoding patterns, etc., while a business performance management ontology would model concepts such as work flow, collaboration, multidimensional data structures, and so on. Figure 78 shows a small and highly simplified portion of a bioinformatics ontology, rendered in UML notation.

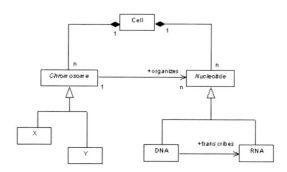

Figure 78: Simplified bioinformatics ontology

The main difficulty in constructing ontological models lies not necessarily in the knowledge acquisition itself, but rather, in how to provide some standard representation of an ontology that is meaningful to non-technical human users (e.g., domain experts), and also consumable and intelligible to automated processes (i.e., software clients and agents). The theory is that, if it were possible to establish ontologies for various domains of interest on the Web, they would be readily accessible and could be used to streamline and improve various services. For example, an ontology-driven search engine is envisioned as being a highly general-purpose tool (non-domain-specific) that could attach to any published ontology, and leverage the encoded, domain-specific knowledge to enhance the accuracy its search results. A user would receive fewer, but much more accurate, hits that were based not simply on matched content, but more likely on domain-specific inferences drawn by the search engine.

Key implementation technologies used today in the development of ontologies for the Semantic Web are the W3C's Resource Description Framework (RDF), and Web Ontology Language (OWL). RDF builds on XML, while OWL builds on both XML and RDF. Ultimately, since both are just specialized ways of using XML, these new languages are readily accessible.

MDA and the Semantic Web

It turns out that there is tremendous synergy between the Semantic Web and MDA, more so than one might initially suspect. This synergy is best described in terms of three key observations regarding the Semantic Web and its concept of an ontology:

- An ontology is essentially a highly domain-specific (vertical) information model.
- An ontology must be capable of having standard representations that are intelligible to both human and software consumers.
- If the Semantic Web is to achieve maximum benefit, there must be some rational strategy for developing new software systems and applications whose architectures are fundamentally ontology-driven. For example, the intelligent web browser described earlier is just one example of such an application.

If you think about each of the above points in light of the basic concepts of MDA, the relationship between the Semantic Web and MDA should become fairly clear:

- Any ontology is essentially a PIM, in MDA terms (although not all PIMs are necessarily ontologies).

- Any ontology cast as a PIM in MDA would necessarily be represented by a UML model. Under MDA, this UML model would be the primary representation of the ontology. As a visual model, it would be better suited for direct human understanding than an equivalent RDF or OWL rendering.

- On the other hand, since the ontology model is an MDA PIM, it can readily be transformed into any of a number of equivalent models in other languages (such as XML, RDF, and OWL).

- From the perspective of MDA, any equivalent XML-, RDF-, or OWL-based rendering of the ontology is a low-level, concrete representation of the ontology that is well suited for direct consumption by a software process. In other words, these are platform-specific models, or PSMs.

Given sufficient tool support, one can readily perform round-trip engineering of ontological models between UML, XML, RDF, or OWL representations. For example, a new ontology could be developed in UML using a visual modeling tool, and then transformed into OWL for deployment on the Web. Similarly, an existing ontology defined in OWL can be transformed to an equivalent UML model, and brought into the MDA framework.

Finally, aligning MDA with Semantic Web standards means that MDA-based software development tools could readily be used in the development of advanced, ontology-driven systems and applications. This is because the software development and knowledge engineering processes are both performed at essentially the same level of abstraction.

What is required to make all of the above happen is to have a standard representation of an ontology in a form that MDA can understand. In other words, a standard *metamodel* of an ontology, expressed in UML. Such a metamodel would serve as the linguistic basis for modeling new ontologies in UML, as well as mappings and transformations between various, standard, ontological representations.

The OMG's Ontology Definition Metamodel

The Ontology Definition Metamodel (ODM) is an effort currently underway, within the OMG, to define just such a standard metamodel of Semantic Web ontologies that, until now, would have otherwise been defined as OWL expressions.

The ODM submission consists of three main components:

290

- An ontology definition metamodel (ODM), developed in UML notation.
- A two-way mapping between UML and OWL DL (OWL Description Logics).
- A UML ontology profile, which enables the re-use of UML notation in ontological definitions.

Since the ODM is defined in UML, it is, by default, consistent with the OMG MOF and XMI standards, and readily fits into the overall MDA framework. What this means is that any MOF-compliant software tool (for example, a visual modeling or repository tool) can readily import, export, and manage instances of the ODM.

There are three variants of the OWL language: OWL Lite, OWL DL, and OWL Full. To ensure maximum expressiveness and basic support for automated reasoning systems, ODM is designed to be consistent with OWL DL. OWL Full, unfortunately, has a number of issues regarding its own computational semantics, so it is currently being avoided by the ODM.

We will not delve into the ODM in any great detail in this chapter. For more information, see the current submission document at http://www.omg.org/docs/ad/2003-03-40. Figure 79 illustrates only the high-level structure of the Ontology Definition Metamodel.

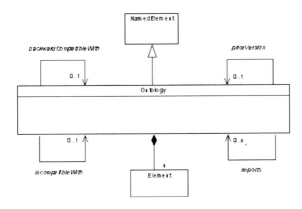

Figure 79: ODM core model

Enterprise Information Integration: A Pragmatic Approach

Key Concepts

1. MDA is focused primarily on three things:
   - The use of formal, visual models to describe systems at different levels of abstraction;
   - Standard transformations of models between various representations;
   - The pervasive use of automated tools in performing these model transformations.
2. The benefit of MDA is that it places visual system modeling at the forefront, and indeed, at all points of the system development lifecycle, ensuring that conceptualization, design, and physical implementation are also mutually consistent and deeply integrated.

Bibliography

1. Arlow, Jim and Ila Neustadt. *Enterprise Patterns and MDA: Building Better Software with Archetype Patterns and UML.* Reading, MA: Addison Wesley, Inc., 2004.
2. Gamma, Erich, Richard Helm, Ralph Johnson, John Vlissides. "Design Patterns: Abstraction and Reuse of Object-Oriented Designs." *Proceedings, ECOOP '93.* Heidelberg: Springer-Verlag, 1993.
3. Gamma, Erich, Richard Helm, Ralph Johnson, John Vlissides. *Design Patterns: Elements of Reusable Object-Oriented Software.* Reading, MA: Addison Wesley, Inc., 1995.
4. Hyperion Developer Network. *Hyperion Metadata Interchange Patterns Catalog.* Hyperion Solutions Corp., 2004. Internet: http://dev.hyperion.com/download/sample_applications/cwm_mip _catalog.cfm/.
5. Java Community Process. *Java™ Metadata Interface Specification, Version 1.0.* Sun Microsystems, 2002. Internet: http://jcp.org/.
6. Kimball, Ralph. *The Data Warehouse Toolkit: Practical Techniques for Building Dimensional Data Warehouses.* New York: John Wiley & Sons, Inc., 1996.
7. Kleppe, Anneke, Jos Warmer, and Wim Bast. *MDA Explained: The Model Driven Architecture – Practice and Promise.* Reading, MA: Addison Wesley, Inc., 2003.
8. OMG. *Common Warehouse Metamodel Specification, Version 1.1.* Needham, MA: Object Management Group, 2003. Internet: http://www.omg.org/technology/documents/formal/cwm.htm.
9. OMG. CORBA, XML and XMI Resource Page. Needham, MA: Object Management Group, 2004. Internet: http://www.omg.org/technology/xml/index.htm
10. OMG. *CWM Metadata Interchange Patterns Specification, Version 1.0.* Needham, MA: Object Management Group, 2004. Internet: http://www.omg.org/technology/documents/formal/cwm_mip.htm.

11. OMG. Data Warehousing, CWM and MOF Resource Page. Needham, MA: Object Management Group, 2004. Internet: http://www.omg.org/technology/cwm

12. OMG. Model-Driven Architecture Home Page. Needham, MA: Object Management Group, 2004. Internet: http://www.omg.org/mda

13. OMG. Unified Modeling Language Resource Page. Needham, MA: Object Management Group, 2004. Internet: http://www.omg.org/technology/uml/index.htm

14. Mellor, Stephen J. and Marc J. Balcer. *Executable UML: A Foundation for Model-Driven Architecture*. Reading, MA: Addison Wesley, Inc., 2002.

15. Mellor, Stephen J., Kendall Scott, Axel Uhl, and Dirk Weise. *MDA Distilled: Principles of Model-Driven Architecture*. Reading, MA: Addison Wesley, Inc., 2004.

16. Poole, John. "The Common Warehouse Metamodel as a Foundation for Active Object Models in the Data Warehousing Environment." ECOOP 2000 Workshop on Metadata and Active Object Models, 2000. Internet: http://www.adaptiveobjectmodel.com/ECOOP2000 or http://www.cwmforum.org/paperpresent.htm

17. Poole, John. "Model-Driven Architecture: Vision, Standards, and Emerging Technologies." ECOOP 2001 Workshop on Metamodeling and Adaptive Object Models, 2001. Internet: http://www.adaptiveobjectmodel.com/ECOOP2001 or http://www.omg.org/mda/

18. Poole, John, Dan Chang, Douglas Tolbert, and David Mellor. *Common Warehouse Metamodel: An Introduction to the Standard for Data Warehouse Integration*. New York: John Wiley & Sons, Inc., 2002. Internet: http://www.wiley.com/compbooks/poole

19. Poole, John, Dan Chang, Douglas Tolbert, and David Mellor. *Common Warehouse Metamodel Developer's Guide*. New York: John Wiley & Sons, Inc., 2003. Internet: http://www.wiley.com/compbooks/poole

20. Tolbert, Doug. "CWM: A Model-Based Architecture for Data Warehouse Interchange." Workshop on Evaluating Software Architectural Solutions 2000. University of California at Irvine, 2000. Internet: http://www.cwmforum.org/paperpresent.html

21. Warmer, Jos, and Anneke Kleppe. *The Object Constraint Language: Precise Modeling with UML*. Reading, MA: Addison Wesley, Inc., 1999.

Core Technology Overview

XML

The eXtensible Markup Language (XML) standard was publicly recommended by the World Wide Web Consortium (W3C) in 1998. XML is a derivative vocabulary of the Standard Generalized Markup Language (SGML), which has been in use since the late 1960's for marking up documents for purposes of automated printing. XML was created as solution to problems associated with the tight pairing of presentation and content in HTML, for Web browser presentation. XML allows content to be described independently of how it will be used, providing for greater reuse. XML's simplicity has been the basis for its rapid ascent in the world of standards. There are some basic things that you need to understand about XML. They are defined here.

The first term we need to know is *element*. In XML, an element is an identifier that embodies a particular piece of information. It is identified by a start tag/end tag sequence, or sometimes, by just a single tag

<TAG>Some piece of unique information</TAG>

Example 1: An element identified by a start and end tag

:

<TAG/>

Example 2: An element identified by just a start tag (also known as an empty element)

XML is a language that is intended to let anyone define and process a markup language of their choosing. For instance, a markup language is sometimes also referred to as a vocabulary, for example HTML. With XML, these vocabularies can be defined ad-hoc, or they can be based on a set of rigid rules, defined in a Document Type Definition (DTD). A DTD tells authoring tools and XML parsers what it elements it should expect, and when it should expect them.

```
<CAR>
        <MAKE>Jeep</MAKE>
        <MODEL>Grand Cherokee/Laredo</MODEL>
        <YEAR>1999</YEAR>
        <COLOR>Bronze</COLOR>
</CAR>
```
Example 3: XML Vocabulary that describes a car

Given Example 3, it is easy to envision the number of ways we could utilize information defined in this manner. We could present it visually in a table, we could store in a database, or we could apply it to a mail merge for an advertising campaign. XML provides us the flexibility to define structures this easily. At the same time, it also provides the power to ensure that certain semantics are preserved.

To use Example 3 once again, we could write a DTD which specifies that a CAR must contain a MAKE, MODEL, and YEAR, and may contain a COLOR. If we remove the COLOR element from this example, it would still be considered to be a valid XML document, from the perspective of a parser. However, if we removed MAKE, then the XML parser would have to report an error since we did not follow the syntax rules for defining a CAR. In addition, using these same rules, if we added VEHICLE_NUMBER, then we would also be breaking the rules, as defined by the DTD.

NOTE: Regardless of whether we follow the DTD or not, our XML documents will be considered well-formed, as long as we follow the XML 1.0 grammar. An XML document that follows both the XML

1.0 grammar and the syntax defined by the DTD is considered to be valid.

Another term that needs to be introduced in reference to elements is *attribute*. An attribute is a named value that is associated with an element's start tag. It defines additional information regarding the element that the XML document's author does not want included in the elements content. In Example 3, we may want to provide a century on the year information to avoid processing problems. The century information does not make sense when viewed as part of the content, especially if we intend to turn it back into an integer representation of itself inside of an application.

<YEAR century="20">99</YEAR>
Example 4: Use of an attribute on an element

Note the format for defining attributes is key="value". It is also important to note that attributes can also appear on empty elements. Like elements, attributes can be applied liberally if there is no DTD for the document. However, if users wish, they can use a DTD to define which attributes are acceptable on which elements, and even force particular value types as acceptable or default.

Entity is another key XML component. An entity defines an alias for a set of character data. Entities can be defined within the XML document, or can point to a source outside of the XML document, also known as an external entity.

Entities are defined within the prolog of the XML document. This is the section that is defined before declaring the first element.

<!ENTITY % address ' 123 Howser Street'>
Example 5: An entity declaration

<TAG>Here is my address: %address;</TAG>
Example 6: Use of a defined entity within an XML document

Example 5 and Example 6 describe how to define and use an entity. Entities are very useful for defining blocks of characters, once, that will be reused multiple times throughout the document. This is a very efficient way to minimize bandwidth when publishing XML documents to the web. This also allows documents to be defined in a very reusable manner. The document described in Example 6 could easily be created once statically, and then attached to a dynamically defined DTD that fills in the fields of the XML document at parse-time.

Two more important terms that need to be well understood are PCDATA and CDATA. PCDATA (parsed character data) represents text that will be evaluated by the parser to ensure compliance with the XML 1.0 grammar, and to identify elements and other XML components. CDATA (character data) is raw data that the parser will read in, but not attempt to process.

RDF

The Resource Definition Framework (RDF) is a standard way to describe metadata. Like XML, RDF is a recommendation of the W3C and was developed as part of the Semantic Web activity. Its purpose is to provide a means of describing metadata in machine understandable format, allowing for more efficient and sophisticated data interchange, searching, cataloging, navigation, classification, etc.

An RDF statement is composed of three components: a subject, a predicate, and an object. These three components combine to create a unique fact. Additionally, the object of a statement can itself be another RDF statement. This design allows traversable graphs to be created to convey meaning and knowledge. Figure 80 below illustrates a single RDF statement, while Figure 81 illustrates an entire RDF graph.

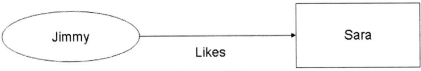

Figure 80: Simple RDF statement

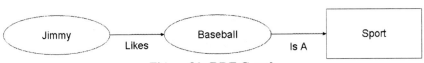

Figure 81: RDF Graph

In Figure 80 the subject is represented by the circle, the predicate by the label on the arc and the object by the box. These are commonly used symbols to express these three facets.

In addition to the graphical representation of an RDF statement, RDF can also be expressed in XML. There are multiple ways to express the RDF statement in XML. However, the most straightforward, albeit verbose, way is called the reified form. In reified form, the subject, predicate and object are spelled out explicitly, and uses explicit RDF XML elements. The example below illustrates the reified statement Figure 80.

```
<rdf:RDF
 xmlns:rdf="http://www.w3.org/1999/02/22-rdf-syntax-ns#">
 <rdf:Description>
  <rdf:subject>Jimmy</rdf:subject>
  <rdf:predicate>Likes</rdf:predicate>
  <rdf:object>
      <rdf:Description>
        <rdf:subject>Baseball</rdf:subject>
        <rdf:predicate>IsA</rdf:predicate>
        <rdf:object>sport</rdf:object>
      </rdf:Description>
  </rdf:object>
 </rdf:Description>
</rdf:RDF>
```

301

RDF Schema

RDF Schema (RDFS) extends RDF so that it can represent with clarity, groups of related resources and the relationships between them. RDF, as a syntax, can describe anything in the world. However, the descriptions are extremely generic and very complex to leverage as part of an application.

RDFS expresses a class and property type system in RDF to provide a more greatly detailed set of rules for defining the metadata that defines a particular set of content. Since RDF is a simple model, it can describe a relationship between resources. However, it does not have a defined mechanism for describing properties or relationships between properties. This capability is introduced through another recommendation called RDF Schema, which is a vocabulary description language.

The following is an example of how the class typing capabilities of RDFS can be used to describe Jet Fuel:

```
<rdfs:Class rdf:ID="A1_Jet_Fuel"/>
    <rdfs:label>A1_Jet_Fuel</rdfs:label>
    <rdfs:subClassOfrdf:resource="#Kerosene_Type_Aviation_Fuel"/
>
</rdfs:Class>

<rdfs:Class rdf:ID="Jet_Fuel_With_Icing_Inhibitor"/>
    <rdfs:label>Jet_Fuel_With_Icing_Inhibitor</rdfs:label>
    <rdfs:comment>
        Fuel, typically aviation fuel, that contains icing inhibitor
    </rdfs:comment>
    <partOrIngredientType
rdf:resource="#Jet_Fuel_Icing_Inhibitor"/>
    <rdfs:subClassOf rdf:resource="#Petroleum"/>
</rdfs:Class>

<rdfs:Class rdf:ID="A1+_Jet_Fuel"/>
```

```
<rdfs:label>A1+_Jet_Fuel</rdfs:label>
<rdfs:comment>A1_Jet_Fuel with icing inhibitor</rdfs:comment>
<rdfs:subClassOf rdf:resource="#A1_Jet_Fuel"/>
<rdfs:subClassOf
rdf:resource="#Jet_Fuel_With_Icing_Inhibitor"/>
</rdfs:Class>
```

In this example, A1_Jet_Fuel and Jet_Fuel_With_Icing_Inhibitor are expressed as atomic entities, but through the means of RDFS we have ways to create a more specific instance of these two types of fuels called A1+_Jet_Fuel.

Web Ontology Language (OWL)

OWL is an example of an RDFS vocabulary that introduces classification, cardinality, (in)equality and set operations. The Web Ontology Language (OWL) is misspelled on purpose in reference to Owl from Winnie the Pooh, who incorrectly misspelled his name in writing to read WOL, which is the proper acronym for the Web Ontology Language. OWL provides a facility that allows us to establish equality between items or entities, even when those items or entities have two different sets of terminology to describe what they are.

The classification scheme provided to us by RDFS enables us to describe things in greater structural form than simple RDF by itself. However, OWL allows us to formulate entire ontologies using the structures of RDFS. Ontologies define terms that describe a particular area of knowledge. They allow people and machines to exchange and share information across a particular information domain. OWL provides us with a very powerful means to describe any domain of objects and to describe them in a manner that is recognizable and comparable.

The following is an example of an OWL document. It is a simple attempt at describing a postage stamp. Notice the definition of a class structure with inheritance as Stamp derives from StampDescriptor.

Also, notice the definition of a class of properties—hasStampDescriptor and hasPicture—that apply to Stamp.

```
<owl:Class rdf:ID="StampDesciptor" />

<owl:Class rdf:ID="Stamp">
 <rdfs:subClassOf rdf:resource="#StampDescriptor" />
</owl:Class>

<owl:ObjectProperty rdf:ID="hasStampDescriptor">
 <rdfs:domain rdf:resource="#Stamp" />
 <rdfs:range  rdf:resource="#StampDescriptor" />
</owl:ObjectProperty>

<owl:ObjectProperty rdf:ID="hasPicture">
 <rdfs:subPropertyOf rdf:resource="#hasStampDescriptor" />
 <rdfs:range rdf:resource="#Stamp" />
</owl:ObjectProperty>

<owl:Class rdf:ID="US_Stamp"/>
    <rdfs:subClassOf rdf:resource="#Stamp"/>
</owl:Class>

<owl:Class rdf:ID="Swiss_Postage "/>
    <rdfs:subClassOf rdf:resource="#Stamp"/>
</owl:Class>
```

While extremely simplistic, we can use the above example to determine that we're talking about the same datatype when comparing US_Stamp and Swiss_Postage. This is one of the primary and most complex tasks in information management—determining the equivalence of mislabeled and poorly organized data.

Web Services

Web Services is a software design pattern that facilitates the design of loosely coupled applications by exposing functionality as well-defined services. Typically, a service is a stateless entity that takes external input and provides some immediate processing. The term "Web Services" originates from the initial design that leverages common Web protocols and technologies, such as XML and HTTP, to implement services interfaces and message transport. However, the Web Services paradigm has now grown to support mature message transport and complex message definitions.

Web Services form the basis of a service-oriented architecture (SOA), which also includes a registry of available services known as Universal Description, Discovery, and Integration (UDDI), a message definition format known as SOAP[18] and a service definition language known as Web Services Definition Language (WSDL). These three technologies form the basis of the SOA. The following sections discuss each of these technologies in greater depth.

SOAP

Web Services is a distributed computing paradigm, which means that services can be located on any hardware or operating system platform anywhere on the network. Therefore, in order to communicate with these services, a standard was defined for the format of the messages that pass between the calling application and the service. This format has become known as SOAP.

A SOAP message is an XML document that consists of two sections: the header and the body. The header section captures typical message header information, such as recipient, routing

---

[18] SOAP used to be an acronym for Simple Object Access Protocol when it was first introduced by Microsoft, however has since lost this underlying representation and is now just known as SOAP

information, timestamps, etc. Applications can extend the header section as needed to capture as little or as much information as might be required. The body section contains the content that is to be passed to the Web Service for processing.

While SOAP is an extremely simple design, newly forming Web Services standards around security, reliability, and routing, specify requirements for the SOAP envelope that allow them to operate properly.

The following is a sample SOAP Message.

```
<env:Envelope
    xmlns:env="http://www.w3.org/2003/05/soap-
envelope">
    <env:Header>
    </env:Header>
    <env:Body>
    </env:Body>
</env:Envelope>
```

Note the three main parts of a SOAP message: the Envelope, the Header and the Body.

WSDL

The Web Services Definition Language is an XML vocabulary that defines the interfaces, bindings, services, and messages that describe a service. Since this information is available in a single, introspective format, the information in it can be used to connect with, and execute services at runtime. This is one of the major advancements of Web Services over other distributed computing technologies, such as COM, CORBA, etc. However, just because a service can be called dynamically, does not necessarily mean that the service can be used in any application. The messages and content that the service requires and provides is still going to be proprietary to the service itself.

SAML

SAML stands for Security Assertion Markup Language and is currently a version 1.1 standard of the Organization for the Advancement of Structured Information Standards. SAML is a framework for exchanging security information between applications in a distributed environment. Since managing security in a boundless universe is an unachievable goal, we need a way for a trusted party to express to other applications and services information about a particular resource.

For example, a trusted authority can express that a request is being made by a machine that has authenticated a user named Bob Smith via a username/password mechanism. It can also tell us that Bob Smith has B-level clearance and belongs to the group "administrators". Based on this information, the manager of a particular application can allow access based on username, clearance level, or role.

This security information is stored in the security assertion that becomes part of the request for access to a secured service. Since the assertion is deemed to be from a trusted party, the information stored in the assertion can immediately be interpreted for authorization policy information. The secured application can also verify the security assertion with the trusted authority, to ensure that the assertion is valid. Figure 82 below illustrates this process.

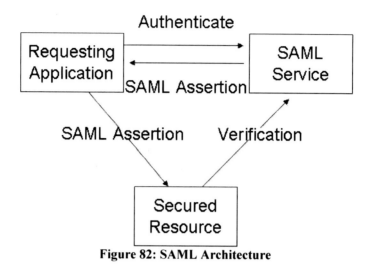

Figure 82: SAML Architecture

Business Process Execution Language

The Web Services Business Process Execution Language (WSBPEL) is a business process definition language based on XML. Currently, this language exists in an accepted form based on the work of BEA, IBM, Microsoft, SAP, and Siebel, entitled Business Process Execution Language for Web Services Version 1.1, which has since been adopted as 1.0 by the OASIS WSBEL technical committee.

The purpose of this language is to be express both executable and abstract processes, whereas an executable process models physical process behavior, and an abstract process models the logical process behavior. An example of an executable process is a withdrawal transaction from a bank account, where money is deducted from the account and transferred to cash or another account. In this example, steps are executed in sequence, they are usually managed within the bounds of a transaction to ensure reliability. and the transaction manages state until it is complete. On the other hand, an abstract process is more closely associated with the conversation of a business-to-business transaction, in which the management of the movement of data between parties is the primary driver and the state and data is managed by each of the communicating partners.

Using BPEL to describe executable processes provides greater opportunity for reuse throughout the organization. Since the processes are described as higher-level constructs, they can more easily be joined together in new configurations, without incurring the overhead of coding. The use of BPEL for abstract processes allows business partners to define a common protocol for doing business electronically, and then share the description of that protocol in a way that will not impact how the process will be implemented within each participating organization.

The following is a subset of an annotated version of a sample BPEL document provided by the OASIS WSBPEL Technical Committee. The goal of providing it here, is to demonstrate some of the capabilities that BPEL provides, and how these operations are represented.

```
<process name="OrderShippingProcess"
   targetNamespace="http://contoso.org/samples"
   suppressJoinFailure="yes"
   xmlns:tns="http://contoso.org/samples"
   xmlns="http://schemas.xmlsoap.org/ws/2003/03/business
-process/">
```

The process document defines a single business process

```
<partnerLinks>
  <partnerLink name="ordering"
    partnerLinkType="tns:OrderingSystemLinkType"
    myRole="OrderingService"/>
  <partnerLink name="orderingresponse"
    partnerLinkType="tns:OrderingResponseLinkType"
    partnerRole="OrderingServiceResponse"/>
  <partnerLink name="shipper"
    partnerLinkType="tns:ShipperPartnerLinkType"
    partnerRole="ShippingService"/>
  <partnerLink name="shipperresponse"

  partnerLinkType="tns:ShipperPartnerResponseLinkType"
    myRole="ShippingResponseRole"/>
```

Enterprise Information Integration: A Pragmatic Approach

```
  <partnerLink name="shippingrequestor"

  partnerLinkType="tns:ShippingRequestorPartnerLinkTyp
e"
    myRole="ShippingRequestor"/>
  <partnerLink name="invoiceprocessor"

  partnerLinkType="tns:InvoiceProcessorPartnerLinkType
"
    myRole="InvoiceProcessor"/>
  <partnerLink name="invoiceresponse"

  partnerLinkType="tns:InvoiceResponsePartnerLinkType"
    partnerRole="InvoiceResponse"/>
  <partnerLink name="orderingconfirmation"
    partnerLinkType="tns:FinalConfirmLinkType"
    partnerRole="OrderingServiceConfirmation"/>
</partnerLinks>
```

This section defines the set of services that will participate in the process.

```
<partners>
  <partner name="Shipper">
    <partnerLink name="shipper"/>
    <partnerLink name="shippingrequestor"/>
    <partnerLink name="invoiceprocessor"/>
  </partner>
</partners>
```

This section establishes the roles that will participate in the process.

```
<variables>
  <variable                         name="order"
messageType="tns:OrderMessageType"/>
  <variable                         name="order_ack"
messageType="tns:OrderAckMessageType"/>
  <variable name="order_shipped"
    messageType="tns:OrderAckMessageType"/>
  <variable name="ship_request"
    messageType="tns:ShipRequestMessageType"/>
  <variable name="ship_request_ack"
    messageType="tns:ShipRequestAckMessageType"/>
  <variable name="pickup_notification"
```

```
      messageType="tns:PickupNotificationMessageType"/>
    <variable name="ship_status"
      messageType="tns:ShipStatusMessageType"/>
    <variable name="ship_history"
      messageType="tns:ShippingHistoryMessageType"/>
    <variable                              name="invoice"
   messageType="tns:InvoiceMessageType"/>
    <variable name="invoice_ack"
      messageType="tns:InvoiceAckMessageType"/>
    <variable name="payment_confirmation"
      messageType="tns:PaymentConfirmationMessageType"/>
  </variables>
```

This section establishes the messages and XML documents that will be used in this process.

```
  <correlationSets>
    <correlationSet name="OrderCorrelationSet"
      properties="tns:OrderID"/>
  </correlationSets>
```

The correlationSets provides the basis for tracking a transaction over multiple documents and asynchronous processes.

```
<sequence name="main">

    <receive name="receiveOrder" partnerLink="ordering"
      portType="tns:OrderingPortType"
operation="PlaceOrder"
      variable="order" createInstance="yes">
      <correlations>
        <correlation            set="OrderCorrelationSet"
        initiate="yes"/> </correlations>
    </receive>
```

The first step in the main sequence is to receive an order.

```
    <assign name="assign1">
      <copy>
        <from variable="order" part="OrderMessagePart"
          query="/OrderMessage/ShippingInfo"></from>
        <to                    variable="ship_request"
part="ShipRequestMessagePart"
          query="/ShipRequest/ShippingInfo"/>
      </copy>
```

```
    </assign>
```

Copy data from the order document and start to populate the ship_request document.

```
    <invoke name="requestShipping" partnerLink="shipper"
      portType="tns:Shipping" operation="PlaceShipOrder"
      inputVariable="ship_request">
      <correlations>
        <correlation              set="OrderCorrelationSet"
pattern="out"/>
      </correlations>
    </invoke>
```

Execute the requestShipping process using the ship_request document.

```
    <receive name="receiveShippingConfirmation"
      partnerLink="shipperresponse"
portType="tns:ShippingResponse"
      operation="GetShipAck"
variable="ship_request_ack">
      <correlations>
        <correlation set="OrderCorrelationSet" />
      </correlations>
    </receive>
```

Handle the receipt of the shipping request.

```
    <switch>
    <case

  condition="bpws:getVariableProperty('ship_request_ack
',
              'Ship_Acknowledged') = true()">
      <assign>
        <copy>
          <from expression="'OK'"/>
          <to                    variable="order_ack"
part="OrderAckMessagePart"
            query="/OrderAckMessage/Ack"/>
        </copy>
      </assign>
    </case>
```

Evaluate if the shipping request was positively acknowledged. If so, set the value in the order acknowledgement document to OK.

```
    <otherwise>
      <assign>
        <copy>
          <from expression="'NOTOK'"/>
          <to variable="order_ack"
            part="OrderAckMessagePart"
query="/OrderAckMessage/Ack"/>
          </copy>
        </assign>
      </otherwise>
    </switch>

    <reply                          name="confirmOrder"
partnerLink="orderingresponse"
      portType="tns:OrderingResponsePortType"
operation="GetOrderAck"
      variable="order_ack"/>
```

Send the order confirmation to party that placed the order.

```
    . . .

    </sequence>
</process>
```

As you can see by this example, BPEL can help manage asynchronous business process orchestration by managing the calls across Web Services, moving data between documents in memory, and evaluating the content of the documents to make decisions.

Glossary

.NET	An application platform developed by Microsoft
ACL	Access Control List
BAPI	SAP Business API
BPM	Business Process Management
CRM	Customer Resource Management
CWM	Common Warehouse Metadata
E/R	Entity/Relationship
EAI	Enterprise Application Integration
EDA	Event-Driven Architecture
EII	Enterprise Information Integration
ERP	Enterprise Resource Planning
ESB	Enterprise Service Bus
ETL	Extract, Transform & Load
HTML	Hypertext Markup Language
IS	Information Services
IT	Information Technology
Java	An application platform developed by Sun Microsystems
JDCB	Java Database Connectivity
LDAP	Lightweight Access Directory Protocol
M&A	Mergers & Acquisitions
ODBC	Open Database Connectivity
OLAP	Online Analytical Processing
O-O	Object-oriented
OQL	Object Query Language
OWL	Web Ontology Language
PUB/SUB	Publish & Subscribe
RACF	Resource Access Control Facility

RDF	Resource Definition Framework
REST	Representational State Transfer
RFID	Radio Frequency Identification
SAML	Security Access Markup Language
SOA	Service-Oriented Architecture
SOAP	The messaging specification for Web Services
SOI	Services-Oriented Integration
SQL	Structured Query Language
UDDI	Universal Description, Discovery, and Integration
UML	Unified Modeling Language
WSBPEL	Web Service Business Process Execution Language
WSDL	Web Services Definition Language
XMI	XML Metadata Interchange
XML	Extensible Markup Language
XQL	XML Query Language

INDEX

Enterprise Information Integration: A Pragmatic Approach

Index

Enterprise Information Integration: A Pragmatic Approach

Lightning Source UK Ltd.
Milton Keynes UK
UKOW01f0017160616

276411UK00001B/252/P